...DING PEOPLE

SOU...

Other books by the authors:

Robert Cockcroft
Rhetorical Affect in Early Modern Writing: Renaissance Passions
  Reconsidered (2003)

Susan Cockcroft
Investigating Talk (1999)
Language and Society (2001)
Contexts (2002)

Persuading People

An Introduction to Rhetoric

Second Edition

ROBERT COCKCROFT AND SUSAN COCKCROFT

To our daughters
Hester, Jane and Laura,
without whom this might have been finished earlier,
and to the new generation

First published 1992 by
MACMILLAN PRESS
Second edition published 2005 by
PALGRAVE MACMILLAN
Houndmills, Basingstoke, Hampshire RG21 6XS and
175 Fifth Avenue, New York, N.Y. 10010
Companies and representatives throughout the world

PALGRAVE MACMILLAN is the global academic imprint of the Palgrave Macmillan division of St. Martin's Press, LLC and of Palgrave Macmillan Ltd. Macmillan® is a registered trademark in the United States, United Kingdom and other countries. Palgrave is a registered trademark in the European Union and other countries.

ISBN–13: 978–1–4039–2182–6
ISBN–10: 1–4039–2182–2

This book is printed on paper suitable for recycling and made from fully managed and sustained forest sources.

A catalogue record for this book is available from the British Library.

10	9	8	7	6	5	4	3	2	1
14	13	12	11	10	09	08	07	06	05

Printed and bound in China

Contents

Preface to the second edition

This second edition of *Persuading People* is driven by two motives. The first is an awareness of the value placed on the earlier edition by many readers, and our consequent wish to make it available again. The second is a need to update and improve the book in the light of our further thoughts about persuasive language, taking into account developments in linguistic (and especially cognitive) theory and rhetorical scholarship since 1992, besides other influential treatments of practical rhetoric.

This revision also seeks to update and extend the range of exemplar materials taken from functional and literary persuasion, which were apparently much appreciated in the first edition. We have added a new final chapter offering opportunities for twenty-first century readers to try their hand at the rhetorical exercises practised in the ancient world, in appropriately updated form. The appendices have been revised, extended and made more accessible, and the reference system has been thoroughly modernised. We also include at the end of each chapter (apart from Chapter 7), a new section offering suggestions for further exploration.

We are grateful to Palgrave Macmillan for their willingness to produce this second edition, and trust that it will prove to be equally as useful, in its revised and extended format, as the first edition.

Acknowledgements

We wish to thank present and former colleagues in the School of English Studies at the University of Nottingham and at Derby College (formerly Derby Tertiary College, Mackworth) who first helped this book to see the light of day. We would particularly like to thank Margaret Berry, Walter Nash, Ron Carter, Peter Stockwell and Doris Crick whose examples of scholarly and critical thoroughness assisted us in our study of the links between language, literature and rhetoric. Professor Alan Sommerstein of the Department of Classics is also owed our gratitude for contributions from his particular expertise, as is Emeritus Professor John Hampton of the University of Nottingham for his happy suggestion of a title, and for Rick Eagles for computer know-how. We also thank our friends and family for their encouragement and support over an unconscionably long gestation, and regestation.

In addition, with our publisher we thank the following for permission to reproduce material. Firstly, for the poetry. Our extract from 'Notes from Underground: W. H. Auden on the Lexington Avenue IRT', from *Days of Wonder: New and Selected Poems by Grace Schulman*, copyright © 2002 by Grace Schulman, is reproduced by permission of Houghton Mifflin Company (all rights reserved) and with grateful acknowledgement to the author. Our short quotations from *Omeros* (1990) by Derek Walcott, and from 'Sweeney Among the Nightingales' (1920) by T. S. Eliot, together with two complete poems: 'Metaphors' from *Collected Poems* (1981) by Sylvia Plath, and 'A Study of Reading Habits' from *Collected Poems* (1988) by Philip Larkin, are reproduced by permission of Faber and Faber Ltd. The justly famous title and climactic line ('Not waving . . .') from Stevie Smith's *Collected Poems* (Penguin, 1985) are reproduced by permission of the Estate of James MacGibbon. 'Henry King', from Hilaire Belloc's *Cautionary Verses*, is reprinted by permission of PFD on behalf of the Estate of Hilaire Belloc, © the Estate of Hilaire Belloc (as printed in the original volume). We are grateful to our friend Ann Parker for her kind permission to reproduce the poem 'Copyrighting the Dormouse' from her collection *The Gasman Dances*, published privately in 2003. The opening and closing couplets of John Betjeman's poem 'A Bay in Anglesey', as included in his *Collected Poems*, are reproduced by permission of John Murray Publishers.

Printed and recorded materials (other than journalism and advertising) that required permission, were as follows. The figure from Gordon Wells (ed.), *Learning through Interaction* (1981) is reproduced with acknowledgements to Cambridge University Press and to Dr Gordon Wells (the author of the figure) for his kind consent to its re-use. The extracts from A. N. Saunders's translation of Demosthenes, *Philippic I*, are reproduced from his selection of *Greek Political Oratory* (1970), by kind permission of Penguin Books Ltd. Parliamentary copyright material from Prime Minister's Question Time, 31 October 1989, is reproduced with the permission of the Controller of Her Majesty's Stationery Office on behalf of Parliament. We also owe acknowledgements to Natasha Bourne for this well-chosen example, which was quoted in her A Level language project for that year. Our transcript of a comment on the British Government's proposed 'top-up' fees for university students, which was made by Nick Brown, the Member of Parliament for Newcastle upon Tyne East and Wallsend and former Government Chief Whip, on Radio 4's 6 o'clock *News* for 2 December 2003, is reproduced by kind permission of the BBC, and with a generous 'no objection' from Nick Brown himself. Our extract from President Kennedy's Inaugural Address (20 January 1961) is taken (with acknowledgements) from the *Public Papers of the Presidents: John F. Kennedy*, as published by the US Government Printing Office. Our quotations from Winston Churchill's speeches are reproduced with permission of Curtis Brown Ltd, London, on behalf of the Estate of Sir Winston S. Churchill. Tony Blair's speech as Leader of the Labour Party, made at the Party Conference on Tuesday, 30 September 2003, is quoted with permission of the Labour Party.

In the category of journalistic material we drew largely on the *Guardian* (broadsheet section, *G2* section, Weekend section, and letter pages) for the following, which are all reproduced by permission of the copyright holders: the extract from Matthew Fort's 'Eating Out' column (*Guardian Weekend*, 15 November 2003), © *Guardian* and Matthew Fort; extracts from Natasha Walter's 'When the Veil Means Freedom' (Comment & Analysis, *Guardian*, 20 January 2004), © *Guardian* and Natasha Walter; part of a Third Leader entitled 'Tony Blair: Open Season', 21 January 2004, © *Guardian*; the concluding paragraphs of Catherine Bennett's article 'Hurrah for Lord Falconer's Supreme Vision!' in *Guardian G2*, 12 February 2004, © the *Guardian* and Catherine Bennett. Other material from this source for which acknowledgement is due comprised the following: Professor D. Piachaud's arguments against the Prime Minister in a letter to the *Guardian*, 6 February 2004, are briefly quoted with acknowledgements to the *Guardian* and the writer, and we are grateful to Timothy Garton Ash for his kind permission to use an extract from his article written on the subject on foreign policy alignments between America and Europe in the aftermath of the Madrid bombings (Comment & Analysis, *Guardian*, 13 March 2004), while the short quotation from George Monbiot's 'An Empire in Denial' (Comment & Analysis, *Guardian*, 1 June 2004) is reproduced with acknowledgements to the *Guardian* and the author. Our extract from a theatrical review by Jeffrey Wainwright (Monday, 6 November 1989) is reprinted by kind permission of *The Independent*, and Brian Hanrahan's memorable eyewitness report from the 1982 Falkland War is quoted with acknowledgements to the BBC.

Finally, we owe thanks for a wide and inventive range of advertising material, from slogans to developed persuasive arguments. The text of an advertisement for the 'First Family' of Toshiba portable computers is reproduced by kind permission of Toshiba Consumer Products, Marketing Division. The slogan featured in an amusing series of Carling Black Label advertisements is quoted with acknowledgements to Coors Brewers Ltd. Another slogan, Ronseal's famously forthright claim on behalf of its product, is quoted by kind permission of the Marketing department at Ronseal Ltd, Sheffield. The similarly straight-forward affirmation in New Heights Furniture's advertisement (current in March 2004) is quoted by permission of New Heights Furniture. Heinz's much more tongue-teasing recommendation of their baked beans is quoted courtesy of H. J. Heinz, while visual and verbal rhetoric in an advertisement for In Focus presentation projection systems is referred to by courtesy of In Focus Corporation (McCann Erickson Agency). A succinct four-word recommendation of the British Airways service to Warsaw, current in March 2004, is quoted with acknowl-edgements to British Airways and M. & C. Saatchi. In contrast, the extended and cleverly angled sales pitch in Saab's 1989 Carlsson CD advertisement is reprinted by kind permission of Saab, Great Britain. Our quotation of graphic language from an advertisement for Neutrogena Moisture Cream (March 1991) is reprinted with acknowl-edgements to Neutrogena UK Ltd.

Introduction: Rhetoric Defined

Rhetoric: a 'Loaded Gun'?

This book has been written in accordance with a very definite order of priorities. Its main purpose in studying persuasive techniques is to encourage you to develop them for yourself. Its secondary purpose is to analyse persuasive practice both written and spoken, because you need to analyse the persuasive language of others before you can adequately synthesise your own. This kind of analysis derives from a long tradition of rhetorical theory, and our third purpose is to enable you to look back and make use of the evolving concepts and practices of rhetoric from its earliest beginnings.

All this will involve the development of a variety of critical skills. In order to form judgements about the effectiveness of any kind of persuasion, we shall need to place it within its functional, structural and socio-historical context. In practice, this means looking at extracts ranging from Shakespeare to the newspaper cookery column, from John Keats's poetry to John F. Kennedy's speeches. Progressing through a range of examples from successive periods, we shall examine how persuasion is used for many different purposes – at one extreme to create the ultimate tragic emotion, at the other to sell us a car. In so doing, readers will have the opportunity to learn to recognise the flexibility of persuasive techniques, and to develop this skill for themselves.

The very word 'skill', however, may seem suspicious to some readers in its cool neutrality. In the context of craftsmanship or technology it has strongly positive connotations (a skilled craftsman, a beautifully made piece of furniture, or machinery): in a language context, however, the idea of 'skill' can suggest manipulation, superficiality, irresponsibility, even cynicism.

The real question should be, to what *purpose* is the 'skill' applied? That expensive handmade chair might be primarily a sign of status in today's machine-made culture, rather than something of practical use.

In this perspective, the 'skill' of making the chair is as problematic as the rhetorical 'skill' employed to sell it. This contrast illustrates the range within which any skill, whether exercised on wood or on words, must operate. We may ask now whether there is anything in the skill itself to govern its use one way or the other? Surely not. Yet it is a recognised fact that, historically, rhetoric has not always been linked to an earnest concern for objective truth, and this has fed an anti-rhetorical tradition which began with Plato and continues right up to the present day. Is it possible to defend the loaded gun of rhetoric against this view by adapting the well-worn words of the Gun Lobby, and claiming that 'It's as good or bad as the people who use it'?

The answer has to be 'no'. There may be a measure of truth in it, but it has to be an inadequate reflection of the true nature and value of rhetorical skills. The conventional mistake is to see the 'skill' in subjective terms, as though rhetoric were simply a manipulative tool with which *A* works on *B*. It is significant that one of the most impressive cases made for rhetoric during the past twenty years, justifies it in terms of *social* psychology. In the second edition of *Arguing and Thinking* (1996), Michael Billig demonstrates the value of rhetoric, not as monologue but as dialogue. He points out how the habit of rigid *generalisation* (categorisation), which is likely to produce prejudice when applied to social groups or to the regulation of social behaviour, may be countered by the exercise of rhetoric in its *particularising* social context. After all, a consciously developed tendency to make exceptions to general rules, to look for arguments on both sides of the question, has always been part of a rhetorician's training. This reflects what actually happens in our society today, at all levels of public and private discussion and debate. Moreover, Billig argues that the structural pattern of rhetoric, with every argument implicitly, if not explicitly, opposed by a counter-argument, offers an exact model of human thinking. The constant movement between *logoi* and *anti-logoi* represents our thought process as we move from example (particularisation) to generalisation (categorisation) and back again.

This *dialogic* model of the human cognitive process is highly relevant to a study of persuasive language for all sorts of reasons (particularly structural), and we shall be referring to Billig's ideas again. If (as he suggests) every argument, every generalisation, invites an exception or a counter-proposal from the individual/group invited to listen, then, whether or not this response is openly expressed, substantial benefits in terms of human freedom and social dynamism will accrue from this dialogue or interaction:

The power of speech is not the power to command obedience by replacing argument with silence. It is the power to challenge silent obedience
by opening arguments. The former result can be obtained by force as
well as by logos, but the latter can only be achieved by logos, or rather
by anti-logos.

(Billig, 1996: 78)

Rhetoric Defined

But we are getting ahead of ourselves, not only in terms but in
concepts. What is meant by 'logos' and 'anti-logos'? What is 'interaction'? More to the point, what is rhetoric? We must establish these basic
definitions, particularly focusing our attention on the nature and character of rhetoric, before describing the methodology of the book. In so
doing, we shall advance each of the three purposes outlined earlier (i.e.
the rhetorical analysis of texts, the practice of persuasion and insight
into the history of rhetorical theory – itself a complex and inherently
controversial area of study). Although most, if not all, of our readers
will be new to this subject, and primarily interested in an introduction
to rhetoric, we also wish to encourage and enable further exploration.
Accordingly, some aspects of our discussion may appeal more to the
potential scholar of rhetoric than to the general reader.

Rhetoric could be very broadly defined as the 'arts of discourse', or,
more precisely, the 'art of persuasive discourse' in that this 'most widely
used and overworked term' refers both to spoken and written language.
As Katie Wales notes (2001: 113), the word 'seems to be used for all
those senses of language, which, in the words of Bakhtin, emphasize its
concrete living totality (1981)'. She offers nine different senses, which
– though important – it is impossible for us to explore. More simply,
we shall use the term 'discourse' in our book to denote a series of
connected utterances or continuous written forms of communication.
The term 'discourse analysis' is similarly complicated; it describes the
structural analysis of spoken language, but can also be applied to written texts in which case it is termed 'text linguistics'.

We therefore use the description of rhetoric as 'persuasive discourse'
advisedly, aware that some readers may have encountered differing
interpretations of the term, as a result of work in other areas of language
study. Rhetoric is one of the oldest surviving systematic disciplines in
the world: its original insights and techniques remain largely valid, and
it has survived precisely because of its capacity to adapt to ideological
and social change. To demonstrate this remarkable continuity, we shall

now quote one of the earliest definitions and descriptions of rhetoric, deriving from Aristotle (384–322 BC), and, later in the chapter, compare this with some modern theoretical accounts of language function.

> Rhetoric then may be defined as the faculty of discovering the possible means of persuasion in reference to any subject whatever. (This is the function of no other of the arts, each of which is able to instruct and persuade in its own special subject; thus, medicine deals with health and sickness) . . . But Rhetoric, so to [speak] appears to be able to discover the means of persuasion in reference to any given subject. That is why we say that as an art its rules are not applied to any particular definite class of things.   (Aristotle 1926: 15)

Rhetoric is thus defined by its unique breadth of application, and (it is implied) by its adaptability to new subject areas as they evolve. There are, for instance, recent studies which explore the rhetoric of science, for example Simons (1989), Gross (1990) and notably Jeanne Fahnestock's *Rhetorical Figures in Science* (1999). As our book will show, the question of subject is intimately related to the situation or context in which persuasion takes place.

Aristotle classifies the 'means of persuasion' in three main categories, and from these categories we derive three permanent working principles of persuasion, which will be used to underpin the structure of our book. These are: *ethos* (persuasion through personality and stance); *pathos* (persuasion through the arousal of emotion); and *logos* (persuasion through reasoning).

But how does Billig's dialogic view of rhetoric mentioned earlier fit Aristotle's definition of rhetoric and its function? This can be demonstrated by drawing an analogy between the art of persuasion and the handling of a chess problem. Both the rhetorician and the chess player will prepare in advance by anticipating counter-strategies from their opponent. Their essential skills will be demonstrated, regardless of the inherent strength or weakness of the argument or the disposition of the chess pieces. And just as the initial layout of the chess problem implies a potential *dialogue* as well as a contest, so the rhetorician's search for 'means of persuasion' implies a potential *counter-persuasion,* before the debate has even begun. Either way we arrive at a dialogue.

Dialogue is not only the technical term used by Billig in his definition of rhetoric; it is also a familiar word used to denote conversation, discussion or debate. Linguists have a more precise and revealing term – particularly relevant for our purposes – which is *interaction.* This term is important because rhetoric (as we have already seen) is a persuasive dialogue, and as such can be described as a *controlled* interaction. The rhetorician seeks to *exploit* specifically the ideological, personal and contextual elements involved in every interaction. Even so, the audience's response can never be entirely predictable, however shrewd the rhetorician's choice of 'means of persuasion' (see Aristotle, above). An audience may not realise they are being persuaded; even if they do, their response can be compliant, resistant, or a mixture of both. On any given topic, something which enables the rhetorician to interact effectively with one audience may not work with another.

It should now be clear that dialogue and interaction are both key terms for our understanding of the nature of persuasive discourse or rhetoric. Returning to Aristotle's definition of rhetoric, we shall now differentiate between the two kinds of rhetorical 'subjects' to be explored in our study. We shall use the term 'functional persuasion' to describe all kinds of persuasive discourse (spoken or written) concerned with everyday life, where real people are being persuaded to a real purpose. We shall apply the term 'literary persuasion' to the techniques by which prose writers, dramatists and poets seek to convince or persuade us of the imaginative truth and emotional significance of their discourse. Our next point concerns the adaptability of rhetorical skills and the conditions governing them, which will necessitate some consideration of the historical context of rhetoric. Thus the reader will acquire a keener sense of how, throughout its history, rhetoric has always been sensitive to and moulded by the social, political and cultural conditions of the moment. We will at the same time indicate several specific areas of enquiry for readers with more specialised interests.

Rhetoric in History

Rhetoric has its roots in the culture of Greece and Rome, as an acknowledged system of persuasive techniques. Our intention, however, is not to put too much stress on historical distance. It is more important for a potential persuader to recognise rhetorical skills as still relevant today. In the following brief survey, two important points will emerge. The good news is that rhetoric is still endlessly adaptable; the bad news is that within any society there seems to be a direct correlation between the erosion of political freedoms and the limitation and degeneration of rhetoric.

Full accounts of the history of rhetoric may be found in Kennedy (1980) and Vickers (1988) among others, with Murphy (1974) and Mack (1993; 2002) providing major individual studies of medieval and Renaissance rhetoric respectively. What we offer here is some brief illustration of rhetoric's changing character and potential.

Rhetoric grew with the democracies, political assemblies and law courts of Greece and Rome, though it received setbacks as a result of imperial autocracy and barbarian invasion. Throughout the Middle Ages, though narrowly channelled and fragmented by both Church and State, rhetoric remained central to medieval culture as it evolved; its spectacular revival as a complete system in the Renaissance was based on rediscovered texts. Since the seventeenth century, although it declined as a taught discipline, rhetoric has continued to flourish as a practical political instrument. Today rhetoric is enjoying a critical revival, not only continuing its political functions but also developing new variants in the media explosion of the twenty-first century.

In the Greek city states and later in Rome, rhetoric served the dual function of deliberation and decision-making. It provided the means of accusation and defence in the law courts, and of persuasion in senates and popular assemblies. Power and prestige were thereby conferred on the orator/rhetorician, and an increasing demand for rhetorical education resulted in the systematisation of rhetoric as an independent academic discipline. Three distinct types of persuasion were developed to serve three specific functions. These were: *political/deliberative debate* (centring on what was expedient or practicable as public policy); *forensic/legal advocacy* (concerned with justice); and *demonstrative oratory* (the oratory of praise or blame, typically employed at funerals or other formal occasions). Unfortunately, the social functions of this last type of rhetoric laid it open to charges of triviality when used in other contexts as a vehicle for display or public entertainment. It is notable, however, that Aristotle (virtual founder of natural and social science in the western world) strongly upheld rhetoric's importance within the polity of Athens.

The runaway success of rhetoric invited counter-attack. This had already appeared in Plato's *Gorgias* (Plato, 1960), where Socrates deplores the skill professed by the Sophists (i.e. rhetoric teachers), describing it as a mere 'knack' of disguising falsehood or ignorance as plausible truth (Plato, 1960: 46). Plato's view is recognisable today in the contempt for 'mere rhetoric' expressed freely by people who exploit it themselves! A more developed refutation of Plato's demonstrably unfair view than we have time for here is given by Crowley and Hawhee in their invaluable guide to rhetorical practice, *Ancient Rhetorics for Contemporary Students* (1999). Like C. S. Lewis (Renaissance scholar, Christian apologist and author of the 'Narnia' tales), Plato tended to be disdainful of rhetoric but used it brilliantly when it suited his purposes. In the *Phaedrus* dialogue (Plato, 1973) he demonstrates what is to him the acceptable form of rhetoric – namely when it is tailored to the 'type of soul' or individual being addressed in one-to-one dialogue. He did not think that rhetoric addressed to groups could achieve anything of value, being inevitably fallacious. He thus creates his own version of the idea of *kairos* (fitness or timeliness) – which is derived ironically enough from the Sophists whom he despised. *Kairos* means the exact matching of language to the addressee's individual situation and needs. We shall be exploring this concept further in Chapter 4.

As Roman society evolved from the Republic to the Empire, the uses of rhetoric changed and diversified. Cicero (106–43 BC) used persuasion in both public and private contexts, in political and legal speeches, in letters, and in dialogues on a range of subjects including rhetoric itself. Whilst recalling other orators' memorable speeches, Cicero (like Plato) also focused on *kairos*, identifying three roles or 'duties' for the effective orator. The enduring importance of these 'duties' places them second only to the Aristotelian proofs. Cicero's formulation had the effect of making people think about how the three roles interact, whether they help or hinder each other, and how they achieve this. Later, Cicero identifies these duties as: *teaching* (or proving): *delighting* (giving pleasure); and *moving* to action or to reaching a decision (Cicero, 1988: 356–7). Cicero's important addition of the 'duty' of *delighting* may seem odd to us. We tend to dissociate pleasure from the immediacy of persuasion: for us it is more likely to be linked at one level with 'reading for pleasure', or reading or rereading at a deeper level. But it is essential to note that according to Cicero *pleasure* has a significant role in the process of persuasion itself. Can we, therefore, glimpse a link between Aristotle and Cicero by trying to square Aristotle's 'proofs' with Cicero's 'duties'? If *logos* (typically) proves and teaches, and *pathos* moves or stirs feeling, does *ethos* (when aptly expressed) generate pleasure? We shall explore these questions further in the next chapter.

Once the authority of the Emperor took precedence over the authority of the Senate, political rhetoric became a matter for behind-the-scenes advice and intrigue, rather than vital public debate; even law-court rhetoric had less scope. Nevertheless rhetoric did continue to be studied and practised. In AD 94 Quintilian, the Spanish-born

Professor of Rhetoric, published his comprehensive work on rhetoric, *Institutio Oratoria* (see Quintilian, 1920–2). He had worked as a barrister in Rome, and acted as tutor to the nephews of Emperor Domitian. Quintilian showed how the discipline of rhetoric drew on other educational studies such as moral philosophy and literature, and in turn, contributed to them. (We shall be discussing later Quintilian's emphasis on the moral qualities of the persuader, his power to stir emotions, and the means by which this was achieved.)

Rhetoric contined to be taught at a high level of sophistication right up to the time of St Augustine (AD 354–430). Theorists and teachers of rhetoric refined techniques for arriving at the essential 'point at issue' in dispute (see Chapter 4) and for generating argument about the issue. They developed sharper techniques to alert listeners and readers to the qualities of style in speech and writing, such as clarity, vigour and simplicity. They also extended the range and usefulness of elementary exercises, well supported by examples for imitation by students. We will provide similar opportunities for exercising practical persuasion in our final chapter, by adapting some of this material. As Christianity spread throughout the Roman Empire and was adopted as the official religion, deliberative rhetoric, infused with new energy and urgency, became the medium of preaching, systematic teaching and disputation, inciting its new audience to *spiritual* rather than political choice and action. Augustine incorporated these techniques and concepts, together with Platonic philosophy and Greek and Latin literary models, into a fully intellectualised Christianity (see Augustine, 1995). For him, sacred rhetoric sought to stir the highest and purest forms of emotion, as it directed the will and intellect towards God.

Despite this Christianising of rhetoric, after the barbarian invasions and the collapse of the Roman Empire in the west, rhetoric entered its Dark Ages. A reduced number of classical rhetorical texts remained in circulation, but although literacy was maintained in the monasteries and their schools, and recovered quite quickly in the evolving feudal kingdoms and city states, rhetoric had largely lost its earlier political, legal and social roles. However, what was lost to rhetoric in one area, was gained in several others. Both reading and writing of texts (old or new, sacred or secular, central or peripheral to European culture) was in effect rhetoricised by the customary provision of scholarly prologues, proceeding along dialectical and rhetorical lines (see Minnis, 1988). These prologues offered ways of analysing the texts, of judging their nature and of positioning them in the universal scheme of knowledge. For example, in the Middle Ages, Ovid's *Metamorphoses* was regarded as an *ethical* text, a direct warning against the very passions Ovid depicts so enthusiastically. Thus, within this Christianised perspective, rhetoric was assigned the task of giving imaginative or emotional weight to authoritative truth, rather than discovering or radically re-interpreting it.

Further specialised forms of rhetoric began to evolve at this time, reflecting new social, cultural and intellectual priorities. The rhetoric of preaching encouraged dramatic and satirical representations, not only in the pulpit but also in literary genres such as drama and satire. One special branch of rhetoric (*ars dictaminis*) was devoted to the writing of letters (a skill vital to contemporary diplomacy); another, the *ars notaria* governed the composition of legal documents; both branches tended to draw on key surviving texts written by (or attributed to) Cicero, such as *De Inventione* and *Rhetorica ad Herennium*, for their style and argumentative method. Modern scholars such as John Ward have also discovered a clear correlation between changes in rhetorical theory and practice, and national and international political conditions. When public speaking once again became part of the political process in cities like Florence, classical rhetoric texts which had been used as preliminary or supplementary guides to composition returned centre-stage as practical handbooks. Unfortunately the subsequent rise of dictatorships inevitably reversed this development (Ward, 2001: 195–218).

Was there, however, a gain for poetry even where liberty was lost? In royal or ducal courts, an increase in wealth and numbers led to a greater need for entertainment (or coded 'in-group' advice). Hence there was greater scope for rhetorical elaboration in poetry, speeches and descriptions. Specialised rhetorical guides to the writing of poetry appeared, serving the purposes of both the political and cultural establishment. Yet it was still possible for anti-establishment dissidents to make use of rhetoric, for example the poet William Langland in *Piers Plowman*. He not only expressed the discontent of the forgotten, the marginalised and the disempowered, but also provided a model for future satirists (see Langland, 1967; Paulin, 1986: 58–9). Clearly the Middle Ages enormously broadened the scope of rhetoric. Whether transmitted, accidentally preserved or invented, it was applied at every significant level of existence from religious and artistic to political and practical. Rhetoric during the Renaissance also enjoyed 'rebirth'. The complete works of Aristotle and Quintilian were disinterred and studied exhaustively; comprehensive new treatments of the subject were published in Latin and various vernaculars; and in Italy (as elsewhere) rhetoric was again studied and practised as an 'art' with universal application. However, a tendency towards political autocracy throughout Europe partially threatened, partly encouraged its revival. In England the spread of printing had made rhetorical texts readily available, having a crucial effect on the rising art form of drama. Marlowe and Shakespeare (products of the Renaissance grammar school) both exploited their rhetorical training, sometimes in ways that were directly subversive of the political, social and religious order of the day (see, for example, Dollimore, 1984; Shepherd, 1986).

Rhetoric had a similarly important role in the religious Reformation of the sixteenth century, one which puts rhetoric itself to the test. The Dutch humanist scholar Erasmus, seeking to discover common bonds of spirituality and morality to counteract the turmoil of outward differences, used the rhetoric of contrasts in his unsuccessful attempt to establish communication at deeper levels than religious division (see Erasmus, 1999). The great Lutheran educator Philip Melanchthon drew on Augustine's rhetoricising of the centrality of emotion in religious salvation, and sought to express his own perception that the transforming emotion of faith worked through the rhythmical, repetitive process of preaching (see Cockcroft, 2003: 63–5).

The teaching of Peter Ramus, logician and educator (1515–72), also must have made it easier for people who lacked a thorough training in academic logic and rhetoric to join in the pamphleteering controversies of the sixteenth and seventeenth centuries. His death in the massacre of Paris made him a Protestant hero, and gave credence to his radical approach. Ramus had developed a simplified method of logical investigation and argument which he regarded as a *dialectical* rather than a rhetorical procedure, and which was supported by a curtailed rhetoric focusing almost entirely on stylistic features. Though some accused him of writing 'idiot's guides' to inevitably complex subjects (see, for example, Leishman, 1949: 110–16), Ramus made it possible for younger and less skilful writers or speakers as well as for practised rhetoricians to think through a topic, rather than blindly following a formulaic procedure (see Brinsley, 1612: 182–3). He demystified the processes of persuasive arguing and writing, making them accessible to a new generation of reformers and pamphleteers, whether self-taught or grammar school-trained.

It's significant that Ramus secured his own appointment as the Royal Professor of Philosophy and Eloquence in the University of Paris. This reflected his strong belief that disciplines *other* than rhetoric, such as logic, ethics and medicine, each had a part to play in achieving

Quintilian's ideal, 'the good man skilled in speaking' (see Henderson, 1999: 43–56). Even within this larger context, his system has its limitations; arguably it fits written persuasion better than the spoken variety, where you are more likely to have to think on your feet, perhaps an easier task for more traditionally educated persuaders. In fact, the narrowing down of rhetoric by Ramus had an effect opposite to what he intended. By insisting on the conceptual separateness of different branches of study, he indirectly encouraged the sixteenth-century critic to go further beyond the bounds of rhetoric (however broadly defined), in the development of critical theory and practice. This meant drawing on a much wider range of disciplines, ranging from rhetoric itself to philosophy, history, medicine etc. This process of combination will be immediately apparent to anybody who studies Sidney's *An Apology for Poetry* (written *c*.1582). Here we see the origins, not just of modern critical and historical reading, but also of the concept of 'literature' itself, as the object of such readings.

Ramus's stress on the contribution of other disciplines to 'eloquence' has particular practical significance for us. However comprehensive a persuader's skills, without real knowledge of the subject area within which an issue has arisen, nobody will be persuaded. This accords with Aristotle's concept of a common technique applicable 'to any subject whatsoever'. Other resources potentially available to persuaders are literature and criticism (both of which often overlap with rhetoric).

As the culture of England (and later, of the new political entity Britain) mutated from the early modern or Renaissance world-view to the more materialistic, science-based culture of eighteenth-century 'Augustanism', rhetoric both contributed to the change and was itself profoundly affected by it. In her study of *Rhetorical Figures in Science*, Jeanne Fahnestock shows how the patterns of thought and perception embodied in the verbal structures of rhetoric promoted scientific observation and understanding. This had already been seen in the early seventeenth century in the use made of *antithesis* by Francis Bacon, the pioneer of scientific methodology (Fahnestock, 1999: 59–65). With the beginnings of systematic psychology based on observation, new conclusions were reached about the relationship between sensory perception, emotion and reasoning, centring on the 'association of ideas'. Rhetoricians such as the Scot George Campbell based their systems on the new philosophy of mind evolved by John Locke and David Hume. According to Hume, 'the qualities, from which . . . association arises, and by which the mind is . . . conveyed from one idea to another, are three, . . . *resemblance, contiguity* in time or place, and *cause* and *effect* (Hume, 1911: I, 19; italics as in original). (In Chapter 3, our strategy for exploring the relationships between ideas using ten 'models' of argument will be seen as a purposive development of this involuntary process 'by which one idea naturally introduces another'.) Hume argued that 'ideas', simple or complex, are derived directly or indirectly from our sense impressions. His word for the way our minds work with these ideas is 'imagination'. Moreover, since this process tends to be accompanied by emotion, the evaluation of emotion became at this time more closely linked to the judgement of ideas, reason being a specific, voluntary and focused activity of the imagination. Accordingly, eighteenth-century rhetoric reflects and promotes a new way of integrating *ethos, pathos* and *logos* by way of 'the sentimental'. Quite contrary to its belittling modern sense, 'sentimental' then signified a capacity for finely tuned, perceptive and sympathetic feeling, occupying 'the middle place between the pathetic and that which is addressed to the imagination, . . . adding to the warmth of the former the grace and attractions of the latter' (Campbell, 1963: 80). Imagination combined rational discernment and moral insight, thus tempering *pathos* into sentiment.

According to Adam Smith, the great Enlightenment economist and moralist, sentiment is particularly intensely felt when we contemplate the mental pain of another person: 'What he suffers is from the imagination only . . . and we sympathise with him more strongly upon this account, because our imaginations can more readily mould themselves upon his imagination, than our bodies can mould themselves upon his body' (Smith, 1976: 29). Such sympathy was most valued when the sufferer showed fine moral qualities, especially if s/he appeared to be restraining rather than indulging emotions! Pleasure (cf. Ciceronian *delectatio*) was also involved, because sympathy for moral heroism of any kind would inevitably be accompanied by admiration, and would then draw further on the imagination for appropriately 'vivacious' or figurative language. This insight is as relevant to literature as to rhetoric; indeed during the eighteenth century rhetoric began to be absorbed into the discourse of literary criticism, to which it had given birth two centuries previously. However, there was an incipient problem: the increasing stress on refined style and 'sentiment' meant that rhetoric's capacity for addressing serious political and philosophical issues might be seriously diminished.

As the nineteenth century unfolded, much of the best and most fruitful insights on persuasive language came not from rhetoricians but from poets and philosophers such as Samuel Taylor Coleridge. In a sharply perceptive essay on 'method', Colcridge (see, for example, Bailcy, 1965: 137–46) shows how clear thought and effective communication depend on a careful balance of generalisation and particularity, keeping everything in a clear frame, sticking to the point and moving forward at the appropriate pace. Shakespeare's characterisation shows what happens when 'method' is lacking. Hamlet's brilliant but melancholy and wayward mind generalises too much, going off at tangents, while the comical, put-upon pub landlady Mistress Quickly rambles on from one irrelevant particularity to another. For Coleridge and his successors, the skill of method (so far as it is a skill, and not the result of innate intelligence), derives from the reading of literary, critical, philosophical and scientific texts, rather than from systematic rhetoric. Here we see an interesting change; Coleridgean method married to the reading of texts and criticism has become the standard way of developing students' writing skills, rather than the study of rhetoric. But as we shall see in the later chapters of the book, this situation is being reversed and rhetoric is once again being taught in centres of higher education.

Herbert Spencer's seminal essay on style (see, for example, Bailey, 1965: 147–72) raises the question of *economy* in speech and writing. Assuming that any audience has finite reserves of energy, a persuader must not demand unreasonable amounts of effort from his listeners or readers, as they follow argument or respond to feeling. For example, he gives guidelines for the appropriate and differentiated use of Anglo-Saxon monosyllables and Latin polysyllables ('grand' should be used to convey an idea of magnitude and 'magnificent' used to convey its emotional impact). Though Spencer leaves some questions unanswered (for example, is it possible for language to build up the energies of its audience rather than simply depleting them), his concern for the effectiveness of lexical choice paves the way for the work of the twentieth-century Czech linguist Jan Firbas and his theory of Communicative Dynamism. He takes the argument beyond word-choice to the choice of word-order (see Firbas, 1992). This has important implications for anybody seeking to combine forcefulness and economy in stylistic choices (thus enhancing rhetorical skill).

In an age of scientific and democratic progress the concept and process of *cause* and *effect*, long recognised as a vital element of the *logos* proof, became crucial. John Stuart Mill (see Bailey, 1965: 173–92) offered a scientifically based critique for determining when phenomena were causally linked and when they were simply contiguous, establishing a standard of rigour still applicable to persuasive language whenever important issues depend on the validity of this link. We shall refer to this when considering the validity of arguments.

The twentieth-century revival of rhetoric as a discipline in its own right was pioneered by such writers as I. A. Richards, Kenneth Burke, C. Perelman and L. Olbrechts-Tyteca. Richards entitled his published lecture series (1936) *The Philosophy of Rhetoric*. It is not by chance that this recalls George Campbell's book of the same title, as Richards and Campbell share a scientific approach to their subject. Richards places metaphor at the centre of rhetoric because it employs images which are meaningful to both persuader and audience, as shown in his fifth and sixth lectures (see Richards, 1965: 89–138). This promotes the ultimate aim of rhetoric which (in his view) is the prevention or reduction of misunderstanding. He introduced the terms 'tenor' and 'vehicle' to his analysis of metaphor, meaning the 'the initial idea to be conveyed' and 'the image chosen to convey it'. These usages are very different from the Hallidayan concept of 'field, tenor and mode'.)

Burke in his *A Rhetoric of Motives*, first published in 1950, went beyond the traditional understanding of rhetoric by introducing (among other factors) the unconscious as an important factor in persuasive effects (see Burke, 1969: 3–46). He linked the strategies of persuasion to the *motives* underlying them, showing how the forms of expression chosen by a speaker or writer modify the deeper impulses driving communication. Rhetoric can provide a way of giving voice to what would otherwise be unspeakable or inadmissible. He suggests that effective rhetoric entails both an 'identification' with the audience's values, preoccupations, characteristic emotions and modes of expression, and an equally powerful appeal to the audience to empathise with the entire persuasive process. Indeed, a compelling 'motive' for the audience's engagement is rhetorical expression itself. Although unconscious motivation might be more characteristic of literary rather than of functional rhetoric, Burke points to comparable ways in which persuaders can unmask their opponents' motives, and examine their own.

Finally, Perelman and Olbrechts-Tyteca's fully systematised *The New Rhetoric*, first published 1958, challenges J. S. Mill's scientific approach to *proof* (see above). Returning to the idea of *kairos*, they exhaustively investigate what makes language actively persuasive, and ask how an audience is taken beyond mere rational conviction to the point of active 'adherence' to committed action or belief. A good contemporary example of this would be the relative failure of the anti-smoking lobby to convince the most committed smokers to give up their habit (they accept the cast-iron proof that smoking damages their health, but they don't stop smoking). *The New Rhetoric* looks at the various means – argumentative, relational and stylistic – through which such obstacles are surmounted. The authors bring the art of rhetoric full circle, showing how the working principles initiated by the Sophists and developed by Aristotle should be applied under modern conditions.

The ongoing revival of rhetoric has involved both of the approaches combined in this book: analysis and composition. Some books (e.g. Leith and Myerson, 1989; Andrews, 1992) have explored the persuasive function within a wide range of genres from lecturing and folk singing to weather forecasts, television news and fashion shows. Over the same period, major books on rhetorical practice have been published, including Corbett's *Classical Rhetoric for the Modern Student* (3rd edition, 1990) as well as Crowley and Hawhee's *Ancient Rhetoric for Contemporary Students* (2nd edition, 1999). Importantly, these thorough-going classroom texts (showing with many illustrations how rhetoric is applied to contemporary issues) promote its restoration not only as a means of enhancing expression, but also as a crucial tool for active citizenship.

Methodology and Procedure

It is now time to indicate in detail what our methodology will be. Perhaps unsurprisingly in view of what has just been written, we shall return to Aristotle. From his analysis we can derive useful structural principles that will enable us to achieve the necessary balance between a practical procedure simple enough to work with, and a theoretical understanding complex enough to constitute a true account of rhetoric.

In his *Rhetoric* (I.ii.3–6) Aristotle distinguishes three kinds of 'proofs' or 'structural principles': persuasion by 'moral character' (*ethos*); persuasion by 'putting the hearer into a certain [emotional] frame of mind' (*pathos*); and persuasion 'by the speech itself, when we establish the true or apparently true' (*logos*). He explains that the 'proof through character' depends on confidence, which 'must be due to the speech itself, not to any preconceived idea of the speaker's character'. He accounts for the 'proof through emotion' by pointing out that 'the judgements we deliver are not the same when we are influenced by joy or sorrow, love or hate'. Aristotle then continues (I.ii.7):

Now, since proofs are effected by these means, it is evident that, to be able to grasp them, a man must be capable of logical reasoning, of

> studying characters and the virtues, and thirdly the emotions – the
> nature and character of each, its origin, and the manner in which it is
> produced.   (Aristotle, 1926: 17–19)

This seems a pretty tall order. By this test nobody can persuade effectively who has not done advanced courses in applied dialectic, moral
philosophy and psychology! In a single short book we can hardly offer
our reader the sort of understanding that Aristotle requires for the full
development of persuasive ability. But we have to make a start somewhere; and by substituting the term 'structural principle' for Aristotle's
general concept of 'proof', we have already achieved something. In
place of an abstract blanket term we have implied a process, combining
method, balance and flexibility. We intend to use the Aristotelian terms
ethos, pathos and *logos* throughout the book as a convenient reminder of
the three 'proofs'. Most importantly, our discussion in the first four
chapters will be based upon these 'structural principles'.

(a)   Personality and stance (or ethos)

We divide the concept of *ethos* into two interdependent concepts,
personality and stance. 'Personality' is recognisable in any spoken
exchange which gives us confidence in the person we're talking to.
Whatever the context, and whoever the persuader might be, he or she
will have impressed us by a range of qualities. These will be comparable to qualities that Aristotle identified as communicating *ethos* within
the cultural context of the Greek city state. Eugene Garver summarises
these qualities in *Aristotle's Rhetoric: An Art of Character* (1994). Trust is
built up progressively by impressions of someone's moral strength
(*arete*), benevolence (*eunoia*) and what we might translate as 'constructive competence' or the ability to offer shrewd, practical but principled
advice (*phronesis*) (see Garver 1994: 132–8). *What* was said to us will
have been less important in giving us a sense of their personality (a vital
aspect of ethos) than *how* it was said. To be able to identify with an
audience, impress them with our individuality (or disturb and reorient
their attitudes by an apparent withdrawal of sympathy) is central to the
communication of personality. In persuasive spoken discourse especially, this interactional skill is essential to the success of the exchange.
How is this success achieved? It results from whatever combinations of
vocabulary, intonation and structural organisation are called for by the
circumstances of the exchange.

Yet *ethos* involves more than contact between speaker and audience, persuader and persuadee. There must also be a wider framework of attitudes, a sense of the persuader's position or viewpoint about what's being discussed (the *issue* giving rise to the interaction). We call this aspect *stance*. Consider the difference between a personal complaint made by an individual, and one made on behalf of a number of individuals constituting a community linked by occupation, social class, culture or nationality. The broadening of stance is measurable: at one extreme is the self-obsessed, boring talker, and at the other, the great public orator.

Interestingly, Aristotle's recommendation to a rhetorician ('study the characters and the virtues') would seem appropriate advice for the persuader keen to make effective use of *personality* and *stance* in persuasion. S/he can achieve this through responding to the psychology and values of the audience, and choosing language that reflects both.

(b)   Emotional engagement (or pathos)

It probably does not require Aristotle to inform the potential persuader that audiences can be persuaded through their emotions. In adding the term *engagement* to our version of this structural principle, we denote the need to orient emotional appeals precisely towards audience and topic, and to found them on sources of feeling accessible to speaker and audience, writer and reader. This link between emotive source, persuader and audience constitutes 'engagement'; and though individual experiences of emotion will vary, most of us can access a wider range of emotion through the power of imagination – for example, the use of powerful imagery creates empathy. We shall see in Chapter 2 how persuasion uses a variety of linguistic means to achieve empathy and create 'engagement'.

(c)   Modelling and judging argument (or logos)

Looking up *logos* in the standard Greek-English dictionary (Liddell and Scott, 1973), one discovers an amazing range of meanings reflecting the Greek genius for conceptual thought. At different periods *logos* has had many senses directly relevant to rhetoric. Senses III.1, 2, 4, 5; IV; V.4; and VI are successively defined as 'plea'; 'arguments leading to a conclusion'; 'thesis'; 'reason or ground of argument'; 'inward debate'; 'speech' (i.e. oratorical discourse); and 'verbal expression'.

As a structuring principle in rhetoric, *logos* includes: the process of identifying the *issues* at the heart of debate; the range of diverse arguments in the discourse; the structure of thought these arguments compose; and the sequencing, coherence and logical value of these arguments. Moreover, in order to be comprehensible, discourse has to be logical; as we shall see in Chapter 2, *logos* structures emotion as well as reasoning. The 'models of argument' that we consider in Chapter 3 represent the various resources available to the persuader; and the processes of judgement which we discuss in Chapter 4 involve the assessment, selection, focusing and ordering of argument.

(d)   Rhetoric and modern linguistic theory

We have used Aristotle's description of rhetoric as a means of presenting the methodology in this book. As another 'way in', we shall also explore the usefulness of modern linguistic theory in our study of persuasive discourse. At this point we shall refer as briefly as possible to these different linguistic approaches (just to list them looks daunting!). The aim is to link them with traditional rhetorical approaches, showing how modern persuasive discourse and ancient rhetorical theory and practice both intuit language as a system of signs functioning within particular social and cultural contexts. Rhetoric, as we will see, exploits the persuasive potential of such sign systems. Indeed, it is increasingly clear that modern persuasive discourse and old rhetoric are not only both part of the same dynamic progression but function in surprisingly similar ways, and are explicable using modern theories of communication.

Certain names spring to mind as key linguistic theorists (Roman Jakobson, Ferdinand de Saussure, Mikhail Bakhtin, Michael Halliday, and the social psychologist Michael Billig); key areas of linguistic theory include discourse theory; the co-operative principles; frame and schema theory; politeness strategies; narrative structure and story-grammar; gender theory; the role of social context; and language and power. All of these in different ways will help us to a better understanding of persuasion, the persuader and the persuadee.

(i)   Jakobson and Saussure (Formalism and Structuralism)

Ferdinand de Saussure (1857–1913) and Roman Jakobson (1896–1982) have had enormous influence on modern literary and linguistic theory. A helpful basic introduction appears in *The English Studies Book* (1998) by Rob Pope, and a more detailed account can be found in Terence Hawkes's *Structuralism and Semiotics* (1977: 76–87). Saussure introduced the idea of the word as 'sign', made up of the *signifier* (sounds/written symbols) and the *signified* (meaning/concept). This exploded the idea that language is a direct representation of reality – it is an arbitrary grouping of sounds (phonemes) or written signs (graphemes) that have culturally agreed meaning. At the heart of all human communication lie multiple sign-systems (e.g. grammar, syntax, vocabulary) whose function is conveying meaning between readers/writers, listeners/speakers. For Saussure, language functions along opposing axes: the *vertical/paradigmatic* axis (where a word is *chosen* from a range of semantic options) and the *horizontal/syntagmatic* axis (which represents the more fixed relationship between words in the sequence of phrase, clause or sentence). The resourceful persuader will exploit the multiple opportunities for word choice in a carefully ordered sequence to achieve maximum effect.

Jakobson's ideas about the poetic function of language are important, but the concept of *binary oppositions* or polarities in language, the concept of *equivalence* and the modelling of the *speech act and its functions* are more relevant to our purposes. The concept of binary oppositions is another version of Saussure's model above; significantly, it also echoes the dialogic/oppositional structure of rhetoric we have already noted. The idea of equivalence (also Saussure-derived) helps us to understand how rhetorical tropes (figures of speech such as *metaphor* and *metonymy*) work in persuasive discourse. If we substitute words because of a perceived/intuited similarity, our trope is based on equivalence or association. Jakobson located this poetic process at Saussure's famous intersection of the paradigmatic and syntagmatic axes, where the speaker/writer *selects* one word (from a range of semantic options) and *combines* it (with other words) into a chosen syntactic pattern. This selection/combination model explains why trope is important to successful persuasion; persuaders can use trope to select, combine and maximise the effects of their persuasive discourse. (For a more detailed discussion, see Chapter 6.)

The third of Jakobson's ideas relevant to our study of rhetoric is his modelling of the speech act and its associated functions. This provides us with a valuable methodology for analysing dialogic structure and function. In Jakobson's view the formula or structure of every speech event or written communication follows the same pattern:

'addresser' > 'message/context/contact/code' > 'addressee'

Moreover, each communicative event is oriented towards a single language function: this function could be *emotive* (oriented towards the *addresser*: 'My best friend won't speak to me'); *referential* (oriented towards the *message* and *context*: 'The next train to York is late'); *conative* (oriented towards the *addressee*: 'Now you listen to me!'); *phatic* (oriented towards social *contact*: 'Hi! How are you?'): *metalinguistic* (oriented towards the *code* or language itself: 'What does this word mean exactly?'); or *poetic* (oriented towards the *message*: 'My love is like a red, red, rose . . .').

In our study of rhetoric, we shall be relating these functions to the Aristotelian proofs of *ethos, pathos* and *logos*. The early theories of Saussure and Jakobson, by modelling how communication works, have drawn our attention to dialogic structure, oppositions in language and the sources of trope.

(ii)   Mikhail Bakhtin (1895–1975)

Mikhail Bakhtin's writings, increasingly important in the latter half of the twentieth century, are of interest to literary and linguistic theorists alike. Particularly useful for our purposes is M. Holquist's collection of Bakhtin's essays called *The Dialogic Imagination* (Bakhtin, 1981). Bakhtin declares that all discourse (whether written or spoken) is *dialogic* or double-voiced, 'echoing other voices and anticipating rejoinders'. Indeed, Bakhtin's own term for what he calls 'multi-layered' discourse is *heteroglossia,* meaning 'many voices'. M. V. Jones (1989: 108) quotes a passage of vital importance for rhetorical *ethos* in its social and political aspects. In every dialogic interaction, Bakhtin observes that 'prestige languages [are trying] to extend their control and subordinate languages [are trying] to avoid, negotiate, or subvert that control'. This 'struggle of voices for dominance' is in many ways comparable to the persuader at work, as s/he prepares for the potential opposition or *counter-persuasion* generated by the persuadee (with or without the intervention of a rival persuader). For Bakhtin, dialogue is a dialectic between an authoritative discourse and an inwardly persuasive discourse, as demonstrated by David Murray in his essay on *Heart of Darkness* (Tallack, 1987: 115–34). (Looking forward to Chapter 2, pp. 69–71, and its discussion of the 'reversal of bias', Bahktin's theories about dialogue and multiple voices will alert us to the ways in which previously repressed 'voices' and emotions can suddenly become dominant.)

(iii)   M. A. K. Halliday (1925–)

Michael Halliday's theory of language as function within a social context challenged the structuralist views of Saussure and (later) Chomsky. Unlike them, Halliday stressed the key importance of *meaning* as the determining factor in all aspects of language function (whether realised through grammar, phonology, lexis or any other system). Although structure remains present in language at a linear level (syntax), Halliday (following Saussure) would argue that every 'language user' has multiple options or paradigms available within the networks/systems of grammar, phonology and lexis. These language choices (whether in spoken or written form) are always determined by audience, context and purpose. Bad rhetoric, however, tends to forget both context and audience in its obsession with its own purposes. Good rhetoric on the other hand has always taken into account the importance of audience and social context. Halliday's reworking of these ideas, however, has provided crucial and generous theoretical support for the modern persuader in maintaining this essential balance.

Halliday's theory of the three language metafunctions (1973: 36–42) is crucial to our linking of new linguistic theory with old rhetoric. Present in any interaction, these metafunctions are: (i) the *ideational* function (expressing ideas about the real world, which we will link with *logos*); (ii) the *interpersonal* function (concerned with social relationships, which we link with *ethos* and *pathos*); and (iii) the *textual* function (the spoken or written enactment/realisation of language choices, which will also be linked with *ethos*). These distinctions will be seminal in our subsequent discussion of rhetorical method, structure and process.

(iv)   Discourse theory

Although (as we saw above) Katie Wales gives as many as nine differing 'senses' of the term 'discourse' (Wales, 2001: 113–15), Rob Pope's helpful explanation may be more appropriate for our specific purposes (1998: 188–9). Three of these 'main meanings' are of particular relevance: (a) discourse as language above the level of the sentence/utterance with the emphasis on verbal cohesion and textual coherence; (b) discourse as dialogue in general or conversation in particular, primarily associated with conversational analysis, but also extended into work on pragmatics and speech acts; and (c) discourse as communicative practices and 'ways of saying' that express the interests of a

particular socio-historical group or institution (i.e. potentially compet-
ing discourses of law, medicine, science, education etc.).

Speech act theory was developed by the philosophers J. R. Searle and
J. L. Austin. Austin described utterances as *performative* (they perform
the action in the words 'I promise to marry you') or *constative* (they
make true or false statements about the world). Communication is 'a
co-operative venture between a writer/speaker and one (or more) read-
ers/listeners', and Austin defines this communication as 'either an illocutionary or a perlocutionary act' (see Steinmann in Nystrand, 1981/2:
296). *Illocutionary* speech acts are expressive, descriptive, directive; they
make statements and convey information; *perlocutionary* speech acts are
intended to achieve certain results in a listener. The persuader will be
able to draw on these kinds of speech act as means of fulfilling Cicero's
three rhetorical 'duties' (to teach, to delight, to move). Whether fully
engaged persuasive discourse constitutes performative or constative
utterances, or includes both, is worth bearing in mind as more examples of persuasion are discussed in each chapter.

Successful conversation happens when 'felicity conditions' are met
and the *cooperative principle* is governing. One of the most accessible
theories about successful speech derives from the 'conversational
maxims' defined by H. P. Grice: 'give exactly the amount of information which is appropriate' (Maxim of Quantity); 'be truthful' (Maxim
of Quality), 'be relevant' (Maxim of Relation), 'be clear' (Maxim of
Manner) (see Grice, 1975; Crystal, 1997: 117). If you violate/flout
these maxims, your communication will be less successful or may even
fail. Persuaders need to be aware of this! Similarly, they need to be
aware of another dimension of the cooperative principle, implied
meaning or *implicature*, where seemingly irrelevant comments are actually relevant ('It's hot in here!' 'Shall I open the window then?'). The
listener has correctly interpreted the implied meaning behind the first
statement. Implicature is an extremely useful instrument in persuasion.

Austin's and Grice's ideas about successful conversation chime significantly with our previous explanations of *ethos* (personality and stance),
and suggest that what holds good for conversation may also apply to
more protracted persuasive discourse. Grice's 'maxims' will be prove
useful not only in Chapter 1, but also in Chapters 5 and 6, where we
shall be analysing the role of persuasive ordering and persuasive style,
as well as exploring how violating conversational maxims may also have
persuasive significance.

Politeness theory began as early as 1967 when Erving Goffman
(1982) noted the importance of 'face' in conversation: positive face

reflects our basic need to be approved of; negative face our need not to be imposed on. (The relevance to persuasion should be clear.) We use positive politeness strategies when we notice/attend to our hearer's wants, exaggerate interest/approval or seek agreement. Using negative politeness strategies includes apologising, being indirect or hedging and being pessimistic (Brown and Levinson, 1978). In successful conversation/persuasion we need to avoid face-threatening acts by respecting social distance/status and avoiding a power imbalance (a neat formulation of this is 'distance + power + rate of imposition = degree of face-threat'). As we shall see in Chapter 1 these factors will be vital in determining stance and undermining the opponent. (See Chapter 1 and especially p. 33 on exclusion/inclusion.)

Structure in spoken and written language can be observed in theories about dialogue and genre variation. We have already noted the dialogic and dialectical nature of rhetorical structure. Conversation analysts Sacks, Schegloff and Jefferson (1974) and exchange structure theorists such as John Sinclair (with Malcolm Coulthard, 1975) and Malcolm Coulthard (1985, 1992) have provided valuable insights into the structure and function of interaction, which is of great value to potential persuaders. Other theorists who have studied the structure of written and spoken language include William Labov (1972) whose *narrative structure* theory has been highly influential. He argues that narrative is central to all forms of spoken and written language (from comic anecdote to the novel) and that it is a 'unit of discourse' with clear boundaries, linear structure and recognisable stages in its development' (Susan Cockcroft, 1999). A narrative starts with the *abstract* (summary of the story). Next is the *orientation* (context in which it takes place); then the *evaluation* (point of interest in the story); the actual telling of the story (*narrative*), followed by the *result* (what actually happened), and the *coda* which signals the end. Some of these 'stages' are obligatory, some are optional. What is important is that the structure is endlessly replicable, and its clarity and familiarity offer much scope to the potential persuader. We shall be exploring the parallel with persuasive order in Chapter 5.

Frame theory (Goffman, 1974; Gumperz, 1982) and *schema theory* (Schank and Abelson, 1977; Schank, 1982, 1999; Tannen, 1993) provide a broader view of the structuring of discourse. Frame theory argues that we use past experience to structure present usage – that is, we pick up contextualising cues or *frames* that enable us to respond appropriately to a linguistic situation; in fact, we have *schemas* (sets of expectations) for a whole range of contexts, and we are disconcerted if they are disrupted (e.g. the doctor tells us about *his* health problems when we go to consult him about our own). A skilful persuader can make use of an audience's *schemata* (plural) to engage or challenge their expectations, as we will see in the course of the book.

Sociolinguistic approaches to persuasive discourse will need to take into account the work of Labov (1972) and Trudgill (1974) on socio-linguistic variables. These include gender (Coates, 1998), age (Coupland et al., 1991) and social context (Coupland and Jaworski, 1997), as well as the role of power and ideology in language (Fairclough, 2001). Fairclough argues that genre can be defined as social action (because it is determined by specific social and historical contexts), and hence discourse/discursive practice in textual form reflects social practice. Hence language is an enactment of ideology and power. The relevance of these theoretical perspectives (and others described above) to our study of persuasion will be more specifically spelt out later in the book.

(e)   Rhetoric: the methodology

Our aim is to cover the first three stages in the process of rhetorical composition, as traditionally conceived. In a book of this length we are not able to treat the fourth and fifth stages, memory and delivery; the latter would, in any case, be served best by a workshop methodology, and the former has closer links today with psycholinguistic theory. The struc-ture of our book will be as follows. We begin by examining the sources of persuasion, with four chapters devoted to the three Aristotelian 'struc-tural principles' (Chapter 1 to *ethos*, Chapter 2 to *pathos*, and Chapters 3 and 4 to *logos*). We then go on to address persuasion in action (Chapter 5, 'The Persuasive Process', and Chapter 6, 'The Persuasive Repertoire'). Finally, Chapter 7 ('Practising Persuasion') uses the traditional rhetorical exercises, the *Progymnasmata*, as the basis for a range of rhetorical activi-ties, some recent, others traditional. We conclude with some suggestions about collaborative projects in persuasion and about applications of rhetorical skill in everyday life. To whet the reader's interest in what is to come, we will end this introduction by demonstrating the role of rhetoric in a major twentieth-century text.

Examplar: The Rhetoric of *Catch-22*

The following extract is from an American novel about the Second World War, *Catch-22*, in which the author, Joseph Heller, urges us persuasively to accept his view of the lunacy of military logic. The narrative voice is partly Heller's own, but mainly we hear the voice of his hero, Yossarian (Heller, 1962: 46):

> There was only one catch and that was Catch-22, which specified that a concern for one's own safety in the face of dangers that were real and immediate was the process of a rational mind. Orr was crazy and could be grounded. All he had to do was ask; and as soon as he did, he would no longer be crazy and would have to fly more missions. Orr would be crazy to fly more missions and sane if he didn't, but if he was sane he had to fly them. If he flew them he was crazy and didn't have to; but if he didn't want to, he was sane and had to. Yossarian was moved very deeply by the absolute simplicity of this clause of Catch-22 and let out a respectful whistle.
> 'That's some catch, that Catch-22,' he observed.
> 'It's the best there is,' Doc Daneeka agreed.

The passage is intended to persuade the readers (with whom the author is in dialogue) that Catch-22 means death. The *ethos* of Yossarian (the one sane man in a world gone mad) is conveyed through the tone of controlled hysteria. Taut, short statements are balanced by conditional clauses ('if he was sane . . .', 'if he flew them . . .', 'if he didn't want to . . .'). Yossarian's colloquial and concrete language ('crazy', 'grounded') is contrasted with more abstract phrases ('concern for one's own safety', 'the process of a rational mind', 'absolute simplicity'), which smooth over the realities of war and death.

Yossarian's use of *pathos* is part of his grimly humorous tone ('Yossarian was moved very deeply and let out a respectful whistle'), though there is relatively little direct appeal to our emotions, except through the cumulative force of logic. Indeed, what is conspicuous in this passage is Heller's masterly use of *logos*. Every statement is immediately undermined, every proposition promptly refuted, in order to hammer home the dreadful futility of Catch-22, ironically described by Doc Daneeka as 'the best there is'.

We can see how the interconnecting networks of grammar and syntax function to enact the mad logic of Catch-22. Modal verbs ('could', 'would') are used to hint at an underlying uncertainty; complex sentence structures mirror the impossibly complex situation of the airmen. Only Orr's apparently simple situation is described in straightforward syntax: 'Orr was crazy and could be grounded.'

There are other linguistic devices here of the kind which we will be introducing later, and which are well known to traditional rhetoric. We encounter the repeated antithesis of 'crazy' and 'sane', and the paradox which results; there are many examples of repetition, particularly of phrases such as 'fly more missions'.

Through this necessarily brief analysis, we have sought to demonstrate a variety of approaches to rhetoric already detailed in this introduction, and which will be spelt out in greater detail in the following chapters. It should be clear to the reader that we have identified the Aristotelian structuring principles, that we have made use of the tools of modern linguistic analysis, and that we have alluded not only to the use of traditional rhetorical devices but also to the dialogic structuring of persuasion described by Billig.

In the section below, we start a practice which will be continued at the end of each chapter, namely, to provide some suggestions for readers who may want to pursue further inquiries about one or more major aspects of the chapter they have just finished. At the end of this Introduction, we are offering readers some ideas for in-depth investigation of one particular topic, the history of rhetoric. Despite the fact that this area of knowledge provides a crucial context for our discussion of rhetoric, the overall balance of the book necessarily limits any more detailed treatment. The key theoretical approaches surveyed above will, on the other hand, be progressively applied in the following chapters, and provided with comparable follow-up under the heading '*Further Exploration: Theory and Practice*'.

Further Exploration: the History of Rhetoric

There are several ways into this topic. One is to start with a survey of the whole history of rhetoric (see Kennedy, 1980). Another way is to focus on rhetoric in a particular period such as the Renaissance in England (see Howell, 1961; Mack, 2002); or readers can go directly to the main classical texts on the subject of persuasion. Interestingly, Michael Billig, an important advocate of rhetoric in the context of social psychology, gives a vivid account of how his own interest began, browsing amongst long-unread volumes in the university library (Billig, 1996: 7–8). His major book provides a model of how to adapt ancient thinking to modern purposes.

Some more specialised areas of interest are the morality of

→

→
rhetoric; the nature of its collective and individual roles; its adaptability; and the question of its demarcation from other disciplines. In her 1984 study of Plato's *Gorgias* and *Phaedrus* (among other texts), Lynette Hunter focuses on the way that 'positive rhetoric' achieves its interactive stance with the persuadee. Eugene Garver's book (1994) is at once a case study of how Aristotle's *Rhetoric* reflects Athenian culture and a source of widely applicable insights into this seminal text.

Readers will find Quintilian surprisingly engaging and accessible in Butler's translation (1920–2). His writing illuminates the relationship between rhetoric and Roman education, shows the influence of reading on persuasive style, and reflects the central importance of Cicero – who was Quintilian's hero and exemplar – within Roman rhetoric.

Debra Shuger (1988) traces the progress of Christian rhetoric from St Augustine, examining its distinctive forms of *pathos* and its characteristic structure and style. James Murphy (1974) demonstrates in a ground-breaking study the innovative achievement, variety and pedigree of medieval rhetoric. Peter Mack (1993) and Walter Ong (1958) examine Renaissance thinking about the relationship of rhetoric and logic (with all its repercussions).

1 Personality and Stance

In the Introduction we emphasised the social and interactional nature of language, and showed how this is relevant to rhetoric. We offered some broad definitions of rhetoric, and focused particularly on the Aristotelian 'proofs' which are central to our argument. We placed rhetoric in its historical context and also linked it with current linguistic theory. In all this, our purpose was to provide accessible ways of approaching rhetoric for everyone who has an interest in the subject (with pointers for further exploration).

In this chapter we shall start with an examination of *ethos*, the first of Aristotle's three proofs, focusing on its main components, *personality* and *stance*, and then considering how these components function in persuasive practice. The term *ethos* (a Greek loan word) has contemporary usage quite different from its traditional rhetorical context. Today we mean the set of values held either by an individual or by a community, reflected in their language, social attitudes and behaviour. When Aristotle used the word, *ethos* meant the proof brought about by the character or virtue of the speaker, and revealed in his speech. Thus modern usage represents a broadening out of the term, and this sense is implicit in what we mean by the stance. In our terms, stance signifies something inherently interactive, reflecting group values, but decidedly subject to the persuader's own control. Personality (deriving from *persona* meaning 'actor's mask') still reflects this meaning in the context of rhetoric. It links a persuader's unique individuality with the act of persuasion, accentuating those character traits best matched to the audience and topic. The more individually engaged a persuader seems to be, the more convincing the persuasion. *Stance* and *personality* constitute the main focus of this chapter on *ethos*, and both will be illustrated in a series of examples selected from literary and functional persuasion.

Before further exploration of the distinction between personality and stance, we need to refocus on interaction. However speakers or writers use paralinguistic features (i.e. body language, gesture, vocal variation) or graphological features (i.e. layout, graphics, illustration) to enhance the appeal of their persuasion, its ultimate success depends on choosing language appropriate to the subject of the discourse, its context and (above all) to its audience. An audience is unlikely to respond favourably if the persuader has not 'tuned in' to them; moreover, he or she will need to maintain this sense of being 'tuned in' to their likely attitudes and responses. Speaker/writer and audience are interdependent in the persuasive process; their reciprocal involvement means that they shape and are shaped by each other.

What do we mean by 'audience'? The answer becomes clear if we look at how an audience actually functions. From infancy onwards, the central medium of communication is language, to which our response may be positive, negative or indifferent. As a child grows, this response will be less *subjective*, and more affected by social experience and attitudes. More complex responses will appear as we become mature users of language; for example, an adult audience may be opposed to the message but sympathetic to the speaker, or vice versa. As readers or listeners we can be persuaded against our better judgement into agreeing with something inherently opposed to our real views; we can also be persuaded to collude with the speaker or writer. Manipulating the audience is, after all, a skill learnt in childhood: then we were arguing for another ice cream; now we might be persuading a friend to come out for the evening instead of studying. In daily life we all play orator and audience by turns. Rhetoric is only a more consciously structured and focused form of manipulative or collaborative verbal interaction, one which requires a particularly astute assessment of the audience.

Personality

We shall now offer a 'camera eye' or cinematic view of the persuasive interaction, periodically stopping the process and presenting a series of 'freeze frames' of persuader and audience. Our first set of frames gives us various shots of the persuader in the act of launching his initial appeal to an audience. Imagine him in the pose of orator (a man of letters? a political demagogue? a head teacher?). What specific features of gesture or expression, what words frozen on the lips, does the imagination pick out? Is the speaker truthful, or merely clever and adept? Isocrates, writing a speech in the character of his former pupil Nicocles, King of Cyprus, claims that 'speaking well [is] the clearest sign of a good mind, which it requires', and that 'truthful, lawful, and just speech [is] the image . . . of a good and faithful soul' (Isocrates, 2000:

171). Following this lead, Quintilian claimed that 'no man can be a good orator unless he is a good man'. Meanwhile (and in sharp contrast) we have Plato's unflattering description of the persuader as a mere 'expert in rhetorical sublety' (*logodaedalos*), skilled in structuring speeches to give the appearance of proof, but without any concern for truthfulness (or indeed any real knowledge of the subject) (Plato, 1973: 83). Like Isocrates, Plato believed that the persuader should be a good man, but unlike him he regarded the persuader as one whose primary gift lay in one-to-one interaction (i.e. philosophical dialogue). Such interaction requires specific insights into the 'soul' of the individual persuadee, with a view to enlightenment and transformation. All this reflects the Idealist philosopher's suspicion of the relativistic and pragmatic persuader. Today's characteristically dismissive use of the word 'rhetoric' inclines more towards the Platonic than the Isocratean view of the persuader.

This may be because the concept of 'image' (a modern version of *ethos*) is at once highly powerful, and also suspect in our society. Personal image (speech, dress, life-style), 'corporate identity' (company logo, house-style, ethos) and political 'charisma' (voice, language, 'grooming', appearance) are all too familiar. The contemporary cult of celebrity commodifies and celebrates everyone in the public eye, from popular culture heroes such as footballers, musicians and film stars to bishops, politicians and even certain kinds of criminals. Public relations has become as admired and essential a profession as law, accountancy or finance, as consultants shape the carefully cultivated 'images' of their clients. In the private domain, because most of us know the falsity of our own 'public image', we also tend to view other people's 'images' with suspicion. In the public domain, national and international figures are less critical, both of their own highly polished images and of the images of fellow 'celebrities', and become even more image conscious as their publicity machines whir faster and faster. Celebrity is achieved by being in some way distinctive, and this distinctiveness is itself persuasive. Therefore it is hardly surprising that persuasive language frequently stresses personality. Particularly in functional persuasion (advertising, political argument, the language of law or religion) success is frequently bound up with the way the persuader's personality comes across. Examples of 'celebrity endorsement' abound; to give examples is almost invidious because celebrity itself is so evanescent. Nevertheless, popular figures who are used to sell products include fashion models, sportsmen and women, film stars, actors and comedians. The nature of the product is less significant than the public's level of recognition of the 'face' selling it. Even out of the public domain, we all recognise the importance of projecting ourselves and our personality in exchanges ranging from the professional (such as teacher/pupil, doctor/patient, social worker/client) to the everyday (service encounters, chats with neighbours and with friends). To sum up: any interaction involving spoken or written persuasion will inevitably start with the communication of personality or image (though the persuader may subsequently modify it, as circumstance and audience dictate).

Stance

Aristotle's view of the orator's personality has been extended today as a result of the media explosion which, according to the 1960s cult book *The Gutenberg Galaxy*, has reduced the world to a 'global village' (McLuhan, 1962: 31). Our opening 'freeze-frame' of the orator still remains the initiating point of the persuasive process. But what of the other side of the persuasive interaction? We shall now look at a second, corresponding set of 'freeze-frames', this time of the audience, as they respond with amusement, cynicism, distrust, unqualified enthusiasm or thoughtfulness to the selected mode of persuasion. Their initial response and ultimate assessment will be substantially affected by what they recognise as the persuader's stance, as much as by 'personality' or 'image'. We might say to a friend making a case for some cause, '*Now* I know where you stand!' We have recognised their stance whether we agree with it or not.

However impressive the personality of a persuader, his or her attitude or stance will be crucial. Stance can be defined in a variety of ways. As we shall see in Chapter 4, a persuader defines his or her position by taking a stand on an *issue*, and by observing the key principle of *kairos* (or timeliness). This means being aware of the current state of opinion, and of any immediate pressures on the audience. Through a recognition of *kairos* the persuader can establish empathy with an audience and choose what to bring to its attention (see Crowley and Hawhee, 1999: 30–43). Observing *kairos* also requires openness and responsiveness on the part of the persuader, a willingness to work with the audience, and a readiness to change. An interesting study by Lynette Hunter, *Rhetorical Stance in Modern Literature*, explores the subject extensively. She argues that stance expresses not *what* someone believes but *how* he or she believes it, and that this will be conveyed variously in relation to topic and audience (Hunter, 1984: 5). A persuader's stance may be open or closed, firm or indecisive, rigid or flexible. It may be highly structured and disciplined, developing a stage-by-stage process of inter-action like a game of chess in which new moves match changes in the audience's response. It may be unpredictable, disorganised, uncon-trolled, even falling apart. What is certain is that stance is dynamic and very much part of *persuasion as a process*. Michael Billig applauds Quintilian's Principle of Uncertainty – that there can be no fixed rules governing success in persuasion (Quintilian, 1920–2: 288–91; Billig, 1996: 92). Both stress the need for pragmatism, flexibility and adapt-ability in the use of persuasive stance, whether in monologue or dialogue. Lynette Hunter (1984: 14) takes the specific example of polit-ical persuasion, and sees stance as crucial in effecting a 'strategic connection' between individual and community. She distinguishes between 'positive rhetoric' (which reveals value, as the persuader's stance shifts or broadens in response to the audience); and 'negative rhetoric' (which hides value and persuades from a single viewpoint). She argues moreover that *naïveté* towards stance, on the part of an audi-ence, results in something even worse: 'incomplete involvement, lack of rigour and passivity, leading to submission to imposed strategies'. Indeed, she asserts that 'the audience needs to assess stance, to deter-mine the strategy and participate in the values revealed in the manner of its mediation' (Hunter: 1984: 64).

So how is stance achieved? Someone may ask the question: 'Where do you stand in relation to this topic, this issue and this audience?' If this query does not provoke an immediate response (reasoned or intu-itive), we will undoubtedly need to deliberate more carefully on our stance, before seeking to persuade an audience on this particular topic. We may feel justified in adopting an authoritative stance in relation to our audience and refusing to yield a single point; or we might choose to veil our stance in irony before the intended disclo-sure of our real position. We may adopt the kind of stance which Lynette Hunter considers preferable, and interact openly with our audience, indicating our initial position on any topic and the progress of any changes in that position. We may even seek to project a consciously rhetorical personality as part of our stance, such as Radical Questioner, Reviser, Devil's Advocate, Mediator, Moderator, Gadfly (or any one of a dozen other roles). From this idea of 'projec-tion' we can move easily to the next question concerning stance in the persuasive process.

How is stance actually communicated? Billig argues (1996: 165)

that 'humans, through their use of language, possess that most important capability which makes rhetoric possible: the ability to negate'.
This is reflected in the choice of rhetorical language, positive or negative, and explicitly signals stance. When, say, a military force crosses a
frontier uninvited, should that situation be described by commentators
in positive or negative terms? Is it a 'liberation' or a 'rape'? Was the
notorious Brinksmat bullion theft a 'robbery' (police) or a 'heist'
(producer of television programme)? (The producer's choice recalls
Michael Caine's world of entertaining villainy in *The Italian Job*, rather
than the reality of criminal violence.)

Similarly, the communication of a persuader's attitudes will represent their stance on any issue, whether political, religious or ethical.
According to Lynette Hunter, drawing on the example of Plato's
Phaedrus, this is a costly process, a kind of death. True positive rhetoric
open to the audience will always involve a 'giving away of self to realise
other . . . a manifestation of loss' (Hunter, 1984: 64). But what is the
gain? The communication of stance to an audience will surrender the
persuader's pre-existent subjectivity in favour of a fresh intersubjectiv-
ity, as the audience responds to the persuader.

Another helpful way of exploring this aspect of communicating
stance is provided via Stephen Levinson's refinement of Erving
Goffman's concept of 'footing' in discourse (Levinson, 1988). As part
of his or her stance, a persuader may emphasise that s/he represents
certain important interests that include the audience in their benefits;
similarly any negative aspects are downplayed, to avoid any possible
feelings of exclusion being aroused in the audience. In an alternative
tactic, when the persuader is in an empowered position, his or her
stance can convey the threat of exclusion from benefits available to
other people. For example, imagine a head-teacher warning, 'Some of
you haven't been showing the level of commitment required for success
in these examinations.' Stance here is linked to *pathos* and to saving
face. A persuader's stance (whether personal or representing others)
often pre-supposes and plays upon human emotional need, from anxiety about exams to hunger for possessions or people's desire to belong
to whatever group is most fashionable. In many real-life situations,
persuasion may involve concealing or down-playing the interests
behind the persuader; for example, a supermarket chain boasts about its
cost-cutting policy but fails to mention how this benefits itself and
disadvantages its suppliers. Again, persuasion may highlight the interests of others (e.g. 'All our profits from tomorrow's trading will go to
the Children in Need appeal').

(a)   The persuader and the self

Contemporary psychological, political and linguistic theory suggests that the self is socially constructed and evolved. Michael Billig would go further than this; he argues that the self is actually constructed through dialogue and dialectic (implying it is located in language). Another view (that of the Freudian critics Jacques Lacan and Julia Kristeva) proposes that an awareness of subjectivity develops as soon as the child becomes conscious of 'otherness' (Jefferson and Robey, 1986: 151–63, 197–9). If social identity begins with entry into the symbolic world of language, this may indeed be the first use of rhetorical stance, because the language acquired by the growing child constantly defines and redefines its position as 'subject'. And, crucially, the child's experience of the world and of its sense of self is determined by gender. It is impossible to discount the effect of gendered experience (both individual and social) on persuader and audience within the persuasive process. Not only is the persuader's own gender likely to have influenced and be influencing everything from language choice to social attitudes, but the audience (whether mixed sex or single sex) will have equally significant gendered experience. Thus a persuader needs to be aware not only of personal experience and attitudes to gender, but also of the ways in which gender is represented in society/media (e.g. gender stereotyping) as well as the crucial area of gender politics. The stance of the persuader must reflect gendered intelligence and perception in order to ensure that appropriate choices are made to differing audiences. Thus a female persuader addressing a strongly feminist (probably all-female) audience would need to ensure that (regardless of her own gendered experience and attitudes) her persuasive stance was appropriate. Indeed, any persuader, male or female, has to be aware that gender is a crucial dimension of intersubjective communication, and that exploitation of gender stereotypes and sexist attitudes can be a double-edged sword in terms of effective persuasion.

Two other important aspects of identity and 'the self' relevant to persuasive stance include the sociolinguistic variables of age and ideology. Although the age/generation of persuader and audience may seem irrelevant, persuaders need to be aware of the potential dangers of stereotyped and/or agist representations. For example, a 'generation gap' between audience and persuader may create an equally difficult 'credibility gap' unless careful attention is paid to potential problems, and action taken. Intergeneration persuasion can be hugely successful but it doesn't happen unless the persuader attunes his or her stance in relation to the audience. Similarly, the ideology upon which a persuader's sense of self is based will be expressed through stance (unless concealment is preferred). An audience may also have a known (or likely) ideological position, and the persuader will need to take this into account.

Whatever approach is adopted, and whether you are engaged in the kind of profound interaction envisaged by Lynette Hunter, or in a relatively superficial contact for a practical purpose, the persuader's attitude to self will be a key aspect of stance. However, 'just being yourself' is not always the best way to start persuading an audience! Rather, you will need to apply a combination of intuition and calculation to determine how much of your 'real self' should be revealed to others in the interaction – and how far this 'self' should risk challenge or suggest the possibility of change in response to audience and context. Your subsequent strategy may be anything from flattery or convergence to outright confrontation. Having selected what aspect of self to present, the persuader must then decide how much ego and 'personality' to inject into his or her presentation. Whilst an over-impersonal stance will seem chilly and bloodless, an 'ego-trip' or flashy display of personality will be just as repellent. Persuasion must project vitality and intelligence, and as Walter Nash, citing Quintilian, puts it, 'at the heart of all writing is *calor cogitationis* – warmth of thought' (Nash, 1989: 215; Quintilian, 1920–2: IV, 94–5). It is this warmth, energy and exuberance of personality which, appropriately channelled, will assist the persuader, finding expression via changing mood and tone. These moods and tones are an inseparable element in stance and its development; they involve the expression of emotion, ranging from extremes of pity, rage or grief to ironic humour. We shall discuss some of these now, in association with *ethos,* rather than waiting till the next chapter on *pathos.*

(b)   The persuader as humorist

Despite its occasional savagery, humour seems a good example of this particular category of *ethos*-linked emotion. It may suggest a detached, non-serious stance; but since humour is a familiar defuser of tension, it may more properly be seen as a signal of serious shared experience. Because it conveys 'warmth of thought' as an indicator of stance, humour must also (if it is to display real vitality) be an expression of the persuader's own personality. Nash comments that '[in] rhetorical humour, as in all other aspects of rhetoric, there is a compact, a presup-positional understanding, between the beguiler and the beguiled' (1989: 167). This 'compact' may be an agreement to laugh *with* some-one, or to laugh *at* someone; it may involve ironic self-deprecation; or, less obviously, it may be a deliberately misleading 'compact', a carefully prepared salutary shock. An audience might suddenly be brought from laughing at others to the realisation that those 'others' resemble them-selves far too closely for comfort. The persuader might be laughing at them, with the intention of jerking them out of complacency into self-reappraisal. (The persuader's real stance can thus be rather different from his assumed one – a breach of Grice's Maxim of Manner [see the Introduction, above]). Conversely, there is the obvious danger that humour may too readily beguile an audience into accepting unexam-ined propositions. Indeed, a more suspect use of humour (from the perspective of *ethos*) is when a persuader adopts a stance towards an important person or issue which uses stereotyping to deflect more detailed examination.

We must conclude then, that in the context of stance, the persuasive resource of humour requires responsible management.

(c) Persuader and topic

Another problem is posed by what we might term 'risk-taking'. This concerns the topic of the persuasive discourse, and the persuader's stance towards it. Although inconsistency of argument is frequently encountered in rhetorical exchanges (and is only a problem if some-body notices!), inconsistency of stance will expose the persuader to damaging accusations of distortion or hypocrisy. An inability to face the demands of the topic squarely will shed a glaring light on the would-be persuader. To be successful, the persuader must address any potentially negative response from the audience, and deflect it. Another risky way for the persuader to cope with inconsistency of stance is to 'change sides', moving adroitly from criticism to justification, or vice versa. Such a shift of position might either be preplanned, or a sponta-neous reaction to the audience (as described by Lynette Hunter). Nothing can be more persuasive to an audience than the sense that, with the speaker, they are deeply involved in the issue, responding honestly to its demands, and jointly reaching a decision. Risk-taking can have its rewards!

We can now consider the next stage in this study of *ethos* in the persuasive process. We will focus on a third set of 'freeze-frames' of audience and persuader, caught in a moment of vital interaction. What will the persuader do now? Having adopted a stance, will he or she choose to maintain it throughout or make a sudden shift?

(d) Persuader and audience

It should now be clear that an effective orator needs to be on his or her toes all the time; as Cicero urged, he or she will require *ingenium* (creativity), as well as *animus* (spirit or talent) (see Cicero, *De Oratore*, I.xxv.113, cited in Nash, 1989: 211–12. The only assumption he or she can make is that the audience are at least willing to be persuaded, because they are there! In the Introduction we noted Austin's term 'perlocutionary', meaning the use of language to change people's attitudes. The changing of attitudes lies at the heart of all persuasion; Kenneth Burke would argue that this is the vital point, whether the persuadee is in a position to take action on this change, or not (1969: 50). According to Burke, this is achieved when the persuader identifies with his auditor: 'You persuade a man only insofar as you can talk his language by speech, tonality, order, image, attitude, idea, *identifying* your ways with his' (1969: 55). This tallies exactly with our view of persuasive interaction, and provides a timely reminder that such 'identification' may oblige a persuader to adjust, relinquish or diversify his or her own 'ways'.

Plainly, a two-way process occurs between the sender and the receiver of a message. But what Burke describes above as a process of 'identification' between persuader and audience may be more complex. Will the pattern of mutual reflection and balance always be the same? If the person we are seeking to persuade is at the same time seeking to persuade us to a different viewpoint, or if we are addressing an audience which is adjudicating a debate between *two* viewpoints, can there be any direct correspondence? Gordon Wells in his essay 'Language and Interaction' offers a model (1981: 69), which we reproduce here by his kind permission, and which may be of particular interest and assistance, as it focuses on an early example of persuasive interaction. Although Wells is studying mother–child interaction, it is convenient to use this model as a simple 'base line' version of adult persuasive interaction.

The Sender/Message/Receiver figure below (Figure 1) is a more complex version of the Saussure/Jakobson model of communication described in the Introduction. It clearly demonstrates the crucial status and position of *topic* in the relationship between persuader and persuadee. Topic provides purpose and creates coherence. The figure also shows how important orientation is in relation to the immediate context of the message as well as the audience's state of mind. The first necessity is that the message should be understood within its context, with expectations of sender and receiver governed by similar *schemata* (as we will show in Chapter 3). In addition, the persuader's orientation towards the audience (which we call stance) will reflect his or her assumptions about that audience. Are we talking down to them, pleading for their help and forbearance, or consulting them as equals?

You will notice that the situations of Sender and Receiver in the figure are similarly patterned, except for an important reversal of over-all direction. Even so, a figure can only represent in a rather drawn-out way what happens in a split second of discourse; and it is approximate in other respects. As Wells is quick to point out (1981: 64), 'it seems unlikely that such a simple, uni-directional model accurately describes what typically occurs'. Compare the relatively straightforward attitude of the mother as Receiver (working hard to understand her child's imperfect communication), with the selective listening of a Receiver more interested in preparing to argue back. Yet more problematic is the situation in which an audience is listening to a debate, and is subject to the contradictory attempts by each persuader to 'talk their language – complicating the process of decoding the messages from both sides.

We must remind ourselves that the most basic features of language have an important part to play in persuasion: they lay the foundations of meaning and human contact. How can the persuader convey his personality and stance most effectively to the persuadee? We will turn to Halliday's theory of language function (see the Introduction) to establish some further criteria that the persuader must observe. First of all, persuasion must fulfil the *ideational* function by using language directly related to the audience's experience. At the same time the *inter-personal function* (linking the sender and the receiver) should be clearly signalled, perhaps through the frequent use of personal pronouns and modal verbs ('I *would* argue . . . *you will* agree . . . *we should*'). The pronouns map out the degrees of distance between persuader and persuadee and reflect changes in that distance; and the use of modal verbs provides emphasis, conveying the speaker's identification with the audience and respect for their judgement. Other grammatical features (such as verb tense, syntax, word order and variation in sentence type) will lend *textual* cohesion and coherence to the persuasion. The dialectic of persuasion, as modelled in Wells's diagram, is now established.

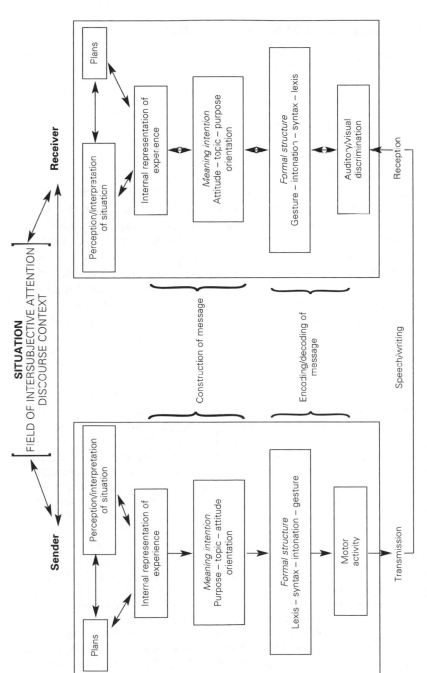

Figure 1 A model of the communication situation

Personality and Stance in Practice

(a) Functional persuasion

All four extracts below focus specifically on the *ethos* of the persuader, though the audiences differ, and we use them to show how the two-way process of persuasion works.

(i) Demosthenes

These extended extracts (necessary to demonstrate the complex presentation of *ethos*) are from a speech by the famous Greek orator Demosthenes to the Athenians, who are being threatened by Macedonian imperialism (1970: 188–9, 198). (Differences between the original Greek and the translator's English are unlikely to distort our impression of Demosthenes' persuasive techniques.) An Athenian himself, Demosthenes wants to arouse the people to action; his patriotism and loyalty to the state (ideology) shine through; later in the speech he will propose the financing of an expeditionary force against Philip of Macedon, in which he intends to be a volunteer.

First, then, we must not be downhearted at the present situation, however regrettable it seems. . . . The fact is that it is plain dereliction of duty on our part which has brought us to this position. . . . Why mention this? To set this fact firmly before your minds, gentlemen, that if you are awake, you have nothing to fear, if you close your eyes, nothing to hope for. . . . [*He goes on to point out their enemy, Philip, has learned far more from the exemplary political wisdom and courage shown by Athens in the past, than they have themselves.*] If then, this country is prepared to adopt a similar outlook and to break with the past, if every man is ready to take the post which his duty and his abilities demand in service to the state, and set pretences aside, if financial contribution is forthcoming from the well-to-do, and personal service from the appropriate group, in a word, if we are prepared to be ourselves, to abandon the hope to evade our duty and get it done by our neighbours, we shall recover what is our own with God's will, we shall regain what inertia has lost us, and we shall inflict retribution upon Philip. You must not imagine that he is a super-human being whose success is unalterably fixed. He has enemies to hate, fear and envy him, even in places very friendly to him. But now all this is beneath the surface. It has nowhere to turn because of the slowness, the inactivity of Athens. . . . When are we to act? What is to be the signal? When compulsion drives, I suppose. Then what are we to

say of the present? In my view the greatest compulsion that can be laid
on free men is their shame at the circumstances in which they find
themselves. . . .
    I have never elected to seek public favour by policies which I did not
believe expedient. On this occasion too I have spoken simply and bluntly
without reservation. . . . May the decision be one which will prove best
for us all.

The presentation of the orator's *personality* is that of a patriotic, loyal
and rational citizen, who wishes to take action to benefit his fellow
Athenians. Demosthenes is careful to identify with them, even when
attacking their inertia, and describes himself as speaking 'simply and
bluntly', a man who is risking unpopularity for his plain speaking. How
does Demosthenes' choice of language communicate this? An obvious
way of seeing how a persuasive text presents the self is to examine the
use of first, second and third person forms, whether in verbal inflexions
or in pronouns. Just prior to the first extract 'I' was used frequently, as
he modestly justifies speaking first. (He implies nevertheless that if they
had listened to him earlier, this speech would not have been necessary!)
The sub-text is 'listen to me and take my advice, and the outcome will
be favourable for you'. More significant for the ultimate purpose of the
speech (and reflective of his *stance*) is Demosthenes' use of the first
person plural pronouns and adjectives. He immediately identifies
himself ideologically with his audience: '*we* must not be downhearted
. . . *our* part . . . if *we* are prepared to be *ourselves* . . . *our* neighbours
. . . *we* shall regain what inertia has lost *us*.' This pattern continues till
the final words of the whole speech: 'May the decision be one which
will prove best for *us all*.' Demosthenes' persuasion depends on standing alongside his audience, recognising common problems and thereby
urging common action. His stance expresses the patriotism they all
share, as he tests the depths and intensity of their commitment.
Interestingly, he makes careful use of the second person when he wishes
to make a point strongly: 'if *you* are awake, *you* have nothing to fear: if
you close *your* eyes. . . . *You* must not imagine that [Philip] is a super-
human being . . .'. And only when confronting his audience with the
ultimate demands of their citizenship and of their situation and showing the penalty of failure, does Demosthenes use the fully detached,
objective third person pronoun: '*his* duty and *his* abilities . . . *their*
shame at the circumstances in which *they* find *themselves*'. At this
moment of critical choice he identifies himself with his hearers by using
the pronoun 'we', and by inviting them to think about what this

implies. If they take the honourable rather than the shameful course of action, he assures them that they will win. Demosthenes' repeated 'big If' pressures each hearer not to exclude himself from an enterprise to which each individual is impelled both by reason and emotion. Paradoxically the very confidence voiced by Demosthenes is based on his citation of Philip of Macedon's political astuteness (which Philip had learned from Athens, as it was in the past). Now Athens must learn from him, says Demosthenes. The cool logic of his stance becomes far more impressive as a consequence, and adds further force to the emotion.

Not only pronominal usage but also lexical choice can be used to convey the orator's personality and stance, and although this is a translation from Greek, we assume a reasonable semantic equivalence. Demosthenes often chooses the typical hedges of casual conversation: 'I suppose . . .', 'In my view . . .' etc. By using modal verbs and subjunctives to suggest potential action, Demosthenes presents himself to his audience in a friendly and positive way. Negative vocabulary reflects the sorry state of affairs in Athens ('downhearted . . . regrettable . . . dereliction of duty . . . inactivity . . . shame') but is not damning since he so wholeheartedly identifies with his fellow Athenians. Stirring words then appear to counteract the negative tone and promise hope: 'best hope for the future . . . awake . . . nothing to fear . . . recover again . . . inflict retribution . . .'.

In this oration Demosthenes needs to present his personality – and arguments – in a highly positive light. He must also convey to the Athenians a willingness to assume a stance alongside them. Even so, he retains the option of ironic or authoritative detachment, as he sees fit. With remarkable skill, the great Athenian orator manipulates *ethos* to change the attitude and behaviour of his audience.

(ii)   Toshiba advertisement

The *visual* impact of this advertisement, closely associated with the *printed* text (which we reproduce here by permission) is of major importance in accounting for its effectiveness. Current in the summer of 1989, it was targeted at a business and finance-oriented audience, its freshness and relevance remain undiminished. The picture is of five men and three women who appear to be satisfied customers, by implication endorsing the product. Three men are in business suits (one in late middle age, one in his late thirties, and the other in his early twenties); two are in casual dress (ages about twenty-five and thirty-five).

The women are all young; one wears an executive business suit, one jeans, one a neat sweater and skirt. All are holding variants of the Toshiba portable computer. The photograph parodies a family group, with the three seated figures relatively static: two standing figures with arms extended, displaying the computer; and the other three (respectively standing, perched, and lying down) all making the thumbs-up sign. The picture conveys activity, liveliness and good humour, balancing youthful enthusiasm and mature commitment. Everyone is smiling! This 'family' seems to represent 'you' in the text below, part of the 'First Family' of computers which 'we' (Toshiba) produce:

A typical Toshiba user needs power, speed, portability, and looks like this . . .

We created the world's first, full line-up of powerful, portable computers. Because we know from experience that every user has different uses and needs. So we've designed models ranging from notebook-sized laptops offering the maximum in portability to powerful office portables that are a match for any desktop. Our super-integrated technology makes it possible – giving you less weight, more power, more speed and more choice. We call them the First Family of Portables. And every one is as individual as you are. Call in at your local Toshiba dealer and see which portable computer we've designed for you.

Can a computer firm acquire personality and stance, and, if so, how and why? Toshiba is choosing to present itself as a firm which takes a personal interest in the individual needs of the computer user, and will provide an appropriate range for all needs. By calling the range 'First Family of Portables', Toshiba jokily recalls the American Presidential family; it also personifies the computers, linking each with an individual 'member' in the 'family group' photograph. Hence the company acquires an image of good humour, status and personalised service, which is enhanced by the text. The very first word is the personal pronoun 'We', occurring four times; 'you' also appears nearer to the end, when all the necessary information about the versatility of the range has been conveyed. 'You' is actually the last word of the advertisement, because it is 'you' (the persuadee) who will be initiating the purchase! Skilful pronominal management is used to create the desired effect, together with strongly positive lexis: *world's first, full* line-up of *powerful, portable* computers . . . we know from *experience . . . maximum in portability . . . powerful* office portables . . . *super-integrated technology . . . less weight, more power, more speed, and more choice . . . as individual* as you are . . . we've *designed for* you'. The final phrase expresses the relationship between consumer and producer, and the orientation of the persuasion. All this (implies the advertisement) is what we at Toshiba, your super-efficient, state-of-the-art, friendly, good-humoured computer company has produced for *you,* our interestingly individualised, perceptive and selective audience. This overall strategy has been described by Fairclough (2001) as 'synthetic personalisation'.

Note that in contrast to the Demosthenes extract, there is relatively little blurring of the 'we'/'you' distinction between persuader and persuadee. Using a time-honoured technique of advertising, potential customers see themselves reflected and prefigured by their peers in the picture. The stance is familiar, attentive, complimentary to the intelligence and vitality of the customer, as well as claiming equal merit and reciprocal respect for the company itself. Everyone feels happy – and the computers are sold.

The sentence structure is uncomplicated: the verb tense mostly simple present, the verbs predominantly active and transitive and the imperative (with tactful restraint) appears only twice in the last sentence. All the Hallidayan functions (ideational, interpersonal and textual) are working very nicely together in this piece of persuasive rhetoric, and so are some other devices from the persuasive repertoire, such as figurative imagery (computers personified as a 'Family'), and the schematic devices of repetition and accumulation (all discussed in Chapter 6). However, the vast majority of persuasive devices functioning in this text are focused on personality and stance.

(iii)   Parliamentary language ('unscripted')

We decided to retain this example (printed in *Hansard*, 31 October 1989) from the first edition of this book, because it features Margaret (now Lady)Thatcher, one of the most distinctive voices in British and international politics over the last twenty-five years, in an exchange with a fellow Conservative at Prime Minister's Question Time.

> **Mr Latham**:   While continuing to implement the policies which have been approved by the electorate on three occasions, will my Right Honourable Friend confirm that successful governments must always be responding and listening to the real aspirations of the people?
>
> **The Prime Minister**:   Yes. That is why under the ten-year-old policies of Conservative governments we have created more wealth than

ever before, have spread it more widely than ever before, have a
higher standard of living than ever before, have higher standards of
social services than ever before, and have a higher reputation than
ever before. Yes, we have indeed been listening. I believe that these
are the real aspirations of the British people.

Although we might expect this oral answer to be unscripted, it
plainly isn't. The question has been set up in advance, to allow Mrs
Thatcher to list, in a highly structured way, the achievements of her
government. Although the pronoun 'we' appears only twice, it nevertheless exists as the concealed subject of four other finite verbs ('have
spread', 'have', 'have', 'have'). The Prime Minister identifies with her
government by using 'we' rather than 'I', conveying a corporate identity (rather different from her well-remembered usage in 'we are a
grandmother'). She is addressing the House of Commons where the
majority was at that time heavily in favour of the Conservative Party: it
seems likely that she is encouraging her supporters and defying the
Labour Opposition by alleging substantial success in a number of areas.
The *personality* of the Government is, it appears, caring and public spir-
ited, wealth-creating and sharing, and worthy of international respect.
Its *stance* of confident pride and implicit defiance (communicated to
the House via the Prime Minister) also reflects its stance towards the
nation and the world. Mrs Thatcher anticipates both support and
hostility from her audience. As a consequence this is a particularly
interesting example of a speaker identifying positively *and* negatively
with her audience. (Although we have a female persuader here, her
gender identity is of little significance in establishing her stance, partly
because of her forceful personality, and partly because in the context of
Parliament, the office of Prime Minister has, by definition, authority
and power.)

This polarisation between potential support and hostility in the
party-divided audience is reflected in the language. The Prime Minister
associates strongly positive lexis with her personality (implied) and
stance (and with her party): 'created . . . wealth . . . standard of living .
. . standards of social services . . . reputation . . . real aspirations'.
Significantly, she uses comparative forms five times ('more' twice,
'higher' three times). These are intended to deflate the Opposition's
potential arguments, and at the end of every comparative clause, the
phrase 'than ever before' is repeated four times (*antistrophe* in traditional rhetoric). One imagines the rising note of the Prime Minister's
voice, pitched against the hubbub of the Opposition benches.

Employing a technique that we shall discuss further in Chapter 2, she progressively builds up emotion through this repeated phrase. Her language seems designed simultaneously to goad and to overbear her opponents, and is powerfully interpersonal in function.

(iv)   Political campaigning (USA 2004)

Readers may like to reflect on the differences between the passage above and a recent piece of American political rhetoric. John Kerry was speaking on his adoption as Democratic candidate (29 July 2004) for the forthcoming presidential election. The repetitive structure of this extract is based on *initial* rather than *terminal repetition*. Kerry implicitly criticises and shames the existing administration by reminding his dual audience (Democrat convention delegates and nationwide television viewers) of the current administration's conduct in office. His authoritative stance reconstructs and reaffirms lost values:

> . . . I will have a vice president who will not conduct secret meetings with polluters to rewrite our environmental laws. I will have a Secretary of Defense who will listen to . . . our military leaders. And I will appoint an Attorney General who actually upholds the Constitution of the United States.

Whatever the outcome of the 2004 election, these words will still reflect the time/audience specificity of Senator Kerry's engagement with his audience (i.e. its *kairos* – see, especially, p. 118 below) and his 'take' on the national mood in the summer of that year. In all these different examples of functional persuasion we have made substantial use of Halliday's theories of language function to demonstrate the communication of personality and stance, and in particular the interpersonal function. In the next set of examples of *literary persuasion,* we shall encounter some different ways in which the author accommodates the idea of personality, stance and audience/reader response within literary texts.

(b)   Literary persuasion

The role of personality and stance in a literary text, where persuasion can be hidden or overt, is quite complex. Kenneth Burke (1969: 50) stressed that the persuader's stance communicates attitude ('attitude [is] an incipient act, a leaning or inclination'). In literary persuasion the writer seeks to 'incline' his or her readers to engage with a particular vision, whether of character, situation or event. The persuasion is much more indirect in literary than in functional contexts. Here the narrative voice, chorus/choric figure or poetic 'persona' are typically used to provide the persuasive focus. The three main literary genres (fiction, poetry and drama) all include narrative to some degree. Recently, a number of important theories have been advanced about the functions of narrative, some of which relate specifically to narrative discourse. Instead of focusing entirely on interaction and lexico-grammatical real-isations of language functions, we shall look at narrative discourse in literature from a broader perspective.

Our particular purpose is to identify the characteristics of literary persuasion in relation to personality and stance. Here the relationship between the teller, the tale and the audience is the key one. We are indebted to Professor Nash for letting us use his diagram (1989: 3) slightly modified. It presents very clearly the 'outer' and 'inner' rela-tionships, which seem to characterise literary texts (see Figure 2).

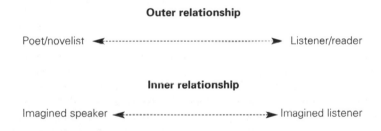

Outer relationship

Poet/novelist ◄--► Listener/reader

Inner relationship

Imagined speaker ◄---------------------------------► Imagined listener

Figure 2   'Inner' and 'outer' relationships between author, text and reader

The actual structure and ordering of literary narrative will be discussed in Chapter 5; in this chapter (because of our chosen focus on personal-ity and stance) we shall concentrate on the way an author presents char-acters within the narrative. Michael Toolan's assertion (1988: 3) that 'to narrate is to make a bid for a kind of power' is important in this context. As a narrative progresses, the narrator gains the reader's 'trust' and becomes a source of authority and powerful persuasion. This can produce an unevenly balanced relationship between author and reader: the narrator may be 'in' his own story (e.g. *David Copperfield*), but may also invite the reader to take an ironic perspective. Again, the reader may be given space to fill in the textual interstices (especially in a fiction such as *Tristram Shandy* where the reader *seems* to have more power than the author himself). So the balance of power between author and reader can be variable, and even deliberately asymmetric.

We shall now turn to our literary examples, anticipating that the features associated with *ethos* in functional persuasion will reappear, modified however by the narrative context.

(i) From Jane Austen, Pride and Prejudice, *vol. II, ch. xi*

In this extract the arrogant Mr Darcy, having (against his better judgement) fallen in love with the witty, beautiful but socially inferior Elizabeth Bennett, makes her a proposal of marriage:

> He sat down for a few moments, and then getting up walked about the room. Elizabeth was surprised, but said not a word. After a silence of several minutes he came towards her in an agitated manner, and thus began,
> 'In vain have I struggled. It will not do. My feelings will not be repressed. You must allow me to tell you how ardently I admire and love you.'
> Elizabeth's astonishment was beyond expression. She stared, coloured, doubted, and was silent. This he considered sufficient encouragement, and the avowal of all that he felt and had long felt for her, immediately followed. He spoke well, but there were feelings besides those of the heart to be detailed, and he was not more eloquent on the subject of tenderness than of pride. His sense of her inferiority – of its being a degradation – of the family obstacles which judgement had always opposed to inclination, were dwelt on with a warmth which seemed due to the consequence he was wounding, but was very unlikely to recommend his suit.
> In spite of her deeply rooted dislike, she could not be insensible to the compliment of such a man's affection, and though her intentions did not vary for an instant, she was at first sorry for the pain he was to receive; till, roused to resentment by his subsequent language, she lost all compassion in anger.   (Austen, 1970: 168)

The very title of the novel suggests the author/narrator's complex ironic stance; this particular passage neatly reflects 'pride' and 'prejudice'. Darcy's reported discourse consists of one short speech, while the rest of the quoted passage is in third person narrative, mainly in the voice of Elizabeth Bennett, whose response ranges from speechless amazement to extreme anger. What is interesting is the way in which Jane Austen manipulates her 'voice'. Sometimes her reported thoughts are heard via internal monologue; at other times Austen will take over the narration, providing ironic distance for the reader: '. . . roused to resentment by his subsequent language, she lost all compassion in anger'.

Persuasion lies at the heart of this passage, and the role of personality and stance is central. Darcy is the initial persuader: his self-presentation, however, demonstrates someone who is uneasy with himself and his situation, indicated by his physical restlessness and lack of linguistic confidence. When he does speak, it is 'in an agitated manner', and the lexis of his proposal reflects this disturbance: 'In *vain* . . . *struggled* . . . will *not* do . . . will *not* be *repressed*'; this tone is only partially counterbalanced by the final noun clause: 'how *ardently I admire* and *love* you'. Darcy's serious failures in understanding are conveyed by his maladroit language, and his offensive assumption that Elizabeth will sympathise with his desire to 'repress' his feelings. The reader, guided by the author in the 'outer' relationship described above, expects him to fail in his persuasion; he does so because he has failed to identify with his 'audience'. Darcy's preoccupation is with himself: and because he is at odds with himself, ruled by the contradictory emotions of pride and love, his *stance* is a failure. Not only is he unable to identify imaginatively with Elizabeth, but he even destroys (at least temporarily) the chance of dialogue with her, by rendering her silent!

In this abortive 'exchange', Darcy's failure as a persuader is directly linked with the *failure of personality and stance*. His 'ardent' love is vitiated by cold arrogance, his candour by insensitivity. Austen conveys this not only by associating him with negative lexis ('inferiority', 'family obstacles', 'degradation'), but also by using oppositional structures. For example, in paragraph 3 we note that 'tenderness' is balanced by 'pride', and 'judgement' by 'inclination'. These oppositions suggest Darcy's emotional confusion, as he risks 'wounding' his 'consequence'. This lexical pattern is continued in paragraph 4, where Elizabeth's 'deeply rooted dislike' is contrasted with her sense of 'the compliment of such a man's affections'. Her emotions, however, gradually change as she moves from being 'sorry for the pain he was to receive' to 'resentment' and 'anger'.

It might be rewarding to analyse the syntactic as well as the lexical structures in the passage: but at this stage it is enough to have identified the reasons for Darcy's failure. Austen has also convinced us to adopt her view of the exchange; in *theory* we are free to dissent, but in practice we are more likely to assent not only to Austen's ironic stance, but also to Elizabeth's angry and alienated one.

(ii)   From Robert Browning, 'My Last Duchess'

This is an extract from a poetic monologue, in which the Duke addresses an envoy from his future wife's father. The Duke has just drawn the ambassador's attention to a portrait of his first Duchess, and as he describes her, it becomes clear to the *reader* that the Duchess's death was not a natural one and that the Duke cannot be sane.

> Sir, 'twas all one! My favour at her breast,
> The dropping of the daylight in the West,
> The bough of cherries some officious fool
> Broke in the orchard for her, the white mule
> She rode with round the terrace – all and each
> Would draw from her alike the approving speech,
> Or blush, at least. She thanked men, – good! But thanked
> Somehow – I know not how – as if she ranked
> My gift of a nine-hundred-years-old name
> With anybody's gift. Who'd stoop to blame
> This sort of trifling? Even had you skill
> In speech – (which I have not) – to make your will
> Quite clear to such an one, and say, 'Just this
> 'Or that in you disgusts me; here you miss,
> 'Or there exceed the mark' – and if she let
> Herself be lessoned so, nor plainly set
> Her wits to yours, forsooth, and made excuse,
> – E'en then would be some stooping; and I choose
> Never to stoop. Oh sir, she smiled, no doubt
> When'er I passed her; but who passed without
> Much the same smile? This grew; I gave commands;
> Then all smiles stopped together.

(Browning, 1940: 318)

This is a poem about the murder by an inordinately proud, jealous and all-powerful husband of a wife who angered him by her simple graciousness to all and sundry. The Duke condemns himself out of his own mouth as the poem progresses and the reader (if not the ambassador in the poem) begins to realise what has happened. Yet the murder is never quite explicit. It is only our reading of the poem which suggests the substance of those 'commands'.

How is the passage to be seen as persuasion? The Duke offers no overt persuasion; he simply assumes the ambassador's understanding and admiration, unconcerned that the conversation will certainly be reported. This suggests a quite extraordinary carelessness about the impression he is making. The distorted 'inner relationship' between the Duke and the ambassador within the poem thus contributes powerfully to Browning's persuasive shaping of our attitude towards the Duke. It adds to the mounting evidence in the text that the Duke has been driven insane by his pride and egoism. By filling in the interstices, the audience reaches this fearsome conclusion. Unlike the Austen passage, the readers in this text are more active in their 'outer relationship' with the text than is the faceless ambassador, listening passively (inside the text) to the Duke.

Browning achieves this by his brilliant manipulation of personality and stance in the presentation of the Duke, using the format of dramatic monologue, with all its complexities. Evidently relishing the challenge of recreating spoken discourse, he shows remarkable skill in handling the 'voice' of the Duke.

In order to communicate personality, Browning uses appropriate lexis to show the Duke's frightening arrogance and anger when he refers to '*My favour . . . My gift* of a *nine-hundred years old name*'; asks 'who'd stoop . . .?'; refers to his '*disgust*'; and at last says chillingly 'I gave *commands.*' Stance is conveyed indirectly; as the Duke recalls disdainfully what trivial pleasures delighted his wife (the 'dropping of the daylight in the West' or 'The bough of cherries'), the reader is attracted by what disgusted him. Our stance is a thousand miles from his. Furthermore, his disintegrating reason is reflected in the increasingly complex syntax, his eloquent use of rhetorical questions serving only to demonstrate his total separation from common humanity.

In this poem we see a different use of personality and stance, with the reader/audience playing an unusually active part in the persuasive interaction. What dominates the poem is the figure of the Duke and, above all, his voice. The irony of the whole poem is that Browning uses his character's eloquence to persuade us not of the justness of his actions, but of his criminal insanity.

(iii)   From J. D. Salinger, The Catcher in the Rye

This is the opening of a novel about a troubled adolescent boy from the East Coast prep-school culture in America:

> If you really want to hear about it, the first thing you'll probably want to know is where I was born, and what my lousy childhood was like, and how my parents were occupied and all before they had me, and all that David Copperfield kind of crap, but I don't feel like going into it. In the

first place, the stuff bores me, and in the second place, my parents would have about two haemorrhages apiece if I told anything pretty personal about them. They're quite touchy about anything like that, especially my father. They're *nice* and all – I'm not saying that – but they're also touchy as hell. Besides, I'm not going to tell you my whole goddam autobiography or anything. I'll just tell you about this madman stuff that happened to me around last Christmas before I got pretty run-down and had to come out here and take it easy.   (Salinger, 1958: 5)

The entire narrative is in the first person; not surprisingly, the personality and stance of Holden Caulfield constitute the central interest of the novel. What is appealing about Holden is his fragile sense of self, his refusal to conform to meaningless rules, and his hatred of 'phonies'. The narrative is addressed as if to a sympathetic listening friend, though the age group of the audience is not entirely clear.

The author has the difficult task of writing as if he were a seventeen-year-old boy, who is 'good at English'. He also has to narrate events, indicate Holden's psychological turmoil, and provide a fresh penetrating critique of American society and its hypocrisies. In this world of adult corruption Holden is the innocent abroad, who despite flunking out of school and being a 'terrible liar' is a more loving and generous person than the people who condemn him.

In the opening paragraph Salinger has to persuade us to be interested in Holden, to like him, to sympathise with him, to find him amusing, and (most importantly) to identify with him. Does Salinger succeed? Before deciding that, we should look at the ways in which personality and stance are communicated. Holden's stance is guarded: he's only going to tell us what he chooses, and he refuses to say much about his parents. At the same time he trusts his listener enough to reveal his pent-up nervousness, conveyed by the tentativeness of the opening conditional clause. It is a very long sentence, but most of it tumbles out in a continuous stream of co-ordinating clauses ('and . . . and . . . but'). As Holden gains confidence in his narrative stance, he uses progressively fewer complex sentence structures, and the conditional tense changes to the more definite future tense: 'I'll just tell you.' His stance towards the listening audience (for the readers are consistently addressed as if they were listeners) becomes more personal and confiding as he explains about his parents. Like the Ancient Mariner, he has succeeded both in gaining the audience's attention, and also in persuading them to identify with him.

Is this achieved just by the sentence structure and syntactic variation already noted? It is perhaps also due to the disarming adolescent slang (for which Salinger plainly has an excellent ear) which signals Holden's rebellion. He talks about his *'lousy* childhood' and 'all that David Copperfield kind of *crap*', exaggeratedly alleging 'my parents would have *about two haemorrhages* apiece . . . touchy *as hell* . . . my *whole goddam* autobiography'. The effect of this hyperbole (see Chapter 6), together with the colloquial usage, is to persuade the audience of two things: his honesty and his vulnerability.

It also locates Holden's stance far closer to his listening audience than his 'touchy' parents. His vulnerability is also conveyed by the repetition of conversational fillers, indicating uncertainty ('. . . and all . . . and all . . . or anything'), as well as defensive parenthesis ('– I'm not saying that –'). This opening paragraph also provides clear illustration of the Hallidayan interpersonal language function, crucial to the whole novel; note that the second word is 'you'. By the end of this paragraph the reader/'listener' is persuaded to a relationship of sympathy and interest with Holden, achieved by Salinger's skilful handling of *ethos*.

Conclusion

In the examples above, we have demonstrated some of the resources of personality and stance available to the speaker and writer when seeking to persuade. It is clear that the way in which the persuader addresses his or her audience is by no means as straightforward as might have been previously assumed. By referring to the sections above, readers should feel confident that they can apply the concepts of personality and stance to the analysis of persuasive texts, and can experiment with different approaches to an audience. Such approaches can range from the immediately practical 'real-time' encounter, to addressing (and thus constructing) the 'implied reader' of a literary text. Readers may ask themselves whether, for example, they would need to start on a personal note with a particular audience. Or should they jump in quickly with a topical reference? Or perhaps they need to begin by setting out some major political or ethical concept? Another question may be whether humour is appropriate, and how it should be used (persuaders may too easily assume that a serious topic automatically precludes any humorous angle). A further concern for persuaders is whether to disguise their real attitudes in engaging with a group of listeners or readers whose known or suspected views differ widely from their own. *Flexibility* has to be the watchword for persuaders, and is entirely consistent with the validity of the principles we have outlined above, which remain more or less unchanged since the time of Demosthenes.

In Chapter 2 we shall look at the ways emotional engagement (*pathos*) is used to enhance and strengthen persuasion.

Further Exploration: the Theory and Practice of *Ethos*

Readers may like to consider Lynette Hunter's distinction between positive and negative rhetoric. This is based on her conviction that meaning is socially constructed and that stance is thus intrinsic to meaning. Relevant texts to explore in this context include the political propaganda of Hitler's regime (see, for example, MacArthur, 1996: 477–80) and any current examples of extremist or fundamentalist rhetoric.

Another topic to investigate is the idea of exclusion and inclusion as elements in the projection of stance. Here Levinson's work on production and reception roles in discourse is relevant (see, for example, Levinson, 1988; R. Cockcroft, 2004). A further topic to explore is the relation between stance and logical argument. In order to do this readers will need to look at Chapters 3 and 4 below, before returning to the key question that concerns the relationship of the *ethos* 'proof' and the *logos* 'proof'. Relevant texts to explore in this context would include feature articles of comment and analysis (cf. broadsheet papers) or didactic passages in contemporary fiction, poetry or drama.

Finally, readers may be interested in exploring the relationship of stance to the *pathos* 'proof' when they have read Chapter 2 below. A striking instance of the handling of emotion (and the lack of it) in relation to authorial and narrative stance can be seen in Mark Haddon's novel *The Curious Incident of the Dog in the Night Time* (2004).

2 *Pathos* and Emotional Engagement

Introduction: Making Emotion Work

The fact that speakers and writers deliberately play on the emotions of their audiences cannot be escaped, and this helps to explain the traditional distrust of rhetoric and its association with insincerity, irrationality and rabble-rousing. Yet it would be odd if people seeking to persuade did not appeal to the audience's emotions! Inevitably, how we 'feel' about an issue combines emotional response with rational and logical judgement. The contradictory assumption is that emotion tends to distort the truth of our perceptions; the real question is whether we can tell the difference between emotion which clouds an issue and emotion which illuminates and deepens our understanding of it. For Augustine the emotion is truthful when the will is properly focused; for Melanchthon, the specific emotion of faith, implanted in the heart, serves to achieve this focusing, whilst prompting the mind to form correct judgements. Contemporary researchers into human consciousness (including psychologists, philosophers, neurologists and linguists) ascribe an equally high truth-value to emotion. For instance, Professor Antonio Damasio argues that humans cannot think properly unless, as a prior condition, they also *feel* (Damasio, 1999). Similarly, William Downes proposes that every new perception, whether it is sensory or cognitive, will be registered simultaneously through intuition, through evaluation and through emotion (Downes, 2000: 102–5).

Whatever degree of emotion is involved in a new perception, we can still have problems in communicating what we feel. This is especially true when engaging with people whose ideas and feelings are (at least initially) alien to our own, compared with the sharing of emotions within established relationships or familiar contexts. Such familiar experiences provide a starting-point for our discussion in this chapter. In exploring the achievement of effective emotional engagement or *pathos*, we shall build on points already made about the functioning of personality and stance in persuasion. We shall analyse this Aristotelian concept of *pathos* in two stages, and will make further use of our 'freeze-frame' technique to sharpen our perception of each stage.

The first stage, before emotion can be communicated by a persuader, requires an appropriate orientation between persuader, topic and audience (we assume that an appropriate persuasive stance is already developing). In the second stage, there must be an *actualisation* of the emotion by the persuader, who needs to arouse in an audience emotions of appropriate intensity, clarity and sharpness of focus. We shall examine the extent to which these stages of emotional engagement are interdependent, using brief examples from functional and literary persuasion, and concluding with some more detailed discussion of examples of successful 'emotional engagement'.

Emotion: Universal and Contingent

What is 'emotion', and how do we harness and set it to work in our persuasion? How, indeed, can we reach a practical understanding of something we all recognise but find hard to define? Further to Damasio's claim that we are incapable of thought unless we can feel, William Downes argues in his discussion of emotion's role in 'felt experience' that feeling must always be accompanied by two other spontaneous processes: *evaluation* and *intuition*. As we feel an emotion, we evaluate on the 'scales of positive and negative' what is happening; at the same time we experience 'a felt urge' to intuit its place within our linguistic scheme of things (Downes, 2000: 102). The felt emotion reflects 'the reality . . . presuppose[d by] our semiotic systems' (meaning the various systems of signs, verbal and non-verbal, through which we make sense of our lives).

Downes's concept of intuition involves several types of instantaneous mental process which include generalisation, deduction and analogy (2000: 105). We have all seen in films such as *West Side Story* or the more recent *William Shakespeare's Romeo + Juliet* what happens when some low-status gang members recognise members of a rival gang in the street. Emotions will range from anxiety or fear to angry hostility, according to their intuitive assessment of personal risk or potential victory. Indeed, any casual street or supermarket encounter can prompt instinctive categorisation of a stranger accompanied by a spurt of positive or negative emotion. (Such a reaction may well disappear when we get a better look at the 'stranger' and respond more rationally.)

Undoubtedly, emotion is the 'raw material' of rhetoric, because without real (or simulated) emotion, effective persuasion is unlikely to take place, whatever the issue involved. The emotions most intrinsic to our various experiences include anger, pity, pride, shame, love, hate, hope, fear, envy, greed, aggression, emulation, vengefulness, indignation, scorn, disgust, admiration, jealousy and generosity. Downes (2000: 101ff.) shares the common perception that emotion as it occurs is conditioned by social experience. Nevertheless, when out of control, emotion can threaten society as well as the individual.

Before developing this further, we must differentiate between *universal* and *contingent* (i.e. socially conditioned) emotion. Such a distinction is vital from the viewpoint of the persuader, with his or her need to evaluate the audience's situation and prepare accordingly. Both kinds of emotion are located along a kind of emotional continuum, but whereas universal emotion connotes emotions common to humanity in general (e.g. joy, sorrow, anger, fear, disgust), contingent emotion connotes their socially constructed manifestation (e.g. acquisitiveness, pride, pity, benevolence, contempt, aggression, indignation, guilt). Both universal and contingent emotions are coloured by what is most or least valued within particular cultures, and are specific to particular societies and historical periods.

From the rhetorical viewpoint, all emotions involve an implicit element of binary opposition (love/hate: courage/fear: joy/grief). Such oppositional patterns repeat and reflect the dialogic structure (*logos/anti-logos*) which Billig described as central to all persuasive rhetoric (see the Introduction). Here we see the structuring importance of emotion within the persuasive process. Nevertheless this binary or dialogic tension is modified by cultural norms (primarily designed to reinforce positive emotions). For instance, major religious festivals are, within their associated cultures, expected to lift the spirits and strengthen the bonds between people, even for those inheritors of the culture who no longer practice the religion. (Indeed, for the majority of the British population, anyone who experiences or communicates the 'opposite' emotions of misery or hatred over the period of Christmas may well feel a complete social outcast.)

Another way of describing universal emotion is to define it as a response to major life experiences (birth, death, religious conversion, love) even though to some extent individual emotion will be affected by gender and ideology. In contrast we can examine an example of contingent or socially constructed emotion – the emotion of 'generosity'. Deriving from Latin, the English word is associated with actions or objects reflecting or characterising an individual of noble birth (Latin accusative form *generositatem*). This link with noble birth has been lost today, apart from when it is applied to a 'generous' action tainted by condescension, as in the Victorian stereotype of the 'Lady Bountiful'. The word evokes a bond seen at its most intense in the relationship between lord and thane in Anglo-Saxon society, and represented by the ceremonial distribution of rich rewards for service. Then, public sharing of wealth implied mutual loyalty and commitment; now, 'generosity' reflects the warmth and self-giving of individuals.

Social history may also be relevant when assessing the function of emotion (universal or contingent) in any persuasive text. We cannot assume that a modern audience will reproduce the same emotional response to a text as its first auditors or readers. This will depend not only on the nature of society, but also on the status of emotion within that society. As we noted in the Introduction, eighteenth-century Augustan culture appealed pre-eminently to reason, and the more extreme forms of emotion and emotional expression were suspect. In contrast, the Romantic period tended to exalt emotion as valuable in its own right. As a consequence in the context of persuasion, the relative status of *logos* and *pathos* differed significantly in the Augustan and Romantic periods. In Augustan literature, the writer's approach to a topic would normally be governed by reason and a sense of natural and social order, before emotion was called upon. The trained and refined 'sentiment' mentioned earlier valued sympathy, but shunned painful expressions of feeling. Emotion was employed via 'vivacious' or 'sublime' imagery to ensure that (one way or another) pleasure predominated. The Romantics, on the other hand, were prepared to engage directly with an issue through emotion. This is famously illustrated in a stanza from Keats's 'Ode on Melancholy', in which the poet advises on ways of coping with this most characteristic 'Romantic' emotion:

> But when the melancholy fit shall fall
>   Sudden from heaven like a weeping cloud,
> That fosters the droop-headed flowers all,
>   And hides the green hill in an April shroud;
> Then glut thy sorrow on a morning rose,
>   Or on the rainbow of the salt sand-wave,
>   Or on the wealth of globèd peonies;
> Or if thy mistress some rich anger shows,
>   Imprison her soft hand, and let her rave,
>   And feed deep, deep upon her peerless eyes.
>   (Keats, 1970: 539–40)

Through the identification and expression of the emotion, and by exploring the oppositions of pain and pleasure, Keats enables us to experience melancholy to the full by actualising it. (Later in the chapter we shall be looking in more detail at the process of actualisation.) An explanation for the fact that 'Ode on Melancholy' retains its appeal after nearly two centuries may be because the poem conveys universal rather than contingent emotion, despite changed social attitudes to women.

What is the cultural status of emotion in society today? In the texts to be discussed shortly we can use our distinction between universal and contingent emotions to demonstrate how important it is. Both kinds of emotion operate within functional and literary persuasion, and both are integral to the persuasive process. Opinions differ about whether the 'universal' or 'empathetic' emotions are the only reliable means of emotive persuasion. Professor Nash (1989: 31) sees universal emotion as best suited to literary persuasion or formal discourse (e.g. a speech by Abraham Lincoln or an Epistle by St Paul). Where contemporary culture is concerned, he suggests that the rhetoric of advertising ultimately debases the imagery it draws on, particularly if associated with 'universal' emotions (ibid., p. 31). A recent example of this is the crescendo of Handel's Coronation Anthem, 'Zadok the Priest', being used to advertise luxury cruises. However, the company commissioning the cruise advertisement might defend this (once the music is combined with visual imagery) as a legitimate arousal of contingent emotion rather than a debasement of the universal emotions of hope and joy.

Emotion and Prejudice

It should now be clear that our emotional engagement with any topic, occasion and audience is culturally conditioned. The way we use emotion in persuasion will demonstrate how skilfully we can handle any audience's response, but it will also expose any prejudices of our own (i.e. generalisations and expectations about people, objects or recurring situations, derived uncritically from our culture). Our prejudices lead us to slot particular people (together with their ideologies and ethnicity) into positive or negative categories, and to make snap judgements based on preconceptions, or (reversing this) to generalise on the basis of an individual encounter. Even worse, on trivial evidence such as dress, accent or eating habits we tend to misidentify and stereotype people we meet! Rhetoric which does not examine the evidence is a primary means of reinforcing such prejudices.

But how important is the link between prejudice and emotional engagement? Here we make a key distinction between 'prejudice' and 'bias', sometimes linked as cause and effect, but always comprising two different categories because bias is broader and more inclusive than prejudice. We may be biased as a result of prejudice; but even so it is not the exclusive cause of bias. For most people, bias is inevitable and may even be admirable. It is typically expressed in the remark 'I'm inclined to think *x* about *y*', suggesting that the speaker is likely to adopt a particular attitude in the light of his or her own observation and that of other people. It is a considered view, yet remains *open* to argument. Prejudice, on the other hand tends to *shut down* argument and rely on established emotional associations. Coping with our own and other people's prejudices can be a disconcerting experience, because emotion as well as reason is involved. An example of this would be a casual remark from a friend expressing a partly shared prejudice. There are several possible responses. Do we just go along with their prejudice without bothering to argue? Do we try to go one better and exaggerate agreement? Or do we ask ourselves how we should really be feeling about the subject of that remark, having recognised our own prejudice embodied in someone else? Will our prejudice become stronger, or will it (after rational reflection) moderate into bias? Another interesting dimension of bias to be discussed in more detail later is the fact that opposing sets of emotions, evaluations and intuitions can co-exist within the mind. This can lead to greater open-mindedness and willingness to change.

Nevertheless, addressing and/or confronting prejudice and emotion in the audience is likely to be an important first step for any persuader in the public domain. The next step will be to reveal alternative viewpoints and their associated emotions and to invite reassessment, enabling the audience to respond with real conviction. Such an audience response is based on understanding, not merely on emotion. Indeed, Aristotle would argue that understanding both controls and focuses emotion as well as intensifying it.

The Orientation of Emotion

The concept of persuasion as an interactive process has already been discussed in some detail. We shall return to the 'Sender/Receiver' model explored in Chapter 1, and use it to investigate a further important aspect of emotional engagement, the orientation of a persuasive text. According to this version of the Formalist model, every message communicated between sender and receiver involves three further elements in addition to those already mentioned: *contact* (psychological or physical), *context* (recognised by both sender and receiver) and *code* (means of expression) (Hawkes, 1977: 116–22). Look again at the diagram first seen in the Introduction:

'addresser' > 'message/context/contact/code' > 'addressee'

Depending on the emphasis of the message, its orientation and function will be focused on one of these six elements. Is this model helpful in our understanding of the role of emotion in persuasion? All persuasive language is conative by definition, since it is oriented to the audience. The diagram below usefully illustrates a hierarchy of function within the persuasive process.

    Phatic ------------>
                        Emotive ----------------->
    Metalingual ------>   ---------> Conative
                        Referential --------------->
    Poetic ------------>

Persuasion involves the sender/persuader as well as the receiver/persuadee, so the emotive function is vital; and because persuasion must have a topic and an issue, the referential function is equally important. (We shall leave the other three functions in the diagram for later examination.) The balance of emotive and referential functions can vary. Inclined one way, the audience *agrees* with the persuader but is not *moved* to act or change its view. Inclined the other way, they *sympathise* with him or her, but see no *grounds* for a decisive response. For example, Demosthenes wanted both agreement and action from his Athenian audience, because if they accepted his arguments they would immediately prepare a task force against Philip of Macedon. The concept of orientation will prove its usefulness when we look in detail at some more examples of persuasion.

Actualisation

(a)   Graphic vividness

Our next question is how exactly does the persuader use emotion to move his audience? It seems to be a matter of representation and perception, whether achieved conceptually, or by evoking sense impressions and using what Quintilian (1920–2: II, 434–5) calls *enargeia* ('clarity' or 'vividness' in Greek). *Enargeia* describes the quality lent to rhetoric by the imaginative and emotional engagement of the persuader with some key aspect of the topic. Quintilian repeats and reinforces Cicero's view that before we can move others to emotion we should feel it ourselves. To achieve this desirable effect through *enargeia*, skilled orators such as Cicero used their imagination (*fantasia*) to create pictures for the audience in which emotion was inherent. If Cicero was pleading a case in court on the issue of fact (e.g. whether or not a man accused of murder committed that crime, either in person or using a hired assassin), he would wish to make the deed more real in the minds of the jury by emphasising its horrific nature. This would involve the use of graphic language (appealing directly to the senses) to recreate the scene. Quintilian's own illustration of this in the passage quoted below is certainly vivid, even gruesome:

> I am complaining that a man has been murdered. Shall I not bring before my eyes all the circumstances which it is reasonable to imagine must have occurred . . .? Shall I not see the assassin burst suddenly from his hiding-place, the victim tremble, cry for help, beg for mercy, or turn to run? Shall I not see the fatal blow delivered and the stricken body fall? Will not the blood, the deathly pallor, the groan of agony, the death-rattle, be indelibly impressed upon my mind?

It would be hard not to respond with horror to this powerful actualisation of emotion, even in this summary form. We can only imagine what its impact would be in the heightened atmosphere of the court room, delivered with appropriate tone of voice, facial expression and body language.

(b) Emotive abstraction

In public oratory, abstract concepts with strongly positive or negative connotations such as liberty, justice, dishonour and tyranny are frequently used. These words reflect communal experience, common values and common aspiration, and when skilfully managed in an appropriate context, will arouse powerful emotions in an audience. But note that whenever we use one of these abstractions, we are arousing emotion through a conceptual process. Whether implicitly or explicitly, we are making a logical argument. If, for example, we protest 'this act would be an infringement of liberty', we imply a further premise or proposition, i.e. that liberty is a condition essential to human life. If we refer to the categories of Schema theory (Schank, 1982), we will recognise liberty as a 'life theme', one of those networks of ideas most central to ourselves and our purposes that establish our long-term or immediate goals (see p. 217 below). It follows, then, that in the example cited above, liberty becomes an 'achievement goal' for all legislators and all responsible citizens. In traditional rhetoric, this further (implicit) premise is a 'commonplace' (i.e. an unchallenged belief providing a foundation for argument and for its emotional appeal). Aristotle shows how such arguments worked in fourth-century Athenian society. He characterises those emotions that had particular social resonance for a male-dominated urban democracy. Recalling Downes's processes of 'evaluation' and 'intuition', both anger and hatred can, for instance, be stirred by invoking abstractions. In the second book of his *Rhetoric* Aristotle claims that 'men are angry with those who speak ill of . . . things which they themselves consider of the greatest importance; for instance if a man speaks contemptuously of philosophy' (1926: 180–1). Moving on to discuss hatred, Aristotle notes the kinds of categorisations that trigger this emotion ('everyone hates a thief or an informer'[1926: 200–1]); familiar to us are similarly emotive categorisations such as 'homophobe' and 'paedophile'. In both cases the emotion of anger or hatred is aroused whenever someone is perceived to belong to the class concerned. But if it can be demonstrated that a particular categorisation has been wrongly applied to the person concerned, the negative emotion promptly evaporates.

(c)   Communication

Persuaders must either feel (or imagine they feel) the emotion they wish to arouse in their audience, whether they achieve this by using graphic lexis, abstract categorisation, figurative language, or any combination of the above. But nobody should assume that their attempt to actualise emotion will necessarily persuade the audience; it might just as easily charm, repel, amuse, enrage or simply bore them. The vital connection depends on the persuader's ability to predict people's likely emotional response and willingness to engage with the persuasion. Interestingly, this confirms our point about the social context of emotion; people can be deeply affected in one age by emotional stimuli that may leave another age unmoved or provoke quite contrary responses (such as ridicule).

Despite these provisos, the persuader needs to use actualisation (graphic or abstract) when arousing and exploiting emotion, whether the emotion is universal or contingent, tragic or trivial. As we would expect, certain features of structure and style will be integral to this process. Professor Nash demonstrates convincingly how the arousal of feeling involves the use of argument and repetition (1989: pp. 29–53); and it is through these means, together with associated stylistic patterns such as antithesis and rhythmic structures, that a powerful emotional interaction is established between persuader and audience (see Chapter 6 and Appendix B). Below are two examples of the actualisation of emotion, one representing literary and the other functional persuasion.

(d)   Actualisation in literary persuasion

We have already seen the actualisation of universal emotion in Keats's 'Ode on Melancholy', achieved through a combination of sensory and suggestive lexis and imagery ('soft hand' . . . 'rich anger'). Keats's extended simile of the 'weeping cloud' contains four metaphors, which redirect the natural image of the cloud towards its human referent ('the melancholy fit'). His lexical choice ('weeping', 'fosters', 'droop-headed' and 'shroud') suggests human action or suffering. This accelerates the to-and-fro of feeling within single lines, transforming the 'sudden' and involuntary onset of melancholy into something refreshing and invigorating, like an April shower. The opposition of seasonal rebirth and human mortality is harmonised and resolved in an 'April *shroud*'. Not only does Keats alternate between the universal emotions of joy and sorrow (reflected in the transient beauties of 'rose', 'sand-wave' and 'peonies'), but he also mediates the discord of 'anger' and 'rave' with the implicit serenity of 'feed deep, deep'. Gathering power from the preceding lines, the ode moves towards the poetic climax of the final stanza, with its rich *enargeia* and complex interplay of emotion, depending on a range of senses other than sight.

A further example of the actualising of emotion in literary persuasion comes from Edgar Allan Poe's short story 'The Pit and the Pendulum'. The narrator, a prisoner of the Spanish Inquisition, graphically describes his horrifying situation, as he lies in the inexorable path of a scythe-like pendulum, bound hand and foot:

> Down – steadily down it crept. I took a frenzied pleasure in contrasting its downward with its lateral velocity. To the right – to the left – far

and wide with the shriek of a damned spirit; to my heart with the stealthy pace of the tiger! I alternately laughed and howled as the one or the other idea grew predominant. . . .

. . . Down – certainly, relentlessly down! It vibrated within three inches of my bosom! I struggled violently, furiously, to free my left arm. This was free only from the elbow to the hand. . . . Could I have broken the fastenings above the elbow, I would have seized and attempted to arrest the pendulum. I might as well have attempted to arrest an avalanche!   (Poe, 1967: 271)

Poe intends to arouse fear and horror, with suspense literally wound to screaming pitch. Graphic actualisation is achieved not only by visual description, but also by creating an imagined sensation of mounting physical tension in the reader, who experiences vicariously the imminent agony of the spread-eagled prisoner. Poe also actualises emotion via sound, comparing the massive blade's whistling displacement of the air to the 'shriek of a damned spirit', and he repeats certain significant words ('down', 'arrest') as well as skilfully contrasting lateral and vertical movement, laughter and terror, the solid steel of the pendulum and the prisoner's fragile flesh. All make their contribution to Poe's powerful actualisation of terror.

(e)   Actualisation in functional persuasion

Similar devices appear in functional persuasion, though often conveying very different emotions. One such contingent emotion is pleasure in food, illustrated by an extract from Matthew Fort's review of eating in a London gastropub (*Guardian Weekend*, 15 November 2003). When discussing one item on the menu, he starts to qualify what has up to now been a highly favourable account:

Cockles I love. They're so much nicer, fatter, plumper, sweeter than chewy bits of clam, I always think. You have to be careful with them, though. They need to be thoroughly washed and checked or they will be gritty with sand. Most of mine, cooked in white wine and onion, were all those things you want cockles to be. Unfortunately, one was full of mud, not flesh, and the fallout contaminated those in the immediate vicinity.

The opening simple sentence inverts normal English word-order, fronting the noun phrase to present the shellfish as a fresh sensory phenomenon, before revealing the author's passionate preference ('I love [Cockles]'). Similarly, the subordinating noun clause precedes its grammatical subject, and the pleasurable experience of eating cockles ('nicer, fatter, plumper, sweeter than chewy bits of clam') is dominant. Fort's actualising adjectives move from 'nicer' (here a term of almost child-like appreciation) to the highly specific taste indicator 'sweeter'. The transition from 'fatter' to 'plumper' also actualises the transition from *mouthing* to *biting* the squashy, juicy shellfish. Grammatically this represents an Aristotelian model of argument, where degree or comparison is making the persuasive point, qualified by the less agreeable 'chewy . . . clam' and confirmed by the grating unpleasantness of an ill-prepared cockle 'gritty with sand'. In the next two sentences the discriminating reader begins to imagine the satisfying taste of these particular cockles 'cooked in white wine and onion', until the image of pure sensory pleasure is literally 'mud[died]' and darkened by the hyperbolic metaphor of contamination and 'fallout'.

To use such rhetorical skills of actualisation to provide a critique of gastropub cuisine may seem at once trivialising and over the top. However, eating in restaurants is as much a part of contemporary culture as sport, theatre and music, and as such is susceptible to similar opportunities for public rhetoricising (see also Chapter 6).

Orientation and Engagement

As we have seen, the process of actualising emotion is neither simple nor straightforward; the orientation of emotion is similarly complex. Orientation suggests the strong directing of a message, and its consequent effect on language function. Emotive orientation, though located primarily with the sender, is nevertheless a constant in every persuasive interaction, as linguistic theory and traditional rhetoric confirm. Despite this constancy, emotion will be subject to variation, refracting and changing in relation to persuader and audience. Just as a laser works in a two-way process, so emotional engagement reflects the emotions on both sides of the persuasive interaction. As a result, we can observe the heightening of emotion in persuader and audience. Managing the force of this emotional charge, and deciding how to aim, focus and intensify its energy, will be a daunting task for the persuader.

As we saw earlier, orientation also involves phatic, metalingual and poetic functions (according to the revised Sender/Receiver model of interaction). We shall now examine them at work in the persuasive process.

(a)   Orientation via phatic, metalingual and poetic language

In this extract from a review of Sue Townsend's play *Ten Fingers, Nine Tiny Toes* by Jeffrey Wainwright (*The Independent*, 6 November 1989), we can see just how these three functions enhance the emotiveness and referential clarity of the critic's persuasive voice.

Shoddy Paintwork

When my father painted the parlour he used to use 'wallop'. It came in large tins, he slopped some water into it, stirred it heftily and with the largest available brush, walloped it on [1]. The result was quick, service-able and covered cracks [2]. Sue Townsend's *Ten Fingers, Nine Tiny Toes*, directed by Carole Hayman, is theatrical wallop, except that it dispenses with anything so painstaking as a brush and leaves chasms in its own argument [3].

The metalingual function of sentence [2] is oriented towards code and, by developing our understanding of the bizarrely old-fashioned term 'wallop', prepares us for the amusing critical judgement: 'Sue Townsend's *Ten Fingers* . . . is theatrical wallop'. Though the prime function of the review is conative (to persuade the reader of the play's shortcomings), Wainwright emphasises its metalingual orientation by explicitly linking the tenor of his discourse to its metaphorical vehicle ('wallop'). This underlines the point of the metaphor, whilst revealing its limitations as a code. After all, even if you apply paint to cover up weaknesses in your home-decorating, you're unlikely to 'dispense with . . . a brush', or 'leave chasms' instead of covering cracks! Wainwright's response to the careless workmanship of Townsend's play is an emotional *melange* of surprise, amusement and indignation, and he exploits the 'wallop' metaphor to the full, as we glimpse not just the play's 'shoddy paintwork' but the equally shoddy 'building' under-neath. There is also some phatic orientation here, which works inter-textually (i.e. the comic music hall song 'When Father painted the parlour / You couldn't see Pa for paint . . .'!). This reference establishes shared contact and creates potential camaraderie between reviewer and reader. In turn, this assists emotive orientation, linking the play's comic clumsiness and self-importance with that of 'Pa'. Poetic orientation further strengthens the comic tone of the review, as Wainwright recalls the rhythm of his own father's painting as he 'slopped . . . stirred . . . walloped it on'. Clearly, phatic, metalingual and poetic functions all contribute to the *enargeia* of the extract; through them Wainwright can convey amused empathy with Townsend's boisterous technique but also a lack of sympathy with its slapdash quality, something that effectively short-changes the audience.

(b)   The emotional laser

Pursuing further the analogy of the laser in relation to emotional engagement, we can see from the example above how the various language functions interweave in a persuasive interaction. The main value of the laser analogy lies in the way it suggests both the unitary strength of emotion and its potential for transformation. We must stress, however, that the analogy is approximate. Just as the progressive build-up of energy in a laser-tube depends on the exact alignment of mirrors at each end, so the emotional charge of the persuasion depends on the persuader's skill in aligning the image of his or her personality and stance with the image of the audience. The laser analogy adds something new, in that it develops the simple idea of reflection (which is ultimately a passive event) into something more emotionally charged and energised. A skilled and attentive persuader will monitor the audience's emotional reaction by 'freeze-framing' the range of facial expression, body language and vocalisation. He or she will thus be enabled to reflect, refine and intensify the feeling. Emotive images function like electric current within a laser, building up an oscillating 'light energy' of emotion, as the persuader is moved more and more powerfully in response to the audience's escalating emotion.

The 'laser' interaction is not necessarily limited to the reflection of simple emotions; it can also mediate between oppositions (as we saw in the discussion of 'Ode to Melancholy'). For example, a persuader might use a kind of emotional refraction, repeatedly referring to the audience's anxieties, and thus restoring their confidence by confronting their fears. The laser analogy could also be used to describe a situation in which the audience is ideologically divided. In any legislative assembly, a significant function of debate is to build up the emotional conviction of one's own side and to demoralise the opposition. Thus members will 'reflect' the emotions of their own side on the topic of debate, whilst goading their opponents to a contrary range of feeling. This usefully illustrates the distinction between sympathy and empathy. Any government supporter empathises with the frustration, anxiety, anger or scorn felt by the opposition, having experienced similar feelings when 'the boot was on the other foot'. But no sympathy is felt because they are ideologically and politically opposed.

Working with Bias and Emotion

The concept of prejudice has already been discussed in terms of its relation to *bias*, but the role of ideology in creating this distinction has not been explored. Originating in Marxist theory (surveyed by David Forgacs in Jefferson and Robey, 1986: 166–203), the term 'ideology' is used to refer to the unconscious conditioning of people's attitudes, feelings and actions by the economic and political structures of society. Today the meaning has been generalised and is applied to any system of beliefs, attitudes, habits of mind and emotions that are potentially influential. Thus a single individual may be influenced by ideologies or codes of conduct linked with everything from family tradition and attitudes to religious beliefs, educational experience and occupational practices. This is not to mention the influence of contemporary culture at every level! Whether unconsciously assimilated or derived from personal experience and rational evaluation, these ideologies bias us in their own distinctive ways. Each ideology or code has its own distinctive language, or what Bakhtin would call 'voice', exerting its own persuasive influence. A single act of persuasion might involve a number of 'voices' (*heteroglossia*) conveying prejudice (covertly) or bias (overtly). In either case, this will have a conative orientation to audience.

Yet, as we recollect the dialectical nature of persuasion, we can see that bias itself is open to change. However biased we think we are on a particular issue, contradictory feelings may unexpectedly rise to the surface, changing our minds temporarily or even permanently. This is especially inclined to happen if a persuader uses such exaggerated bias that the audience feels a sense of revulsion. The persuader has miscalculated. Such 'reverse bias' switches the polarity of their emotional engagement. A persuader needs to avoid producing this undesirable response by careful anticipation. Genuine dialogue where objections based on bias are openly anticipated is very different: here the persuader deliberately seeks to energise and transform 'reverse bias' into a rational and emotionally consistent dialectic.

A classic example of successful 'reverse bias' is Mark Antony's manipulative address to the Roman mob (*Julius Caesar*, III.ii.70–249) following the killing of Caesar, and Brutus's speech of justification. Brutus has pledged his own honour (cf. Aristotelian *arete*) as a guarantee of his truthfulness, and having expressed the goodwill he feels towards the citizens of Rome (addressing them as 'lovers', i.e. 'dear friends'), concludes by offering to die for them, placing only his love of liberty above his duty to them. For Brutus the issue of the preservation of liberty is more important than his own love and loyalty to Caesar and respect for his military eminence. The crowd momentarily see themselves cast in the same noble mould, and share Brutus's seeming idealism – until Antony starts to speak. Playing on the refrain 'Brutus is an honourable man' (a term Brutus used of himself moments earlier) he skates over the issue of liberty, and begins to stir up indignation in the crowd at Brutus's breach of friendship. He appeals to their sentimental pride in Caesar's victories and to their gullible eagerness for his huge legacy of money and public amenities. As these self-seeking emotions erupt, nobler feelings are forgotten. Antony tantalises the crowd by referring to Caesar's will but refusing to disclose the contents (a rhetorical ploy discussed in Chapter 7); this feeds their desire to find out what has been concealed. He pretends to hesitate: 'I fear I wrong the honourable men / Whose daggers have stabbed Caesar; I do fear it' (ll. 148–9). No one would expect the sinister word 'daggers' to follow the noble epithet 'honourable', and this juxtaposition demonstrates Antony's skill in the reversal of bias, replacing the deliberations of a democracy with the emotive seesaw of a mob. (Significantly, the word 'mob' is derived from the Latin *mobile vulgus*, meaning 'inconstant crowd'.)

In sharp contrast to Antony's aristocratic and cynical manipulation of those whom he despises, our next example again uses the issue of liberty, in a way that does not infantilise the audience but dignifies it. Here *logos* and *ethos* work together to create a new constituency united by a shared political consciousness, and drawn from two previously opposed political groups. This extract is from *The Bloody Project*, a pamphlet by William Walwyn (a 'Leveller' seeking to extend the franchise) and written at the height of the Second Civil War in England. Printed in August 1648, it addresses all participants in the 'wars', whether royalists or parliamentarians:

> I beseech you (you that are so forward and active to engage in the defence of the King's, Presbyterian, or Independent interest, and yet know no just cause for either) consider, was it sufficient that the King at first invited you in general terms to join with him, for the defence of the true Protestant Religion, his own just Prerogatives, the Privileges of Parliament, and the Liberty of the Subject; but never declared in particular what that Protestant Religion was he would have defended, or what Prerogative would please him, what privileges he would allow the Parliament, or what Freedoms the People?
>
> Or was it sufficient think you now, that the Parliament invited you at

first upon general terms, to fight for the maintenance of the true Protestant Religion, the Liberties of the People, and Privileges of Parliament; when neither themselves knew, for ought is yet seen, nor you, nor any body else, what they meant by the true Protestant Religion, or what the Liberties of the People were, or what those Privileges of Parliament were, for which yet nevertheless thousands of men have been slain, and thousands of families destroyed? (Erskine-Hill and Storey, 1983: 90–1)

Emotive abstractions such as 'Liberty of the Subject' and 'Liberties of the People' are equally questioned; Walwyn intended his words to be read and heard by individuals and by groups of people who were (or had been) each others' bitterest enemies. Designed to stimulate both thought and feeling, his text is at once referential and conative. It attacks prejudice and exposes his readers' seemingly absurd inclination to fight, kill or be killed for grand and insubstantial ideas, which arbitrarily attract the most extreme of universal emotions. Instead, he invites both sides not only to judge these ideas for themselves, but also the leaders who manipulated them for their own ends. Walwyn's scorn and suspicion underlie his repetition of 'in *general* terms', and hammer away ('*what* . . . *what* . . . *what*') as he pursues the missing details of each side's manifesto. Unlike Demosthenes who set out precisely what should be done to resist Philip of Macedon, neither side in this conflict has offered specific and achievable images of liberty, religion or civic obedience that would inspire rational conviction and truthful feeling. Thus Walwyn shifts the bias of his audience from blind loyalty to increasing distrust, shame and horror, which in the paragraph we quote culminates in the image of 'thousands of men . . . slain, . . . thousands of families destroyed'.

We have shown above that orientation is the focusing mode in any interactional situation, selecting, organising and focusing emotion within the central dialectic. Emotional engagement is always oriented to Sender/Persuader, since unfelt emotion cannot persuade; at the same time it is oriented to Receiver/Audience, since persuasion is void without an intended effect on the persuadee. And this is not all. Persuasion deploys all the language functions involved in interaction, from conative, referential and emotive to phatic, metalingual and poetic. With its insistent quest for missing particulars, the last example shows us how crucial the referential function can be in the refinement of emotional effect.

Emotional Engagement in Functional Persuasion

(a)   Unscripted emotion

The following passage is taken from a BBC news bulletin (Radio 4, 6:00p.m., on 2 December 2003) and concerns the government's proposal to introduce top-up fees for university students, to be repaid after graduation. The Prime Minister's alleged claim that 'top-up fees would be socially just' is challenged by his former Chief Whip, Nick Brown:

> I don't think social justice comes from loading young people from fami-
> lies of ordinary means with a large amount of debt; I don't think social
> justice comes from, putting obstacles in the way of youngsters from the
> very poorest households; I don't think social justice comes from allow-
> ing the . . . er . . . most privileged of higher educational institutions to
> increase their fees and just take in rich people.

The rather ponderous repetition of the emotive abstraction 'social justice' contrasts with the grudging and negative terms 'loading', 'putting', 'allowing', giving Nick Brown space to organise his own argu-ment and contradict the Prime Minister's. The seemingly tentative 'I don't think' (cf. Chapter 7, *litotes* or 'playing down') adds ironic force to his indignation at what he perceives as irrational and callous govern-ment policy. The 'laser effect' is exploited to include the audience in his own concern that a great social ideal is drifting further and further away. Though the unscripted extract has its weaker moments (the patronising term 'youngsters' replaces the simple description 'young people', and 'obstacles' is never explained), Brown does communicate what was (at that time) his rebellious stance, made more pointed by his previous 'party-line' approach as the Chief Whip.

(b)   Political oratory

The following passage is taken from John F. Kennedy's Inaugural Address (20 January, 1961):

> Now the trumpet summons us again – not as a call to bear arms,
> though arms we need – not as a call to battle, though embattled we are
> – but a call to bear the burden of a long twilight struggle, year in and year

out, 'rejoicing in hope, patient in tribulation' – a struggle against the common enemies of man: tyranny, poverty, disease and war itself.

Can we forge against these enemies a grand and global alliance, North and South, East and West, that can assure a more fruitful life for all mankind? Will you join in that historic effort?

In the long history of the world, only a few generations have been granted the role of defending freedom in its hour of maximum danger. I do not shrink from this responsibility – I welcome it. I do not believe that any of us would exchange places with any other people or any other generation. The energy, the faith, the devotion which we bring to this endeavor will light our country and all who serve it – and the glow from that fire can truly light the world.   (John F. Kennedy, in *Public Papers of the Presidents*, 1962: 2–3)

These paragraphs provide an emotive blend of graphic imagery (light/darkness, space/time) with abstract concepts ('hope', 'tribulation', 'freedom', 'responsibility', 'endeavor'). Kennedy's claim that his fellow Americans would not wish to 'exchange places with any other people' echoes Henry V's words before Agincourt (*Henry V*, IV.i.113–15; IV.iii.64–7), as well as St Paul's exalted ideal of a people 'rejoicing in hope' (*Romans*, 12:12). His speech employs familiar persuasive strategies ranging from repetition, inversion, alliteration and contrasting structures to accumulation of emotive lexis, climax and interrogatives (see Chapter 6). Its overall purpose is to achieve a reciprocation of emotion between audience and persuader, prompting American citizens to active participation in worldwide humanitarian effort. Kennedy presents himself as a twentieth-century warrior king (emotive orientation), and actually reworks his own battle metaphor ('the trumpet summons . . . not as a call to bear arms . . . but a call to bear the burden . . .') in order to persuade his audience.

(c)   Political writing: the 'Comment' page

In this edited article from the *Guardian* (20 January 2004), Natasha Walter examines the issues associated with an imminent French law banning the display of religious symbols in schools (including the Islamic female headscarf, the *hijab*):

When the Veil means Freedom

. . . Many women in the west find the headscarf deeply problematic. One of the reasons we find it so hateful is because the whole trajectory of feminism in the west has been tied up with the freedom to uncover ourselves. . . . Taking off their covering clothes, gloves and hats as well as painful corsets and long skirts was tied up with a larger struggle [for women] to come out of their houses, to speak in public, to travel alone, to go into education and into work and into politics, and so to become independent. . . . When I visited Afghanistan, I spoke to many women who were desperate to take off the burka, including one who had been almost beaten to death by the Taliban for showing her hair. These women wanted to take the same path that women in the west took . . . to be free of such hampering laws, despite the anger of the men around them and taunts of immodesty and irreligiousness. . . .

Women who have fled such brutal patriarchal regimes and come to the west have become some of the most vociferous supporters of the new French law. But good intentions do not necessarily make a good law. . . . And we should not be too easily seduced into believing that a law which makes women take off their headscarves is a feminist law. It is absurd to argue that the decision of a Muslim woman to cover her hair is inherently evidence that she is oppressed, any more than a Sikh man's turban – also among the religious symbols to be banned in French schools – is evidence that he is being oppressed.

. . . For some women, in some societies, the veil enables them to feel freer to move into work and education. In Egypt, Leila Ahmed argued [that] . . . the veil – far from being some kind of throwback – has actually become a symbol of their possible 'entrance into modernity'. And at the demonstration in London I certainly met many women who had taken to wearing the headscarf out of choice . . . 'It doesn't restrict me at all, why should it?' ask Salma Yaqoob, the chair of Birmingham Stop the War Coalition. She is a vocal supporter both of Islam and of women's rights. . . . ' I think that Muslim women who wear *hijab* often feel that they are valued for their intellect rather than their looks, which is actually very liberating . . .'

It is hard for me to accept such views, since I personally find even putting on a headscarf when I visit Muslim countries a deeply uncomfortable action. . . . But if we really believe in tolerance, then that . . . must include tolerating behaviour we find alien. . . . The great achievement of feminism has been to offer women freedom of choice in their personal lives, together with political equality. If we hold to that ideal, then, paradoxical as it may seem, we should take a stand against those who would force women to wear the headscarf – and those who would force them not to wear it.

The last sentence quoted above typifies the balancing act that Natasha Walter contrives between differing emotional responses (hers and others') throughout her article. The fact that she can overcome her

own culturally conditioned aversion to any form of physically restrictive clothing demonstrates her respect for the opposing point of view,
which finds it 'liberating' to wear the headscarf.

The first paragraph in her argument conveys a sense of irksome
restriction and cowed conformity felt by women ('gloves . . . hats . . .
corsets . . . skirts'); in her account this is negated by the liberating burst
of energy that carries women 'into education and into work and into
politics'. The repeated prepositional phrases communicate an exhilara-
tion and an eagerness to subvert or unmask the status quo. From the
restrained beginning, abstract words ('problematic', 'trajectory', 'freedom') work in dynamic combination with concrete terms and with
words expressive of extreme feeling ('painful', 'hateful', 'struggle') to
build this polarity of confinement and release. Walter's negative
response to 'covering clothes' is made even more pressing in the next
paragraph, where male violence (commonly blamed by feminists for
such restriction) bubbles to the surface in the account of an Afghan
woman 'almost beaten to death . . . for showing her hair', representative of the 'many women' who resisted men's attempts to control them
emotionally through guilt, fear and shame.

Against this, Walter invites the reader (assumed to be sympathetic to
women, whether from a female or a male perspective) to resist being
'seduced' by this emotion into accepting the 'new French law' that
prompted her article. Using the compressed logical form of *enthymeme*
or implicit premise argument (see Chapter 4), she denies that feminism's opposition to all forms of restriction on women necessarily rules
out the *hijab*, and notes that, on the contrary, its wearers can find it
'liberating'. To counterbalance her own emotional aversion, she is
stressing *ethos* more than *pathos*. According to influential Muslim
women in Egypt, Birmingham and London, the ethos of the *hijab*
embraces moral and educational status as well as political activism. By
specifying their professional and leadership roles, Walter takes care to
indicate how these women, like their western sisters, have moved 'into
education and into work and into politics'. Unlike them, the *hijab*
wearers have done so by adopting more (not less) 'covering'. Their own
words are used to convey the emotional satisfaction of being 'valued for
their intellect'. With this stress on the power and innate authority of
mind, irrespective of gender or religion, *pathos* is not only validated by
ethos, but also reflects it.

In the final paragraph, Walter's 'uncomfortable' and alienated feelings are outweighed by the emotions attached to self-determination:
'freedom . . . choice . . . equality', values acknowledged by feminists of

all persuasions. The firm stance of her final position with its resolute, quasi-military tone ('take a stand'), rules out complicity with 'force' from any direction, religious or secular.

Emotion in Literary Persuasion

(a)   Drama

In this extract from Act II of Shakespeare's tragedy (II.iii.105–15), the eponymous Macbeth gives an elaborately mannered account of Duncan's horrific murder. This account differs significantly from Quintilian's version of a similarly gruesome event, already cited. Quintilian addresses a single audience (the Roman law court) on a particular occasion; the actor playing Macbeth addresses a fictional audience of Scottish nobles as well as the actual Jacobean audience in London:

> Who can be wise, amaz'd, temp'rate and furious,
> Loyal and neutral, in a moment? No man.
> Th' expedition of my violent love
> Outrun the pauser, reason. Here lay Duncan,
> His silver skin lac'd with his golden blood;
> And his gash'd stabs look'd like a breach in nature
> For ruin's wasteful entrance; there the murderers,
> Steeped in the colours of their trade, their daggers
> Unmannerly breeched with gore. Who could refrain,
> That had a heart to love, and in that heart
> Courage to make's love known?
> > (Shakespeare, 1997 [1606]: 2582)

Having described the corpse, Macbeth immediately turns the spotlight on himself and his pretended emotion, and explains his killing of Duncan's grooms on the grounds that 'violent love' outweighed his sense of justice. He describes the scene so graphically and extravagantly that the horrific physical image is overlaid by opulent images associated with kingship ('silver', 'lac'd', 'golden') instead of a hideously butchered body. Macbeth thus manages to blunt rather than sharpen the horror, investing the corpse with a weird beauty, and reducing the hearers' emotion from the universal horror of murder to the contingent horror of an affront to monarchy. He describes the unfortunate grooms as 'unmannerly' and bloodstained by their 'trade'. Here the emotion of horror is transformed to aristocratic disgust at the coarse brutality of the lower orders. By *orienting* emotion at Duncan's death as a terrible insult to order, Macbeth seeks to signal to the peers – who will shortly elect him King in Duncan's place – his loyalty to the ideal of order and his fitness for kingship. Throughout the passage we can see how skilfully Macbeth manages the orientation of emotion, both in relation to the Scottish nobles whom he is addressing on stage and to the original royalist audience in the theatre.

(b)   Poetry

Below are the three opening stanzas from Grace Schulman's 'Notes from Underground: W. H. Auden on the Lexington Avenue IRT'. First published in 1994, it recalls the days of the Vietnam War when Schulman was living in New York and recognised the much-admired English poet commuting regularly on the same subway line.

> Hunched in a corner seat, I'd watch him pass
> riders who gaped at headlines: '300 DEAD',
> and, in their prized indifference to all
> others, were unaware that he was one who heard
> meter in that clamor of wheels on rails
>
> Some days I took the local because he did:
> He sank down into plastic, his bruised sandals
> no longer straining with the weight of him;
> there, with the frankness of the unacquainted,
> I studied his face, a sycamore's bark
>
> with lichen poking out of crevices.
> His eyes lifted over my tattered copy
> of his *Selected Poems*, then up to where
> they drilled new windows in the car and found,
> I guessed, tea roses and a healing fountain.
>   (Schulman, 2003: 83)

The first stanza marks out Schulman (the aspiring poet) and Auden (the established poet) from the other subway 'riders', who remain emotionally detached from the railcar setting and from each other. They even register the news of day-to-day carnage with 'indifference'. Schulman alone is vividly aware of another person (Auden) and imagines his delight in the subway train as in all such machinery. She recalls the pleasure famously expressed in his poem 'Night Mail', where the reader or listener does indeed hear 'meter in that clamor of wheels on rails'. Throughout, Schulman's poem achieves graphic vividness through a blend of manmade and natural imagery. Auden is presented as awesomely separate, through her evocation of his extraordinary lined face, like lichened treebark. This contrasts with the colour and freshness of the visionary 'tea roses' with which Schulman's own poetic imagination endows him. There is also an echo of the 'healing fountain' in Auden's poem 'In Memory of W. B. Yeats'. Here, this imagery interacts with the 'plastic' cushions of the car, the poet's 'bruised sandals', and the 'new windows . . . drilled' by the movement of Auden's gaze, which crosses the poet's own as she stares across at him. (Only at the end, not quoted here, do their glances meet in unspoken communion.) In the wider context of the poem, which repeatedly conveys the noise of metal on metal, the verb 'drilled' seems to retain the force and direction of a power tool without its sound. It conveys an impression of purely mental energy. Emotionally, the quoted lines project a physical empathy with Auden's weight and weariness; but tiredness is turned to light and upward movement, the assertion of mind and spirit over matter – a sense of confidence and relief perhaps more securely located in Schulman's mind than in Auden's. The subtlety of this poem is seen in that fact that it recalls our 'laser' image of the mutual reflection of feeling – without fully confirming it.

(c)   Fiction

In this extract from *Our Mutual Friend* by Charles Dickens, we meet a repellent group of people, most of whom Dickens intends us to dislike thoroughly. They are pictures of superficiality and hypocrisy.

> The great looking-glass above the sideboard reflects the table and the company. Reflects the new Veneering crest, in gold and eke in silver, frosted and also thawed, a camel of all work. . . . Reflects Veneering; forty, wavy-haired, dark, tending to corpulence, sly, mysterious, filmy – a kind of sufficiently well-looking veiled prophet, not prophesying. Reflects Mrs. Veneering; fair, aquiline-nosed and fingered, not so much light hair as she might have, gorgeous in raiment and jewels, enthusiastic, proprietory, conscious that a corner of her husband's veil is over

herself. Reflects Podsnap; prosperously feeding, two little light-coloured wiry wings, one on either side of his else bald head, looking as like his hair-brushes as his hair, dissolving view of red beads on his forehead, large allowance of crumpled shirt-collar up behind. . . . Reflects mature young lady; raven locks, and complexion that lights up well when well-powdered – as it is – carrying on considerably in the captivation of mature young gentleman; with too much nose in his face, too much ginger in his whiskers, too much torso in his waistcoat, too much sparkle in his studs, his eyes, his buttons, his talk and his teeth.   (Dickens, 1952 [1864–5]: 10)

The graphic quality of this scene is striking. How does Dickens not only achieve this, but also manipulate our emotional response? This extract from a much longer paragraph acquires its structure and power from the increasingly ominous repetition of 'Reflects', reminding us of the 'great looking glass' which coldly mirrors them all. Dickens uses this structuring device to progressively withdraw his (and our) sympathy from people who have themselves withdrawn from reality and become (at least for the moment) nothing more than reflections in glass. Through ironic lexical contrasts (e.g. 'raiment'/'mature young lady') Dickens reveals the horror of their narcissism, infecting everything from conversation to appearance and behaviour. In each descriptive sentence the accumulating details inflate and deflate the subject, ending with the grotesque disarray of Podsnap, 'feeding' like an animal, and the predatory 'teeth' of the 'mature young gentleman'. Readers may find that Dickens has managed the emotive orientation and emotional engagement so successfully here, that their feelings of scorn and disgust verge on a nightmarish sense of horror.

Conclusion

In the extracts above we have demonstrated the use of emotion (both contingent and universal) in order to persuade. Intentions on the part of the persuader have ranged from urging high ideals (Kennedy) to conveying devastating scorn (Dickens); from visionary intensity (Keats) to carefully poised *pathos* and *ethos* (Natasha Walter); and from a universally recognisable pitch of horror and suspense (Poe), to culturally conditioned shock and revulsion (Macbeth acting out his horror at Duncan's death). The aim has been to suggest the infinite variety of purposes, whether practical or artistic, to which the basic principles of emotive rhetoric can be applied. Although *pathos* may be used to distract the persuadee from making a rational judgement on a specific issue, it may equally be used to give force and focus to rational argument. The extract from William Walwyn is an outstanding example.

Further Exploration: the Theory and Practice of *Pathos*

Readers wishing to develop their understanding of emotional engagement will benefit greatly from exploring a range of emotion from positive to negative, from the most 'base' to the most 'exalted', and in all kinds of writing. Literary texts in which varying emotion is powerfully conveyed include *Paradise Lost* by John Milton, *A Long Day's Journey into Night* by Eugene O'Neill and *Middlemarch* by George Eliot. Specific strategies to identify include the 'emotional laser', emotional orientation and the reversal of bias.

Two particular techniques not included in the above chapter (but well worth developing as ways of intensifying *pathos*) are the use of *deixis* (see Jones, 1995; Semino, 1997; R. Cockcroft, 2004) and the management of sentence perspective (see Firbas, 1992; R. Cockcroft, 2004).

---

3 Reason: the Resources of Argument

We now come to *logos*, the third structural principle of persuasion. As always, we want to emphasise its integral relationship with *ethos* and *pathos* in the persuasive interaction. It is also important to remember that our tripartite division of the sources of persuasion should be seen not as a linear *sequence*, but as a simultaneous *process*. Our earlier 'freeze frame' analogy is also worth recalling; a speaker, framed momentarily as an attitude is being conveyed, may simultaneously be projecting emotion and preparing an argument. In other words, he or she may even be using *logos* to control emotion.

We know that the persuader's personality or stance, together with his or her emotional engagement with the audience, determines the choice and development of persuasive arguments. However, as the persuasive interaction proceeds this may change, depending on whether the persuader is in active dialogue with the audience, or simply watching or listening for other signs of audience response. If logical objections are raised (or seem likely to be raised) by the persuadees, these will exercise a reciprocal influence on the persuader's stance and emotional orientation.

We shall now focus our attention on the resources of argument available to the persuader. It will be easier to understand this structural principle of *logos* if we differentiate between the two stages traditionally known as *invention* (Greek *heurisis*) and *judgement*. We shall focus our attention on *invention* in this chapter and *judgement* in the next. By 'invention' we mean a method of thinking up arguments on any given topic, and by 'judgement' we mean the evaluation of these arguments as they bear on the issue in hand. In the course of this symbiotic process of invention and evaluation, some arguments will have to be discarded and others developed, depending on the audience's likely response to the persuasive argument, its relevance and credibility.

As Billig has demonstrated (1996: 74–80, 119–20, 161–4), every persuasive argument must attract a counter-argument, every generalisation a particularisation or exception. Every kind of persuasive interaction must take place within the larger framework of a social dialectic, centred on some issue. This means that each of the distinctive resources of argument has to be available to all parties in the dialectic to enhance their case. However assertive our use of such arguments, we may reflect that as *anti-logoi,* they can equally be turned round and used against us! The next question is how many ways of arguing exist? Are we able to make full use of the range of argument available?

When asked to prove a point, most of us adopt a surprisingly small set of structured arguments. For example, when explaining why something has happened, or predicting what will follow when some proposal is implemented, we invoke the argument of *cause and effect.* We use the argument of *similarity* to point out similarities between objects or ideas and draw deductions from that resemblance. In classifying arguments of this kind, rhetoricians and logicians distinguish between the small number of general models of argument, and the much larger range of specific models. Aristotle, for example (*Rhetoric,* I. iv–viii) identifies a whole set of argument-types peculiar to political argument, in which he lists goals motivating political action such as happiness and security, describes the means available for achieving them, and identifies ways of arguing about their desirability or otherwise (1926: 38–89). Furthermore, he identifies three classes of argument employed in all the major rhetorical genres (1926: 264–73). The persuader may argue: (a) that something is possible or impossible; (b) that it has occurred in the past or may occur in the future; and (c) that it is greater or smaller than something else (*Rhetoric,* II. xviii.2 ff).

In this chapter we are concerned with similarly general arguments (ten in total). These arguments may be applied to an even wider range of purposes than Aristotle's common topics; several of these are recognisable as modes of reasoning used by everyone on a daily basis. In the context of rhetoric these kinds of everyday argument are extended, refined, co-ordinated and used with stronger persuasive focus.

Classical rhetoricians used the term *topos* (meaning 'place' in Greek, *topoi* being the plural form) to denote any kind of standard argument, such as the general models referred to above. The metaphoric use of *topos* for a model of argument is significant; it clearly implies that there is a real 'place', somewhere where anyone can go to look for an idea. Thus a persuader might glance through the *topoi* for possible arguments, just as someone might run through a mental checklist when preparing for some activity or event. For example, remembering the general *topos* of *cause and effect,* the persuader might wonder how specific arguments about the source and purpose of anything relevant to the discussion could be used to strengthen the persuasion. However, we shall not ourselves use the term *topos* but will simply refer to models of argument. 'Model' suggests an adaptable, even flexible concept, which matches our overall case for the relevance and practicability of rhetoric in modern persuasion. Indeed, drawing as they do on involuntary and universal thought patterns (see Appendix A), models of argument offer systematic and coherent methods of 'thinking through' a topic, and of selecting and organising the most effective arguments. They are arguments for everyday use! Whenever there is a controversial issue, persuaders are likely to ask themselves a series of questions about it, which will help to marshal their arguments:

1. How do we *define* whatever is being argued about? *Definition model of argument*
2. What caused it and what effects will result? *Cause and effect model of argument*
3. What is similar to it? *Similarity model of argument*
4. What is in any way opposed to it? *Oppositional model of argument*
5. Is it less or more than something else cited? *Degree model of argument*
6. Can a witness or witnesses be cited? *Testimony model of argument*
7. How is the subject categorised, broadly or narrowly? *Genus/species model of argument*
8. Is it a whole in itself or a part of something else? *Part/whole model of argument*
9. What are its associations and qualities? *Associational model of argument*
10. What is the origin of the words used to refer to the subject? *Root meaning model of argument*

How does the persuader best learn when and how to use these arguments? In effect they comprise an invaluable 'bank' of resources readily accessible to any persuader. Even more advantageously, these arguments can be selected, matched and adjusted to the likely concerns and expectations of a specific audience.

One new approach to selecting and organising arguments can be found in *schema* theory, a methodology which enables the persuader to focus on cognitive approaches to argument. This methodology means that there is no need to consult lists of special *topoi* (such as those devised on Aristotelian lines by Perelman and Olbrechts-Tyteca [1969] for contemporary use) or to commit them to memory.

Recent developments in cognitive theory have drawn attention to the way in which memory is based on networks or interconnections in our brains. R. C. Schank and others point out that human beings make sense of experiences *not* by referring to specific memory traces from particular happenings, but by relating each new event to recurring experiences of a particular kind, echoed in a distinctive pattern within the memory (i.e. a *schema*). Moreover, each individual perception may be linked with other perceptions in a variety of ways. Each set of 'links' constitutes a distinct schema, which in turn has its part to play in a range of more complex *schemata*. For example, encountering a receptionist 'figure' is a situation (or schema) everyone recognizes. This 'figure' has different roles to play depending on the context and the particular *script*. Examples could be anything from a doctor's surgery to an airport check-in or a hotel reception desk. Such is the flexibility of schemata, that they can just as readily be reinforced, challenged or modified by human responses to changing experience – including our personal experience as persuadees (see Schank and Abelson, 1977; Schank, 1982, 1999; Semino, 1997).

Through these neural networks, patterns of expectation are aroused every time we use or respond to language (both spoken or written) in situations we have previously experienced and remember. Such patterns of expectation relate to our recognition of types of arguments, as well as the patterning of familiar social interactions such as consulting the doctor, buying stamps, or asking for directions. In the field of persuasion, an awareness of these networks of schemata can help us to 'guestimate' the mind-set and susceptibilities of our audience, thus increasing our persuasive opportunities as well as responsibilities. Such deliberate *cognitive engagement* with the likely patterns of memory and expectation in any given audience enables the persuader to adapt general models of argument to particular circumstances. In Appendix A, we provide a brief and comprehensive account of the main classes of schemata to which we refer readers; in the meantime we draw attention to individual cases of cognitive engagement, whenever relevant and easy to follow. Our aim is to demonstrate that there is no need for lengthy checklists of *topoi*. By using cognitive engagement, the persuader can make a focused application of the general models of argument to the particular circumstances of the persuadee. Thus the *kairotic principle* (see Chapter 4, below) is enacted in a distinctive response to the specific situation.

In the next section we shall review in more detail the ten models of argument described above. We shall also link these models with whatever schema or schemata seems to fit most appropriately. We followed the sixteenth-century educationist and populariser Peter Ramus in our choice of ten models, slightly modifying his selection (see Ramus, 1968 [1574]) to match our sense of current rhetorical usage, and in pursuance of our overall aim to make rhetorical skills as broadly applicable as possible. Even Aristotle's three general topics (*koina*) used across the whole range of rhetoric, and noted by Crowley and Hawhee (1999: 82), have their characteristic uses (i.e. the *greater or lesser* for the rhetoric of praise or blame, the *past* for legal rhetoric, and the *possible or impossible* for political deliberation.) Our purpose in focusing on ten models of argument is to explore the role of rhetoric in a wider range of contexts, as diverse as advertising and poetry. Taking this broader perspective, we shall start our consideration of the ten models with the definition model of argument.

The Definition Model of Argument

We put this first because it is vital to cognitive engagement. It reflects a general characteristic of schemata, because definition is inevitably part of every act of cognitive engagement, as each particular combination of schemata is recognised and acted on.

'Define your terms' is an exhortation frequently encountered both in discussion and written contexts, especially by those in a learning situation. It means we are required to narrow down the generalisation into a precise meaning. This process is exactly what Aristotle's model of definition entails: first, any idea or thing requiring definition must be assigned to some general category (*genus*); next, its *differentia* (the unique feature that makes it essentially distinct from other members of its *genus*) must be identified (see, for example, Luce, 1958: 27–30, 129–30). Famously, Aristotle's definition of 'man' was 'animal' (general category) and 'rational' (unique feature). Twenty centuries later, Swift, less optimistically, redefined 'man' as 'animal' (general quality), modifying 'rational' to 'capable of rationality' (unique feature) (1932: 429). This bitter redefinition confirms that in persuasive argument, every definition may prompt a counter-definition. To Swift 'man' was an animal characterised by a unique degree of irrationality, who, though capable of reason, more often chose not to exercise it.

(a)   The definition model of argument in functional persuasion

(1)   Ordinary conversation

This model is frequently employed in collocations such as: 'What it boils down to is . . .'; 'By definition he's a . . .'; 'She's the sort of teacher who . . .'; 'In the last analysis what sets him apart is . . .'.

(2)   Journalism (invented examples)

'This is the political party that seeks to make vegetarianism compulsory'; 'Not so much the Green as the Greens Party!'

(b)   The definition model of argument in literary persuasion

Our examples (from *Middlemarch* by George Eliot and the modern epic poem *Omeros* by Derek Walcott) use the definition model to introduce their heroines. Dorothea Brooke is rich but looks 'poor'; Helen is poor but has the hauteur of the 'rich'. This is the very first line of Eliot's novel:

> Miss Brooke had that kind of beauty which seemed to be thrown into relief by poor dress.   (Eliot, 1965 [1872]: 29)

A little further into his poetic narrative (comparatively speaking), Walcott's narrator sees through the noonday dazzle of a tourist beach on the island of St Lucia, what at first appears to be a 'padding panther':

> Now the mirage
> dissolved to a woman with a madras head-tie,
> but the head proud, although it was looking for work.
> I felt like standing in homage to a beauty
>
> that left, like a ship, widening eyes in its wake.
> 'Who the hell is that?' a tourist near my table
> asked a waitress. The waitress said, 'She? She too proud!'
> (Walcott, 1990: 23–4)

In the Eliot extract we have an exact process of definition through differentiation. Dorothea is beautiful in one specific way, which is not unique to her personally (we recognise her contemplative and unselfconscious 'kind of beauty'), but it is used to define her predicament. These opening lines, through the use of definition, prepare the reader for what will follow – Dorothea will find herself torn between her principled humility, her own emotional needs and society's expectations. In cognitive terms, the definition reflects Dorothea's guiding life theme schema, and also engages the social role theme schema of her high status as a gentlewoman in nineteenth century England.

In contrast with Eliot's precise definition, Walcott introduces his Helen with a looser set of defining and distinguishing characteristics. Definition here is part of a complex of imagery and observed detail that also involves the models of comparison and cause/effect. Helen's beauty is implied through the pride that accompanies and perfects it; this pride is differentiated in social and economic terms ('the head proud, although it was looking for work'). A further distinguishing characteristic is the effect and intensity of her beauty; even in the casually exploitative context of a Caribbean beach bar, the narrator feels like 'standing in homage'. This 'definition' is assisted by Walcott's cognitive engagement with the reader. Within the physical and social *scenes* of the bar and beach, tourists lazily pursue their *enjoyment goals* (schema), while the waitress has her *instrumental goal* (schema) of keeping the customers happy, and Helen hers of 'looking for work'. Each of these elements 'defines' itself with a series of specific indicators, including some not quoted here. The scene, and the climax of the waitress's *script* (schema) as she tells the customer what he wants to know, helps to 'define' the subsequent progress of Walcott's tragic epic. This is to be a Helen 'with a difference'. A third defining characteristic plays on the famous description of Helen of Troy ('the face that launched a thousand ships'), and contrasts Homeric grandeur with the beach bar environment. Moreover, Walcott's Helen is 'like a ship' herself. In her 'wake' we see her effect, as the poet observes eyes 'widen' with desire.

The Cause and Effect Model of Argument

Cause is at once a simple concept, and a highly problematic one. Its larger processes are so multiple and random that they lead to the most profound scientific and philosophical questions. However, we shall limit our discussion to cause within the context of persuasive language. *Cause/effect* is the model of argument absolutely central to all persuasive discourse, used in all contexts both public and private. It is important to note that its structure is inherently dialectical (suggesting as it does a two-way process of argument).

We can break down this complex model into manageable parts if we analyse the way in which our minds work to isolate or inter-associate the processes of cause and effect.

- A *simple cause* usually produces a *simple effect* (I drop an egg: it breaks). But it could have a *complex effect* (it is the last fertilised egg of a rare species, which becomes extinct, causing irreparable loss to the gene pool)
- A *complex cause* may have a *simple effect* (oversleeping and missing bus leads to late arrival at work; trying to catch up all day means shopping forgotten: *simple effect* – cat goes hungry).
- A *complex cause* may have a *complex effect* (German militarism, British jingoism, naval arms race, colonial rivalry, economic and nationalistic tensions plus other incalculable factors lead to: *complex effect* – the First World War).

Looking at these combinations, we can see how differently a persuader might use the cause and effect model of argument by changing its orientation (see Chapter 2). For example, the conjectural issue of a murder trial (see Chapter 4) would be oriented referentially, determining cause of death by identifying the murderer. The task of persuader/prosecuting counsel would be to focus the jury's attention on this task. In the context of a political speech, the persuader would use conative orientation to address the supposed interests of the audience, identifying the beneficial *effects* of his or her policies. Thus the murder trial could be described as cause-dominated argument, and the political speech as effect-dominated argument. Both types can produce rhetorical oversimplification and imbalance, something which easily happens whenever people are seeking to claim credit or pinpoint blame.

There are several varieties of the cause and effect model of argument regardless of orientation or degree of complexity. Aristotle's distinction between four types of cause (see, for example, Lloyd, 1968: 57–62) may not match modern scientific and evolutionary criteria, but it remains rhetorically useful in its representation of how a particular state of affairs has come into being. The four types of cause are:

(a) *Final cause*: the purpose for which something exists, or the end to which an action is directed.
(b) *Formal cause*: what makes something 'itself' (a *single seat* and *back* together compose a *chair*, which makes it *different* not only from a *stool, form* or bench but also from an *armchair*).

(c)   *Material cause*: the physical materials or conditions essential for existence generally sustain a given state of affairs or individually produce an object or an action.

(d)   *Efficient cause*: the agency that brings something about, possibly involving the agency of a subordinate or *instrumental cause*.

(a)   The cause and effect model of argument in functional persuasion

The following extract is the penultimate paragraph of a third leader (*Guardian*, 21 January 2004). Despite its conventionally lighter tone, it nevertheless makes a serious political comment about the Prime Minister's willingness to engage in public debates and interviews outside parliament. The leader headline is 'Tony Blair: Open Season':

> He evidently regards such sessions as useful; if he did not, then he would not do them. Presumably he does them because he is confident that he can change sceptics' minds. Or perhaps because he thinks that his readiness to defend himself in public impresses the voters that he is a strong leader with guts. But it must be doubted whether they are really as positive as he believes. Are they accountability or spectacle? In the age of reality TV the line between the two is growing thinner. How long before Mr Blair appears on 'I'm a Prime Minister – Get Me Out of Here', or is voted off the island?

The leader writer is dealing with the public's perceptions of Mr Blair, and the tangible consequences of these perceptions in terms of the effects he hopes will follow from these 'sessions', if he 'does them' diligently enough. That he considers them 'useful' for a variety of purposes is clear from the fact that he always finds room for them, in what writer and readers both know to be a very crowded schedule (the wording and the choices here seem to echo Heller's *Catch-22* – see pp. 24–6 above). Note that the definition model of argument is also involved here, as the writer asks where is the 'dividing line' (*differentia*) within the 'public perception *via* the media' (general) that separates 'accountability' from 'spectacle'? The paragraph ends with a humorous fantasy about a Prime Ministerial 'reality TV' show. The cognitive engagement or schema we note here ('a strong leader with guts') invokes role themes associated with leadership, the projected *effect* being heightened public confidence. The paragraph as a whole reveals that the schema most clearly involving a perceived link of cause and effect is the instrumental goal.

Perhaps Mr Blair has discovered a particularly effective mode of public communication through which to achieve his objectives – or perhaps not. (If he veers too far towards 'spectacle', this will produce a distinctly undesirable effect).

(b)   The cause and effect model of argument in literary persuasion

The following passage turns on the idea of final cause or motivating purpose. In Alice Walker's *The Color Purple* (1983) the metaphor of growth is used by Shug Avery, much-admired friend of the heroine, to describe her understanding of God:

> . . . It sort of like you know what, she say, grinning and rubbing high up on my thigh.
> *Shug*! I say.
> Oh, she say. God made it. Listen, God love everything you love – and a mess of stuff you don't. But more than anything else, God love admiration.
> You saying God vain? I ast.
> Naw, she say. Not vain, just wanting to share a good thing. I think it pisses God off if you walk by the color purple in a field somewhere and don't notice it.
> What it do when it pissed off? I ast.
> Oh it make something else. People think pleasing God is all God care about. But any fool living in the world can see it always trying to please us back.   (Walker, 1983: 167)

No longer is God an 'old white man' ('God ain't a he or a she, but a It'), but a creative spirit manifested in human love as well as in nature. Liberation comes to Celie through enlightenment about what motivates God (the final cause of 'Its' actions), and about the effect humanity has on God. The cognitive engagement here depends on the reader's schema (recollected or imagined) of a flowering field (physical scene) enriched by 'the color purple'. The general script of a stroll through the country is activated by Walker, as Shug reminds Celie that her 'country walk' should include a sense of wonder at any kind of beauty met on the way. To perceive this is the effect of a motivating cause, namely God's intention 'to please us back'.

The Similarity Model of Argument

Similitude is important not merely for its imaginative or figurative use, but also as a strictly logical mode of argument. Both kinds of use depend on an intuitive process integral to language as communication. In debate or discussion, before an argument can proceed, and irrespective of its ultimate objective, it is often vital to establish whether A is comparable with B. Furthermore, it makes sense that this model of argument should be closely associated with the models already discussed, since definition and cause and effect must be used to determine comparability. Equally, the similarity model will have links with our next two models, opposition and degree. Cognitively, the intuitive perception of similarity enables us to link every object, situation or event we encounter with one or more of our memory-based schemata; in the context of persuasion we may need to examine, qualify, assert and/or exploit this similarity. Having perceived similarity, we may also recognize thematic qualities (*thematic organisation points* or TOPS). This mental process of identifying similarity underlies every act of comparison from metaphor through logical analogy to children's acquisition of grammatical structures.

(a)   The similarity model of argument in functional persuasion

An invaluable model of argument for political orators, this is typified in Churchill's witty response ('Some chicken! Some neck!') to the Nazi boast in 1940 that Britain was about to have 'its neck wrung like a chicken'. Without entirely rejecting the comparison, Churchill transforms the script and the implied farmyard scene so that listeners imagine an enormous chicken towering over the puny farmer!

(b)   The similarity model of argument in literary persuasion

Comparison is one of the dramatist's basic resources, especially when criticising contemporary society, where an audience may be invited to compare their own situation with that represented on stage. Bertolt Brecht's *The Resistible Rise of Arturo Ui* parallels Chicago gangsterism with Hitler's rise to power. As he puts it in one of the alternative prologues to the play:

Friends, tonight we're going to show . . .
. . . Our great historical gangster play . . .
. . . we'll give you for your betterment
DOGSBOROUGH'S CONFESSION AND TESTAMENT.
ARTURO'S RISE WHILE THE STOCK MARKET FELL
THE NOTORIOUS WAREHOUSE FIRE TRIAL, WHAT A SELL!
THE DULLFEET MURDER! JUSTICE IN A COMA!
GANG WARFARE: THE KILLING OF ERNESTO ROMA . . .
. . . we've decided to put on
A story in these parts little known
That took place in another hemisphere
The kind of thing that's never happened here . . .

(Brecht, 1981: 105–6)

The capitalised lines refer to specific stages in gangster Ui's rise, paralleling equivalent stages in Hitler's career, and including an ironic disclaimer. As a process of cognitive engagement, Brecht invokes a network of schemata familiar from gangster movies such as *The Godfather* ('the Killer's Rise to Power'). A series of TOPs links the distinctive feature of each stage to a corresponding phase in Hitler's fanatic opportunism. Because the audience knows what will happen, Brecht focuses their political and moral awareness upon the substance of his comparison. Elsewhere, in his *Jottings* (quoted in Brecht, 1981: 109), he explains precisely how the similarity model is being used in this 'parable play', what are its limitations and what final cause it is being shaped to serve ('the aim of destroying the dangerous respect commonly felt for great killers').

Like Brecht, the imaginative exploration of poetry also draws heavily on the logical resource of similarity. The reader thinks as well as feels. Stevie Smith's well-known poem 'Not Waving but Drowning' points to the similarity between the physical state of an isolated, exhausted swimmer and the psychological state of people isolated from society ('Oh, no no no, it was too cold always'). In both cases, observers find it convenient to interpret the waving arms as cheerful insouciance, though in fact the 'swimmer' is 'not waving but drowning' (Smith, 1985: 303). Moving between these two painfully contrasted scripts we move from one instantiation (as it is termed in cognitive theory) of the familiar 'sea-bathing' *scene* to another instantiation, both literally and metaphorically.

The Oppositional Model of Argument

Appropriately, this model of argument is the opposite of the previous one, and is easy to recognise and use. We employ it, for example, when one personal commitment becomes incompatible with another equally pressing one (e.g. a friend needs support when an essay is due to be handed in), or when new priorities are changing old-established patterns of behaviour or affiliations. A typical conversational expression of this will be 'You can't do **A** and at the same time keep on doing **B**.'

In Marlowe's play *Faustus* (II.ii.67–73), the eponymous doctor, having sold his soul to the Devil for power, pleasure and knowledge, asks Mephistophilis one vital question: 'Now tell me, who made the world?' Refusing to answer until Faustus's indignant protest ('Villain, have I not bound thee to tell me everything?'), Mephistophilis snaps back 'Ay, that is not against our kingdom, but this is' (Marlowe, 1969: 287). In cognitive terms, this question threatens Mephistophilis's instrumental goal of keeping Faustus on the Devil's side. So, in broader terms, using the oppositional model of argument can expose incompatibilities between our goals.

Another common use of the oppositional model of argument is demonstrated in the frequently adversarial nature of contemporary public debate. There is a common assumption today that any action in the public domain has a single dominant motive (if one opposed motive is accepted, the other motive must be ruled out entirely). When this kind of oppositional thinking becomes adopted generally, not only does it seem to reflect deeply rooted mental and spiritual assumptions, but it also transforms them into syllogistic ('either/or') patterns of thought. Less oppositional views of motivation ('why not both?') lose credibility. Nevertheless, the oppositional model of argument can be a valid way of stirring up debate through deliberate provocation. There are also some well-known sub-varieties of the oppositional model of argument, such as *contraries* (good/bad); *contradictions* (good/not good); *privatives* (sighted/blind); *relatives* (parent/child).

(a) Oppositional models of argument in functional persuasion

The rhetorical usefulness of the contrary is obvious and appears frequently, especially in political argument where characteristically it is integrated with the cause and effect model of argument. Typically it is

used in advertisements where a painfully unfashionable figure effectively recommends a product by opposing it. Here new cognitive
scripts are applied in a familiar social scene – but reverse expectations
(e.g. fashionable young woman learns about healthy bacteria from
geeky young man in coffee shop). An example of contradiction is the
acerbic comment of the French philosopher Voltaire who described the
ramshackle 'Holy Roman Empire' (constituted by the assorted states
and mini-states of eighteenth-century Germany) as 'Neither holy, nor
Roman, nor an empire'. Familiar idioms and proverbs provide examples of other sub-varieties: 'Don't blame the children, blame the
parents' (relative opposition); 'There's none so blind as them that will
not see' (privative opposition). In *The Tenure of Kings and Magistrates*
of February 1649, written to justify Charles I's execution, John Milton
uses relative opposition to prove that those Presbyterians who are now
protesting at his death had already effectively deposed the king by
disobeying him. Once a king's subjects stop behaving as 'subjects', he
effectively ceases to be a king (1974: 274–5).

An effective example of opposition argument in contemporary journalism may be seen in an article by George Monbiot, the campaigner
against global capitalism ('Comment and Analysis' page of the
Guardian, 1 June 2004). In a piece entitled 'An Empire of Denial' he
attacks a book by an old friend, Niall Ferguson, in which Ferguson
urges the United States to face up fully to its responsibilities as a *de facto*
imperial power, and learn from the best practice of the former British
Empire. Monbiot questions whether there was ever any good practice
to emulate:

> But he asks us to remember only in order to persuade us to forget. He
> seeks to exchange an empire in denial for an empire of denial.

The second opposition here is subtler than the first one: a contrast
between wilfully forgetting one's own responsibility to exercise power,
and forbidding others to remember the true awfulness (in Monbiot's
view) of any imperial precedent.

(b)   Oppositional models of argument in literary persuasion

Shakespeare's Sonnet 66 displays a bravura series of oppositions, involving many vivid personifications of the qualities at war within his society (with the bad ones always winning):

TIRED WITH all these for restful death I cry:
As to behold Desert a beggar born,
And needy Nothing trimmed in jollity,
And purest Faith unhappily forsworn,
And gilded Honour shamefully misplaced,
And maiden Virtue rudely strumpeted,
And right Perfection wrongfully disgraced,
And Strength by limping Sway disabled,
And Art made tongue-tied by Authority,
And Folly, Doctor-like, controlling Skill,
And simple Truth miscalled Simplicity,
And captive Good attending captain ill:
   Tired with all these, from these I would be gone –
Save that, to die, I leave my love alone.

Shakespeare's unstated oppositional premises are that vice should not be accorded the honours and power appropriate to virtue, nor virtue, the dishonour and disempowerment appropriate to vice. Eleven lines give alternating instances in which one of these things is happening in the world of the poet. The primary effect is emotional, built on a sense of *unfitness* long since identified as a major key to *pathos* (see Mack, 1993: 208–9). Here, indignation is beaten down into bitter exhaustion by grinding repetition. Any reading of the poem will be enriched by greater understanding of its context, but it still speaks powerfully to us through its sharp oppositions; the universal emotions 'translate' readily into today's contingent emotions, scripts, scenes and frustrated goals.

Two and a half centuries later, Charlotte Brontë in *Jane Eyre* (1847) attacks the false oppositions (reason/passion, body/spirit, male/female, grace/nature) inherent in the oppression of women. The hypocritical and tyrannical clergyman Mr Brocklehurst reproaches Miss Temple, Superintendent of Lowood School for extravagance. In a half-page diatribe he uses rhetoric opposing the achievement goal of religion to the preservation goal of adequate nourishment (two things not normally thought of as incompatible). Recalling to the reader the common scene (school dining room) and its characteristic script (school meal), Mr Brocklehurst concludes:

Oh, madam, when you put bread and cheese, instead of burnt porridge, into these children's mouths, you may indeed feed their vile bodies, but you little think how you starve their immortal souls! (Brontë, 1996 [1847]: 74)

The Degree Model of Argument

This model relates closely to the two preceding ones. Referred to earlier as one of the three 'common topics' assigned to deliberative or political rhetoric by Aristotle, its various formulations are quickly recognised. Qualitative arguments claiming that A is fairer/more profitable/more practicable/cheaper/better value/more ecologically sound/safer/more fun, etc. than B, are frequently applied to anything from politics to holidays. We compare two things or people possessing the same quality but to differing degrees ('You think he's clever? Wait till you meet her!'). The degree model of argument can be applied to the desirability of one goal when compared with another, and to the instrumental means of achieving an agreed goal. It reflects the inbuilt dynamism of the processes of cognition, constantly modified as we meet new circumstances. We conceive better or different goals, construct new instrumentalities for achieving them, and 'write' more effective scripts for ongoing scenes. The terms 'more' or 'less' are inevitably fraught with feeling as well as cognitive perception.

In discussion, the degree model of argument works both ways. If a friend praises film A, we may claim that it's not nearly as good as film B on the scale of directorial achievement. Conversely, should the argument turn on probability, we might cite a greater (and more improbable) achievement, arguing that whoever could do that, will certainly manage our much easier task ('If she can recapture that constituency, she can certainly organise a village fete!').

(a)   The degree model of argument in functional persuasion

Advertising makes much use of this model, to the extent that illustration seems almost superfluous. We are more than familiar with the claim that car A has more X than car B, more Y than car C, and more Z than car D – and costs less! For examples of this model in political persuasion see Mrs Thatcher's parliamentary reply (pp. 44–5).

(b)   The degree model of argument in literary persuasion

An effective and mutely tragic example of this model appears in Nadine Gordimer's short story 'The Last Kiss', in which she presents the decline of an Afrikaaner pioneer from his earlier financial success and mayoral dignity:

The town outgrew Van As. As he got older, it got younger, more vigorous and brash, became more and more of a show-off. He was all right for Masonic gatherings and Dutch Reformed Church bazaars and the Sons of England ball, but would he have done to open swimming galas, judge beauty queens, or welcome a visiting Hollywood film actress making an appearance in person?   (Gordimer, 1983: 192)

The passage continues with further hypothetical instances of social and rhetorical occasions which would overtax the old man's skills, in the degrees to which he had developed them ('His English was not very good; his Afrikaans, though that was his mother tongue, was not much better'). Cognitively, the reader recognises the townspeople's new goals of enjoyment and relatively trivial achievement, and the different and more demanding social scripts entailed. By these means Gordimer seeks to persuade us of the inevitability of his decline and disgrace.

The Model of Testimony

This model was always regarded as the weakest of the *topoi*, because it depended on the credibility of a witness and was not inherently reliable. The value of testimony is likely to be highest either when based on genuine specialist knowledge skilfully deployed, or when it is a first-hand account of material events perhaps validated by searching cross-examination in a court of law. When *testimony* is part of a persuasive message, the authority's way of thinking should be made so apparent that the audience feel themselves to have applied his or her logical approach in reaching a conclusion, rather than passively relying on the *ethos* or prestige of an expert's name. *Witness* in this sense should function in the same way as teaching, enlarging awareness, extending method and presenting a recognisably practical *plan* (see pp. 216–17 below) for solving a problem or resolving an issue. Otherwise, testimony must be assigned to *ethos* rather than *logos*. Indeed, any persuader seeking to use this model of argument should be mindful of the way in which all testimony (knowingly or unknowingly) is susceptible to ideological shaping and orientation (see Chapter 2).

(a)   The testimony model of argument in functional persuasion

Appearing everywhere, this model of argument bombards television viewers throughout advertisement breaks with endless images of talkative

and satisfied consumers. Testimony is also a stock feature of party political broadcasts, where interviewees declare their support for a particular party because opportunities have been afforded or needs met, shown
in *scenes* familiar to the viewer. This model of argument can be strik-
ingly exemplified in news reporting, as when the BBC television
reporter Brian Hanrahan denied that any British aircraft were lost in
the first raid of the 1982 Falklands War ('I counted them all out and I
counted them all back').

(b)   The testimony model of argument in literary persuasion

In John Donne's poem 'The Ecstasie' (11.69–76), the reader of the
poem is invited imaginatively to testify to the power of spiritual love –
an unexpected script for the personal and physical scene of love-making
anticipated by the male voice and recommended to the reluctant
woman:

> To our bodies turn we then, that so
>   Weak men on love reveal'd may look;
> Love's mysteries in souls do grow,
>   But yet the body is his book.
>
> And if some lover, such as we,
>   Have heard this dialogue of one,
> Let him still mark us, he shall see
>   Small change, when we'are to bodies gone.
>   (Donne, 1990 [1633]: 123)

The poetic voice does not seriously ask us to become *voyeurs*; rather,
any lover who reads this poem is invited to witness and imaginatively
empathise with Donne's own testimony of love.

In fiction, since the concepts of narrative voice and multiple narrative began to be exploited, witness has played a vital part. In *Wuthering
Heights,* for instance, Emily Brontë makes full use of the differing testi-
monies of Lockwood, Nelly Dean and Isabella to unfold a mysterious
ambiguity in Cathy and Heathcliff's relationship.

The Genus/Species Model of Argument

This dialectical model of argument (still used regularly in discussion and debate) is recognisable in Greek philosophical dialogues well before Aristotle's time. Typically, the pattern of argument starts with Speaker 1's generalisation, functioning as an opening statement ('all juvenile delinquents come from a deprived background') or with an assumption ('we'll never get anywhere with this problem until we improve housing and youth employment'). Using the same model of argument, Speaker 2 may counter this by citing exceptions ('but wait a minute, records show that some delinquents come from prosperous and loving homes'). Speaker 1 might counter this new generalisation with a further exception ('but perhaps those particular delinquents are deprived in another sense – morally and culturally?'), and so on. This genus/species model of argument is like a set of Chinese boxes, with the argument moving from *genus* to *species*, from *species* to *sub-species* and even to *sub-sub-species*. In terms of cognitive networks, *generalisation* (grouping things together) is used to predict characteristics, and *particularisation* works to limit this predictability. The value of this interplay is stressed very persuasively by Michael Billig (1996: 148–85).

It is also vital to note that any deliberate attempt to engage with the cognitive schemata of an audience will have to take account of the interplay between general ideas or values (typically what Schank calls life themes), which for most people change very little once established (e.g. a commitment to honesty), and the constant re-categorisations that rise from direct experience, with its demands on human adaptability. As Schank puts it in his *Dynamic Memory Revisited* (1999: 2): 'Our memories are structured in a way that allows us to learn from our experiences. They can reorganise to reflect new generalisations – in a way, a kind of automatic categorisation scheme – that can be used to process new experiences on the basis of old ones.' The persuader who is sharing the new experience of his audience (e.g. a politician facing an unexpected turn of events touching everybody; or one of two friends, intuiting what some new personal experience means to the other), may well go on to link this sudden re-categorisation of experience and expectation to old-established ideas – to appeal to 'unchanging values' as guides in a new situation, or to challenge their relevance.

(a) The genus/species model of argument in functional persuasion

This model is often used in casual conversation: in this exchange ('Can't James have his thirtieth birthday party at home?' 'Not likely:

he's still living with his parents!') the initial generalised expectation (that James owns a house or flat) is countered by an observation reflecting a current social trend (property is too expensive for young people). In a written context, this model was used to searching effect by Jonathan Swift in his letter to Alexander Pope (29 September 1725), where he attributes nothing but evil to the human species, as well as specific groups within that species, differentiating only in favour of the individual:

> I have ever hated all nations, professions, and communities, and all my love is towards individuals: for instance, I hate the tribe of lawyers, but I love Counsellor Such-a-one, and Judge Such-a-one . . . But principally I hate and detest that animal called man, although I heartily love John, Peter, Thomas, and so forth.   (Swift, 1932: 429)

Through his cognitive *thematic organisation point*, Swift links lawyers as a species to the barbarism, rapacity and exclusiveness which (for him) characterises a 'tribe'. However, while retaining his reference to sub-specified legal roles (Counsellor and Judge) he singles out certain exceptional and amiable lawyers who really care about justice.

(b)   The genus/species model of argument in literary persuasion

In literary persuasion this model is often used to address possible bias in the reader, or at least to undermine their expectations. It can also be used to present a character's thought-processes. In this passage from Ralph Ellison's *Invisible Man* (1952) a young black student (working in a paint factory after being unfairly expelled from his Southern black college) is attacked by Brockway, an elderly fellow-worker, for attending a Union meeting:

> 'I'LL KILL YOU, THAT'S WHAT!'
>   He had said it again and something fell away from me, and I seemed to be telling myself in a rush: *You were trained to accept the foolishness of such old men as this, even when you thought them clowns and fools; you were trained to pretend that you respected them and acknowledged in them the same quality of authority and power in your world as the whites before whom they bowed and scraped and feared and loved and imitated, and you were even trained to accept it when, angered or spiteful, or drunk with power, they came at you with a stick or a strap or a*

cane and you made no effort to strike back, but only to escape unmarked. But this was too much . . . he was not grandfather or uncle or father, nor preacher or teacher.   (Ellison, 1965 [1952]: 184)

Ellison's protagonist remembers how he was trained to accept any kind of bullying authority (*genus*) embodied in black or white (the dominant white *species*, its imitators, and the *sub-species* of father, preacher, leading hand, etc.). He learns 'in a rush' to change his deferential social script, to differentiate and reject such false, second-hand authority in all its forms. By challenging Brockway, the protagonist breaks with 'authority' for the first time in his life.

The Part/Whole Model of Argument

It is not easy to differentiate the *part/whole* model of argument from the genus/species model; the key is to remember that parts are normally dependent on their wholes, whereas the species comprising a genus can exist separately. The *parts* of a living body or a machine can only be understood fully in relation to the *whole*. In our increasingly complex society, we acquire extended cognitive schemata (Meta-MOPs, see p. 218) that 'package' multiple scripts and scenes to describe complicated entities. For example, the word 'module' (applied to a taught course) implies a free-standing unit; in fact, any one 'module' will include multiple scripts of administration, course materials, teaching and assessment, *each* of which has its own separate constituent script. These are the parts that make up the whole. To evaluate any one part requires relating it to the whole. A more politically dubious version of this model of argument is when a society as a whole is judged on the basis of one individual *group*, with other groups marginalised and forgotten.

(a)   The part/whole model of argument in functional persuasion

A classic example of this model of argument is provided in St Paul's letter to the first-century citizens of Corinth (I. Cor. 12: 14–20, Jerusalem Bible translation). Using the analogy of the human body, Paul is arguing that followers of Christ, though individuals, together are Christ's body.

Nor is the body to be identified with any one of its many parts. If the foot were to say, 'I am not a hand and so I do not belong to the body', would that mean that it stopped being part of the body? If the ear were to say, 'I am not an eye, and so I do not belong to the body', would that mean that it was not a part of the body? If your whole body was just one eye, how would you hear anything? If it was just one ear, how would you smell anything? Instead of that, God put all the separate parts into the body on purpose. If all the parts were the same, how could it be a body?

Not only is Paul using the part/whole model of argument, but he is also using the similarity model, comparing the human body in its numerous parts to the distinctive, mutually supportive relationship between the Church and the people.

A rather different question about the part/whole is posed by D. H. Lawrence in his essay 'Nottingham and the Mining Country':

England has had towns for centuries, but they have never been real towns, only clusters of village streets. Never the real *urbs*. The English character has failed to develop the real *urban* side of a man, the civic side. Siena is a bit of a place, but it is a real city, with citizens intimately connected with the city. Nottingham is a vast place sprawling towards a million, and it is nothing more than an amorphous agglomeration. (Lawrence, 1950: 121)

Lawrence implies that 'village streets' are too much alike to be effective parts of a whole and hence Nottingham (with its 'amorphous agglomeration' of streets) is not a city worthy of the name.

(b)   The part/whole model of argument in literary persuasion

In 'To his Coy Mistress' (written *c*.1651) Marvell uses the emotive force of *enargeia* in a witty and hyperbolic variation on the conventional *blazon* (or amplification) of beauty. He launches into a part-by-part evocation, thus creating a composite picture of overwhelming impact:

A hundred years should go to praise
Thine eyes, and on thy forehead gaze.
Two hundred to adore each breast:
But thirty thousand to the rest.
An age at least to every part,
And the last age should show your heart:
For, lady, you deserve such state;
Nor would I love at lower rate.
(Marvell, 1990 [1681]: 24)

Such 'building up' had become a contemporary poetic convention (see Edmund Spenser's description of the bride in 'Epithalamion' [Spenser, 1992: 348–9]). Marvell energises the device by making the fantasising lover 'adore', successively, each component of the coy mistress's infinitely desirable beauty, thus taking that infinity of desire quite literally. The sum total of the 'time' he longs to spend in loving her, 'part' by 'part', far exceeds the totality of time itself. At this date, the beginning of time was calculated at around 4000BC, with the creation of Adam and Eve. Marvell's 'amatory arithmetic', as J. B. Leishman called it, adds up to more than the whole sum of time. Marvell bends the 'literal' back towards the 'metaphoric', preparing the reader for the shock of real time – and death – in the next stage of the poem. Rapidly losing patience with his carefully constructed pretence of infinite patience, Marvell sweeps reader and mistress into the climax of the poem, in which time itself is made to 'run' after the lovers.

The Associational Model of Argument

This model of argument is suspect on the grounds that it tempts the user to make false logical and ethical assumptions. Nevertheless it is frequently employed in argument over qualitative issues (see Chapter 4). Although it has affinities with the figurative device of metonymy, discussion of this will be deferred till Chapter 6. We now distinguish four main varieties of this model of argument: *subject/adjunct, lifestyle/status, place/function* and *time/activity*. A slightly different pattern will be followed in this section, providing examples of both functional and literary persuasion in our discussion of each variety.

(a)   Subject/adjunct association model of argument

Although Peter Ramus used the terms 'subject' and 'adjunct' to denote the whole category of associational argument (see, for example, Ramus, 1968 [1574]: 30–5), we shall apply them more narrowly. Adjunct means an adjoined attribute, quality or condition associated with a definable subject (this could be anything from a person to an activity or concept). In the context of persuasion, we might call such an adjoined attribute an 'indicative quality', because it shares a feature in common with the subject. As we tend to interpret descriptions of people or things on the basis of expected themes or goals (e.g. characteristic motivation, behaviour, personal qualities), persuasion with a positive spin will assure us that the proper indicative qualities are in place (our soldiers are brave and compassionate, our government ministers principled and politically adept, our judges just). In negative persuasion such expectations will be reversed, as Winston Churchill did in 1945, when trying to dissuade the British people from electing a Labour Government. He warned them that under Attlee 'we shall have civil servants who are neither *civil*, nor *servants*'. Another example might be when we argue that a given quality cannot properly belong to somebody, as in this example: 'I don't know why you call her generous: it's not *her* money she's giving away, it's ours!' The aggrieved speaker's argument turns on who can be described as generous, the treasurer of the club or the club members. In Ramist terms, the club is the subject to which the quality of generosity is attributed as adjunct.

(b)   Life-style/status association model of argument

This particular association model operates widely throughout our consumerist culture and its assumptions are well-documented by sociologists. Status is accorded to an individual on the basis of everything from house, car, clothes and occupation to diet, drinking habits and leisure activities. Conversely, the briefest indications of a person's status will prompt predictions about their life-style. Evidence of this *life-style/status* association occurs not only in everyday conversation, but especially in that kind of advertising that uses dialogue as part of its persuasion. The slogan 'I bet he drinks Carling Black Label!' appeared throughout the 1980s in a seemingly endless series, successfully condensing the association in an amusing two-way process. Various instances of way-out 'macho' behaviour invariably triggered off the slogan, the implication being that any drinker whose life-style included the beer, would be accorded similar status by his masculine peer group. In stark contrast, a more recent beer advertisement shows a destitute French prisoner, bound for a penal colony, maintaining status in his own mind by the seemingly endless pursuit of an elusive bottle of Stella Artois.

Chinua Achebe's novel *Things Fall Apart* offers an interesting example of this lifestyle/status model of argument functioning in an African context, positioning his hero in readiness for the subsequent tragic narrative:

Okonkwo's prosperity was visible in his household. He had a large compound enclosed by a thick wall of red earth. His own hut, or *obi*, stood immediately behind the only gate in the red walls. Each of his three wives had her own hut, which together formed a half moon behind the *obi*. The barn was built against one end of the red walls, and the long stacks of yam stood out prosperously in it.   (Achebe, 1958: 10)

In *The Castle*, Franz Kafka makes a very different use of the life-style/status model. In his surreal and oppressive world there are minimal indicators of status, yet even here people obsessively use dress to confirm status and identity. They have no other way of defining their position in relation to the Castle, seat of all power:

Well, he might be one of the lower grade servants . . . but these always have an official suit, at least whenever they come down into the village, it's not exactly a uniform . . . you can always tell castle servants by their clothes . . . a peasant or handworker couldn't do with them. Well, a suit like that hasn't been given to Barnabas and . . . it makes us doubt everything. Is it really Castle service Barnabas is doing . . .?   (Kafka, 1959 [1926]: 165)

(c)   Place/function association model of argument

This association model is embodied in the following sharp comment by a teacher to a lazy pupil: 'You don't come to school to stare out of the window! You come here to get on with your work!' A holiday postcard from the French Riviera is a written example of the *place/function* model; against a romantic image of a couple in the sunset the legend reads 'St Tropez' and 'Love'.

(d)   Time/activity association model of argument

This kind of association model of argument typically reflects people's expectations ('What, me? At my time of life?') and social rituals ('After Eight Mints'). As his end approaches (v.iii.25–6), the murderous usurper Macbeth laments being written out of the script and scene of 'that which should accompany old age' for a revered monarch, namely 'honour, love, obedience, troops of friends' (Shakespeare, 1997: 2611).

The Root Meaning Model of Argument

This is another model of argument which is open to all kinds of manipulation (and further undermined by recent theories about the social construction of language). Nevertheless, the *root meaning* model of argument retains some persuasive mileage, and – uniquely – does not merely express logical concepts through the received meanings of words, but seeks alternative meanings and arguments in the origins of words themselves.

A few examples will suffice to demonstrate its use in functional and literary persuasion. A dubious teaching technique is revealed in this comment:

> *Teacher*: 'Nice'? Can't you think of any other word? Do you know what it meant originally? 'Ignorant' – just like you!'

Focusing on the root meaning of a word can help us to expose unexamined assumptions on which an argument is based. For example, a female politician might challenge a male opponent: 'You talk about the nature of society as if it was something that just happened! Unlike nature, society was made by men – and we're trying to make a better job of it now!'

A different use of the root meaning model appears at the end of Shakespeare's late comedy *The Winter's Tale* (V.ii.133–7). The entertaining rogue Autolycus is pardoned at the instigation of the Old Shepherd, whose graciousness matters more than his logical and etymological naïveté.

> *Autolycus*: I humbly beseech you, sir, to pardon me all the faults I have committed to your worship. . . .
> *Shepherd*: Prithee, son, do, for we must be gentle now we are gentlemen.
>
> (Shakespeare, 1997: 2611)

This concludes our analysis of the resources of reason (or *logos*) available to a persuader. As an exemplar of *logos* at work, we offer a passage which remains as topical to this second edition as it was in the first.

An Example

> The National Health Service should be a completely adequate system for the health-care of the nation, provided at public expense (*definition*). It

means precisely that: not some kind of nationally available system you can pay for, or a nationally available but second-rate service if you're poor and ill and can't afford anything better (*genus/species*). Today it is under threat from forces opposing these public ideals and wishing to promote private care for the sick (*opposition*). The result is demoralisation for those who work in the NHS, and confusion for those who need to use it (*cause/effect; whole/part*). Building up a structure of legislation to 'improve' the Health Service, which in fact damages it, is like asking the fireman to put petrol on the fire instead of putting it out (*similarity, opposition*). Only in this instance the fire is being lit all across the country! (*Degree*). If you doubt this, ask anyone who has recently been in hospital or who works for the NHS (*testimony*). What do we mean, we might ask ourselves, by the terms *National Health Service*? Surely 'National' implies the good of the whole nation, not just those able to pay; 'Health' means 'wholeness', not division; and 'service' means caring and protecting, not destroying (*root meaning, opposition*).

Conclusion

In this chapter we have 'pulled out' the ten models of argument to outline and illustrate, rather as if they were rabbits coming one by one out of a hat. In other words we have taken them out of their rhetorical contexts, in order to see how each one works. In so doing, our aims are to show readers how to recognise the *logos* element in any kind of written or spoken argument or discourse, to tune in more precisely to logical signals, and to make confident use of a wider repertoire of logical models. Readers may also find that – recalling Chapters 1 and 2 – the preponderance of a particular model of argument in any given persuasive text will provide a strong clue to its ideological slant.

We shall be looking in Chapter 4 at the process through which these models of argument are combined more or less overtly with other propositions or implied ideas, and used to make individual logical deductions. We shall also consider the wider framework of argument to which individual models contribute, strengthening a persuader's position regardless of whether the issue has just been raised with the persuadee, or is already under debate. As we shall demonstrate, this activity involves the persuader in a careful selection and prioritisation in his or her choice and combination of models – a process traditionally known as 'judgement'.

Further Exploration: the Theory and Practice of *Topoi*

Readers who are interested in exploring the more complex ancient systems of particular *topoi* should start by looking more closely at Aristotle in Lawson-Tancred's accessible modern version (1991) or at Kaplan's translation (1954) of the anonymous *Rhetorica ad Herennium*. Lanham (1991: 167–8) provides a summary of topics adapted from Aristotle and suitable for modern use. An even more detailed treatment of *topoi* (strongly supported by reference to other modern commentators) will be found in Corbett (1990: 94–155).

Readers who have an interest in teaching rhetoric in post-16 education may find the following texts useful. Robert Cockcroft (2004) writes about encouraging students to experiment with models of argument as a means towards cognitive engagement. He also analyses a range of early modern and contemporary texts (both literary and critical), making use of schema theory integrated with models of argument (Robert Cockcroft, 2003).

4 Reason: Choice and Judgement

Introduction: the Context of Judgement

We now come to the moment of truth in our study of the sources of persuasive language. How will the audience (or indeed the persuader) *judge* the persuasion? Judgement will certainly be exercised at both ends of our familiar diagram (Sender > Message > Receiver). The persuader as Sender will judge stance, emotional engagement and choice of argument before beginning the persuasion, having assessed the audience. In spoken persuasion it will be possible to monitor audiences minute by minute, adapting techniques accordingly. In writing, however, final judgements about how the reader is likely to respond have to be made before the book is published, the essay submitted or the advertisement printed.

The audience as Receiver will also exercise judgement. In spoken persuasion especially the audience will be affected to some extent by *ethos* and *pathos* as well as *logos*. Depending on the occasion, any one of these principles might come to the fore. For instance, as seen on archive film in Ludovic Kennedy's programme *The Gift of the Gab* (BBC2, 15 August 1989), Hitler swayed his audiences by personality and stance, waiting silently for their total attention before speaking. Another example is Mark Antony's speech which, as we saw above, makes much use of cunningly oriented emotional engagement and reversal of bias. Again, in our imaginary speech about Health Service cuts at the end of Chapter 3, reasoning is central to the persuasion.

In summary then, judging persuasion is more complex than might at first appear. There are many variables to be considered when analysing the central interaction between persuader and audience. Recalling Chapter 1 and the discussion of dialectic and persuasion, we must note that at all times the persuadee retains the options of counter-argument or even rejection. These hidden but ever-present possibilities must inform our understanding of judgement.

109

We shall now consider specific questions asked by persuaders about their own rhetoric, and by persuadees about their responses. On both sides of this interaction, our judgement should by guided by the *kairotic* principle, with its constant reference to what occasions the persuasive interaction. Crowley and Hawhee (1999: 42) note that 'A rhetor (i.e. a persuader) attuned to *kairos* should consider a particular issue as a set of distinct political pressures, personal investments and values, all of which produce different arguments about an issue.' Thus an 'issue' can be described as a common point of focus within such a 'set'. The key questions to be asked here are: What is the issue? How urgent is it? How close to the audience's concerns? How relevant are the arguments likely to be used on both sides? Are these arguments valid – or at least probable?

What is the Issue?

We need to consider how the models of argument described and illustrated in the previous chapter are to be employed. To use them effectively, the persuader needs a vital point of confrontation. This is called the point of issue, and it will define the persuader's specific stance in any individual situation. Earlier we considered stance in relation to *ethos* (the values, personality and trustworthiness of the persuader); in this chapter we emphasise the relation between stance and *logos*.

Unexpectedly, the point of issue has proved to be a key feature in a popular television series (*Sex in the City*) set in the sophisticated world of New York. The heroine writes a weekly column for a fashionable journal about life and love in Manhattan, and every week she raises a 'point of issue' or generalised question based on her own or her close friends' experiences. Each episode, at some stage, includes an image of Carrie's laptop screen as she types (with voiceover), the words which formulate the issue. (Indeed, one of the last episodes of the final series put as the 'issue' question: 'When is it time to stop asking questions?'!) In this chapter we shall demonstrate how such questions are formulated, confronted and resolved.

A persuader must inevitably 'take a stand' on a particular issue. To make any real progress, the persuader must also be *in stasis*, as Crowley and Hawhee put it (1999: 45) with his or her opponent. By agreeing to differ on the same issue, they can each present focused arguments and a decision can be reached by the audience (e.g. a jury). According to Quintilian (*Institutio Oratoria*, III.vi.72–3) the *question* precedes the issue (his term for this is *basis*). If a man accused of murder denies the charge, the question is whether he has, in fact, killed anybody. Thus the issue is factual. Such factual issues are in the rhetorical sense of the word '*conjectural*' issues. On the other hand, if the accused man admits to a killing but claims justification, there is no factual issue, and argument will centre on the motive for his action (see below). In the first scenario there is already a point of stasis over a factual issue; in the second there is not.

Stasis is still important in the context of persuasion, even where there is no active opposition. For example, if a politician is addressing an audience of the 'party faithful', there is still an issue of some kind between them (e.g. the level of support, the right strategy or the prospects of success). The politician and the audience are thus in stasis over these unresolved issues. This demonstrates our differentiation between the politician's stance as a persuader, and the issue. The terms equivalent to issue are *stasis* (Greek) and *status* (Latin). (Interestingly, these terms are both recalled in the modern English words 'status' and 'stance'.)

To identify something as an issue, we need either to be familiar with the ongoing progress of a debate, or to reflect on the essentials of some entirely new topic (for example, a barrister with a new brief; an advertiser with a new client; a new head teacher faced with a culture of bullying; or a back bencher promoted into government). If a writer wishes to apply persuasive techniques to his or her writing, he or she will need to think of an issue or series of issues on which to focus the tensions and perceptions of the chosen genre, whether poetry, drama or fiction. Arguing that issue has its part in literary persuasion means that, in one sense, our treatment is broader than that of Crowley and Hawhee (1999: 44–74), and narrower in another. One of the clearest passages dealing with this complex and much-debated theory is to be found in Book III, Chapter 6, of the *Institutio Oratoria*:

> We must therefore accept the view . . . followed by Cicero, to the effect that there are three things on which enquiry is made in every case: we ask *whether a thing is, what it is,* and *of what kind it is.* Nature herself imposes this upon us. For first of all there must be some subject for the question, since we cannot possibly determine *what a thing is,* Or *of what kind it is,* until we have first ascertained *whether it is,* and therefore the first question raised is *whether it is.* But even when it is clear that a thing *is,* it is not immediately obvious *what it is.* And when we have decided what it is, there remains the question of its *quality.* These three points once ascertained, there is no further question to ask. . . .

One or more of them is discussed in every demonstrative, deliberative or forensic theme.   (Quintilian, 1920–2: I, 450–1)

This 'natural' order of enquiry can, as Quintilian states, be applied to all three persuasive genres, i.e. to praise and blame, politics and the law. We would argue that this can be extended to include imaginative writing as well as other genres of practical persuasion. Our outline of issue will cover the three divisions of whether it exists (the *conjectural* issue), what it is (the *definitive* issue), and of what kind or quality it is (the *qualitative* issue). In extending the issues into imaginative writing we take our cue from Sir Philip Sidney, who claims that 'to imitate . . . true poets . . . borrow nothing of what is, hath been or shall be, but range, only reined with learned discretion, into the divine consideration of what *may be* and *should be*' (Sidney, 1973: 102; our emphasis). We will now look at conjectural issue, definitive issue and qualitative issue in selected texts, typifying how models of argument are activated by issues.

(a)   The conjectural issue – does it exist?

In the context of persuasion, there are several ways in which the actual or potential existence of an entity, such as a crime, a political crisis or a workable policy becomes manifest to everyone. The most obvious models here are cause/effect and testimony. In examining the events leading to a trial, the jury considers the motives, actions and methods involved in the alleged crime as possible causes. Legal textbooks call this 'the chain of causation'. However, the oppositional model ruling out the commission of a crime by somebody with a convincing alibi, will negate the 'chain' in the prosecution's case – unless the chief instrumental cause of the crime can be shown to be human (e.g. a 'hit man' or hired thief). Especially in murder cases where there is no direct evidence relating to the killing (e.g. when no body is ever found) the prosecution will make use of the part/whole model, assembling all the pieces of the puzzle except the missing one (e.g. motive, time and place of the victim's disappearance, evidential value of the defendant's subsequent actions etc.) in order to argue the case.

Where political rhetoric is concerned there is a striking recent example of the conjectural issue (*whether it is*). Were any Iraqi weapons of mass destruction (WMD) in existence just before the

2003 Gulf War? If any such systems (in whole or part), or any direct evidence of their production (cause/effect) had been discovered, the resolution of this issue would have led to profound consequences, both nationally and internationally. As it turned out, the continuing political controversy surrounding WMD centred on other issues. The issue of fact remained for a long time on the 'back burner', showing the importance of past *events* (or non-events) as durable sources of disagreement. Failure to find concrete evidence of Iraqi WMD has continued to advantage opponents of the war.

Political rhetoric also applies the models of argument to current 'factual issues' in society. Has a particular policy made any measurable difference? Opinions will vary according to the perspectives of the contending parties. Similarly disparate conclusions will be reached by political journalists. With respect to future political action as assessed by the electorate, the conjectural issue switches from 'whether it *is*' to 'whether it *will* be'. Thus argument focuses on probability. Cause/effect argument is used to demonstrate the *likelihood* or *unlikelihood* of success. The policy announced in February 2004 by the British Conservative Party for cutting taxes while improving public services, has been attacked using the oppositional model, and defended using the cause/effect model (elimination of wasteful practice, freeing of funds, concentration of effort etc.).

Other more familiar persuasive approaches turning on this issue include the 'factual' claims of advertising, from the blunt, hugely successful Ronseal slogan, 'It does exactly what it says on the tin!' to the carefully modulated statement that a particular skin cream can make wrinkles less apparent (even if it can't get rid of them altogether).

The literary equivalents of this conjectural issue range from the use of demonstrably factual settings for imagined characters (as in the naturalistic fiction of Zola) to the representation of impossible events as 'real' to the senses and the emotions (as in magic realism, fantasy or science fiction). Being believable is the first step in literary persuasion; if the reader is not convinced about character situation or plot, an issue of credibility has arisen. The writer cannot then go on effectively to raise other issues. But 'factuality' can itself become important within the story. For example, the 'factual issue' of what did or did not happen in the Malabar caves moulds the whole development of E. M. Forster's *A Passage to India* (1924). Questions of 'fact' loom equally large in Conrad's *Lord Jim* (1900), to which we shall refer later in exemplification of all three types of issue.

(b)   The definitive issue – what is it?

In legal rhetoric, the definitive issue arises when the connection between a particular action and an accused person has been established or agreed. The most crucial and familiar kind of definitive issue addresses the question of whether a particular homicide should be defined as murder or manslaughter. The stock definition of murder is 'unlawful killing with malice aforethought'. This conforms exactly to the Aristotelian model of *genus* and *differentia*. However, in the jury's consideration of malicious intent, final and instrumental causes will come into consideration (e.g. carrying a gun, interfering lethally with equipment). Moreover, the degree and motivation of 'malice aforethought' might be questioned, changing the issue to one of quality. This demonstrates the importance of this legal issue as a general standard for the handling of definitive issue within other, non-legal rhetorical genres.

Where political persuasion is concerned, the WMD controversy described above provides a straightforward illustration of the definitive issue in another context. Granted that the British government and security services were fully persuaded of the weapons' actual existence immediately before the 2003 war, what kinds of weapon were they thought to be? An obvious definitive issue arose in January 2004 over whether Iraq's alleged chemical or biological weapons were short range or long range. Only in the latter case would they constitute a threat to neighbouring countries. Was it important that the British Prime Minister was aware of this difference? A letter to the Editor of the *Guardian* from Professor D. Piachaud (6 February 2004) turned on this issue. The writer asserted that if Tony Blair didn't know that battlefield weapons were meant, his ignorance was 'shameful'; or if he did know, he was embroiled in a 'grossly deceptive and false' series of misstatements and omissions. In either case the Prime Minister 'should resign'.

The definitive issue will always be involved when politicians seek to prove the distinctiveness and efficacy of their approach to policy, whether applied in the form of individual measures, or as an all-embracing political philosophy defined by some specific priority (e.g. economic efficiency, social justice, a 'green' approach, Europeanism, nationalism etc). The task of definition will in either case be assisted by the use of the part/whole model: showing how a particular philosophy will touch every area of national life, or how particular organisations will be reshaped to 'deliver' planned improvements. The similarity model of argument can also be used in political persuasion when parties seek to define their intrinsic differences. A typical format is when opponents of a particular governmental policy use the similarity model to illustrate ministerial ineptitude or failure. For example, government concerns about welfare, safety and public health (i.e. obesity and alcohol abuse) lead to accusations that a 'nanny state' is being created.

When the definitive issue of value is not agreed or resolved, and a disagreement arises over a specific problem, debate is effectively stalled. The disputants are not *in stasis* if they are facing what amounts to a complex issue. One group, for example, might insist that immigration should be dealt with in accordance with economic expediency, and another, that social justice should be the priority. The first group will call it 'an economic issue', and the second 'an issue of social justice'. A third group might argue that neither of these concerns should resolve the issue by itself, without reference to the other. Nobody will be persuaded unless they agree to a redefinition which may be either a reversal or a broadening of their ideological stance. Moreover, they still have to find a solution to the immediate problem occasioning the dispute. Thus they have two questions to answer, not one.

In other areas, the issue of definition has a clear part to play, notably in advertising, which often seeks to persuade people of the distinctive character of a product by claiming it is 'in a different class'. The product is not simply better or worse, it's better because it's fundamentally different, like the dustbag-free Dyson vacuum cleaner.

In literary persuasion, the definitive issue has been detected at the very core of the creative impulse. For instance, it is implicit in Harold Bloom's famous theory of 'the anxiety of influence', according to which every 'strong poet' is not only brought into imaginative being by his or her great 'precursors', but also driven to define his/her difference from them (see Bloom, 1973, 1975). Artistic output in any medium (for example, film) draws attention to itself in the first place by belonging to a familiar genre (road-movie, film-noir, western, thriller, epic, bio-pic) but the director and the distributors will emphasise its definitive difference from all other examples of the genre.

(c)   The qualitative issue – of what kind is it?

Although in a legal context this is known as the *juridical* issue, the common term is the *qualitative* issue. In its most developed form this issue involved a complex series of sub-distinctions, which we will look at briefly. They raised questions about motive and responsibility, which might lead to the exoneration of an accused person, or the lessening of his/her guilt in the eyes of the court. The modern persuader might follow a similar course in uncovering the motives behind an action. An example of how this works is Malcolm Heath's interpretation of the work on issue by the Greek rhetorician Hermogenes (*c.* AD 160–225). He brings the process to life with a made-up example of how to shift the issue:

> First you demonstrate the innocence of your intentions; then you effect the transfer of blame . . .; next you minimize the wrong done in comparison to the constraint you were under; then . . . you recharacterize your action in such a way that you no longer appear to have done anything wrong after all. So a student who claims that he failed to submit an essay . . . because of the constant demands of his elderly, bedridden landlady . . . could argue . . .: it was not the result of idleness (*intent*); it is all because of my old landlady (*transference*); my obligation to be kind to the elderly and infirm outweighs the obligation to produce the essay (*relative importance*); so my default is more dutiful than negligent (*forcible definition*).   (Heath, 1995: 21)

The process involved here is *counterposition*, where what appears to be 'an acknowledged . . . wrong is defended as justifiable or excusable in the circumstances'.

A similar use of counterposition will be found outside the legal context whenever motive is being uncovered. As 'persuasion may involve *concealing* or 'down-playing' the interests behind the persuader' (see Chapter 1), modern investigative journalists may follow the same tactic in uncovering suspect motives and interests. The quality of these interests and motives is being scrutinised. For example, this might mean emphasising business or trades union influences behind a political party, or calling attention to a 'whistle-blower' with a vital message. The tactic exemplified above foreshadows the 'extenuating circumstances' argument advanced by the British and American governments in relation to WMD. The qualitative issue of *transference* is invoked, with a stress on *intent* (both governments sincerely believed that the information provided by their intelligence services could be relied on).

Another major resource employed in relation to the qualitative issue is the degree model of argument. When people are considering what action to take on any matter (e.g. choosing which one to buy of two equally suitable cars), they are not concerned with issues of fact or definition but with the qualitative issue. Different scales of evaluation may apply in different situations, but all will involve less or more of a quality. Other models of argument, such as cause/effect, association, and similarity may also be invoked to persuade us of the relevant quality.

(d)   Conjecture, definition and quality in Lord Jim

Literary persuasion inevitably engages with issues of quality; in Conrad's novel these are powerfully combined with issues of fact and definition. The book takes the reader through all three issues in the company of the hero, Jim. Put very briefly, Jim loses his honour when as a young officer he deserts his ship, and regains it when he keeps a promise to a friend, although this involves his death. As a result, he abandons not only his lover, Jewel, but also the community of Patusan, which has come to rely on him as its protector. Jim's first 'issue' in the modern sense is conjectural: he finds it hard to admit that he did jump over the side of the *Patna* into a lowered boat. He gives a mesmerising account of the experience to Captain Marlow, the novel's narrator, and finally tries to face the fact:

> 'I had jumped . . .' He checked himself, averted his gaze. . . . 'It seems,' he added. His clear blue eyes turned to me with a piteous stare, and looking at him standing before me, dumfounded and hurt, I was oppressed by a sad sense of resigned wisdom, mingled with the amused and profound pity of an old man helpless before a childish disaster.
> 'Looks like it,' I muttered.
> 'I knew nothing about it till I looked up,' he explained hastily. And that's possible too. You had to listen to him as you would to a small boy in trouble. He didn't know. It had happened somehow.   (Conrad, 1986 [1900]: 125)

The issues involved actually intertwine (i.e. they are not linear) and are debated internally throughout the narrative. *What* is it that Jim does, and *why?* As an officer charged by the code of duty with the safety of his ship and her passengers, he is by definition guilty of desertion; yet his account makes him seem hypnotised by the cries of the renegade officers he is to join in the boat. He never admits to a moment of wilful choice, but invites us qualitatively to explore all his excuses. Later in the book, duty itself becomes a complex issue, variously definable and never really resolved. Do we admire Jim for his stoicism in sticking to a more personal code of honour and remaining loyal to his friend (for

whose safety he has pledged his own life)? Or do we deplore his failure
to see that a much more binding duty lay elsewhere?

Argument, *Kairos* and Relevance

(a)   Relevance and the issue

Relevance (or appositeness) in argument will be judged according to: (i)
the relationship between the proffered argument and the point at issue;
(ii) the narrower and wider contexts of the persuasion; (iii) the relationship between persuader/audience (see Grice's relevance maxim
[p. 22 above]). In the context of practical persuasion there will also be
a distinction between arguments of theoretical relevance and those with
topical or personal significance. Relevance is primarily a logical concept
and controls argument; appositeness, on the other hand, is required in
the handling of emotion (*pathos*) and interaction (*ethos*) in the persuasive context. The appositeness and relevance of any persuasive approach
should be judged not only by an assessment of the immediate audience,
but also in response to current public attitudes. Every *issue* subject to
public debate will be affected by what people are prepared to believe at
any particular moment. We have mentioned *kairos* on several occasions
earlier in the book, but it is particularly important here. As a rhetorical
concept denoting 'timeliness' or a 'window of opportunity', the fleeting
quality of *kairos* is symbolised by a winged figure (see Crowley and
Hawhee, 1999: 32–3, for illustrative examples). *Kairos* reminds the
persuader to seek an apposite 'solution' to whatever issue has been
raised, thus reflecting the fleeting quality of the moment. In the example we cite below (pp. 124–6), *Guardian* journalist Catherine Bennett
will be seen to make a conscious estimation of the response of her read-
ership at the time of writing.

If a persuader can redefine or shift the point at issue in an argument,
he or she will stand a better chance of convincing an audience of the
irrelevance of an opponent's argument. Something like this may occur
even when the debate is not adversarial. Where two or more parties
have set out to reach a common view, there will be shared satisfaction
in any progress achieved. Where the issue is clearly defined, and
supported by relevant arguments, the confidence of the participants
will grow further, and reservations felt by waverers will dissolve. At this
point, non-adversarial discussion acknowledges 'the feeling of the meeting'. However, there remain two possible ways of resisting this consen-

sus. One possibility is to shift the issue, thereby undermining the major premise agreed by the majority. The other way is to agree on this premise but to claim that the argument so far has no connection with it. The following examples illustrate these two kinds of counter-attack.

(i) Shifting the issue

A striking example of this will readily be recalled by anybody who is familiar with the boudoir scene in Shakespeare's *Hamlet*, III.iv.128ff. His father's ghost has appeared and spoken to him a second time, unseen and unheard by his mother, and interrupting his denunciation of her behaviour in marrying Claudius. Gertrude begins once again to doubt his sanity and attribute his searing rebuke to madness, rather than her own conduct:

> *Queen Gertrude*:   This is the very coinage of your brain.
> This bodiless creation ecstasy
> Is very cunning in.
> *Hamlet*:   Ecstasy?
> My pulse as yours doth temperately keep time,
> And makes as healthful music. It is not madness
> That I have uttered. . . .
> . . . Mother, for love of grace
> Lay not a flattering unction to your soul
> That not your trespass but my madness speaks.
> (Shakespeare, 1997: 1723)

From the very beginning of this scene (III.iv.9–10), the issue between them has been in dispute. For Gertrude ('Hamlet, thou hast thy father much offended') it is about *his* behaviour; while for the Prince ('Mother, you have my father much offended') it is about *hers*. Who is being undutiful to whom? As Hamlet, after his impulsive killing of Polonius, continues his verbal onslaught, his mother (not having seen the ghost) questions the *quality* of the charge against her. It's not a matter of her own disloyal and lustful yielding to Claudius, but of Hamlet's insane accusation. In the full legal development of stasis theory, this would constitute a *counterplea* (Heath, 1995: 33, 72, 75). Despite seeing her own degradation in Hamlet's graphic account – 'Thou turn'st mine eyes into my very soul' (III.iv.79) – Gertrude seeks to shift the issue by questioning its rational basis. In the last line of the extract Hamlet shifts the issue back to the intrinsic quality of Gertrude's 'trespass'.

(ii) Proving irrelevance to the issue

Here we cite *Rhetorica ad Herennium* (II.v.8) to show how what seems to be a convincing argument may, after all, fail to prove the point:

> For Subsequent Behaviour we investigate the signs which usually attend guilt or innocence. The prosecutor will . . . say that his adversary . . . blushed, paled, faltered, spoke uncertainly, collapsed, or made some offer – signs of a guilty conscience. If the accused has done none of these things, the prosecutor will say his adversary had . . . so . . . calculated what would actually happen to him that he . . . replied with the greatest self-assurance – signs of audacity, and not of innocence. The defendant's counsel, if his client has shown fear, will say that he was moved, not by a guilty conscience, but by the magnitude of his peril; if his client has not shown fear, counsel will say that he was unmoved because he relied on his innocence.   (*Rhetorica ad Herennium*, 1954: 72–3)

There is evident agreement on the issue (did the accused commit the crime or not?) between the prosecution and the defence. The opposed arguments and counter-arguments reflect disagreement over what the evidence suggests. Both sides claim that the behaviour of the accused supports their case. In effect, the very ambiguity of the 'evidence' proves its irrelevance.

(b) Appositeness to audience

If persuasion is to be effective, both the issue and the arguments bearing on it must be of immediate relevance and concern to the audience. For an audience made up of disparate groups, *kairos* might require a mixture of issues if attention is to be held. Unless these are skilfully linked, the response will be equally mixed. For example, when a prospective parliamentary candidate seeks adoption by a constituency association, she has to square the concerns of the local party with national policy, however difficult this may be, and present herself in such a way that she appeals to a disparate and critical audience.

The relevance of argument and illustration tends to broaden in direct proportion to the importance of the issue. A profound issue will require a more fully developed context. For example, the religious concept of reward and punishment is placed in a socio-historical frame by the great poet–preacher John Donne, in his last sermon, *Death's*

Duel. He draws a parallel between the immediate situation of his hearers and another situation remote in place and time. The sermon was delivered 'before the King's Majesty, in the beginning of Lent 1631' 'in a faint and hollow voice', according to eyewitnesses, as the dying preacher invited the congregation to share his meditation on the Passion of Christ:

> I dare scarce aske thee whither thou wentest, or how thou disposedst of thyself, when it grew dark and after last night: If that time were spent in a holy recommendation of thy selfe to God, and a submission of thy will to his, it was spent in conformity to him . . . I will hope that thou didst pray; but not every ordinary and customary prayer, but prayer actually accompanied with shedding of teares, . . . puts thee into a conformity with him. About midnight he was taken and bound with a kisse, art thou not too conformable to him in that? Is not that too literally, too exactly thy case? at midnight to have bene taken and bound with a kisse? (Donne, 1967: 390)

Donne addresses a sophisticated congregation whose observance of Christian rites was belied by notoriously loose sexual mores. He indirectly attacks their behaviour during the most penitential season of the Church's year (when even marital relations were thought wrong). Donne's ironic questions twist the meaning of 'conformity', and link the betrayal of Christ with the self-betrayal of the sensual believer. He uses the intimate form 'thee', thus pointing the finger at each member of the congregation, not excluding the king himself. The 'kisse' becomes only too apposite! Donne is playing on the definitive issue by showing what kind of 'conformity' this is. To receive the kiss of sensuality (invoking memories of the Judas kiss) betrays a sinful 'conformity', diametrically opposed to true spiritual 'conformity' with Christ.

Argument and Probability

We shall now consider logical form, the credibility of argument in particular contexts, and its validity. We begin with a brief demonstration of how arguments are put together.

(a)   Introducing syllogism

In Aristotle's *Topics* (his work on logical invention), the philosopher distinguishes between the force of *analytics* or scientific demonstration (which reaches incontrovertible and purely rational conclusions) and *dialectic* (whose conclusions are based on probabilities rather than certainties – see Aristotle, 1984: I, 167). A common resource for analytics, dialectic and rhetoric is the argumentative form known technically as *syllogism*. This word, first used by Aristotle and meaning 'a putting together of two propositions', denotes the deliberate, rule-based and formalised employment of a deductive mode of argument. This occurs whenever two statements or two intuitive mental processes, each of which connects *two* ideas together, have *one* idea in common which makes it possible to link the other two ideas in the form of a conclusion. It is a process intrinsic to cognition whenever, matching any new perception to an existing schema in our memories, we look further for what belongs to that schema. A much fuller treatment of syllogism than we have space for will be found in *Classical Rhetoric for the Modern Student* (Corbett, 1990: 43–59). This includes the 'Square of Opposition', a diagram which regularly occurs in older textbooks of logic. This provides a means of evaluating the truth or falsity of statement in the premises from which syllogisms are constructed, as well as other relevant factors.

In reasoning and persuasion this process is more or less overtly verbalised. In our next example we introduce fully formalised argument in a context that intriguingly bridges the gap between academic usage and popular controversy. Syllogism was much used in drama and pamphlet literature in the sixteenth and seventeenth centuries. In *A Muzzle for Melastomus* (1617) Rachel Speght attacks an anti-feminist pamphlet by Joseph Swetnam ('the Baiter of Women'). Brought up in an academic family, she skilfully turns the weapon of scholastic logic back on its male proponents. She does this (in the mode of a confrontational 'disputant' at university) when she rebuts Swetnam's claim that 'God had . . . made women only to be a plague to men':

> Although I have not read Seton or Ramus, nor so much as seen (though heard of) Aristotle's *Organon*, yet by what I have seen and read in compass of my apprehension [i.e. within the limits of my understanding] I will adventure to frame an argument or two, to show what danger, for this your blasphemy, you are in.
>
> > To fasten a lie upon God (i.e., to claim that God tells lies) is blasphemy: but the Baiter of Women fastens a lie upon God:
> > **ergo**, the Baiter is a blasphemer.
> >
> > The **Proposition**, I believe, none will deny; the **assumption** I thus prove:

> Whoever affirms God to have called women 'necessary evils',
> fastens a lie upon God: for from the beginning of *Genesis* to the end
> of the *Revelation* is no such instance to be found. But the Baiter
> affirms God so to have called women: **ergo**, the Baiter fastens a lie
> upon God.

> *The reward according to Law Divine due unto the Baiter of Women:*

> Whoever blasphemeth God ought by his law to die: the Baiter of
> Women hath blasphemed God: **ergo**, he ought to die the death.
> *The Proposition is upon record* (*Levit.* xxiv: 14, 16).
> *The Assumption is formally proved.*   (Speght, 1985 [1617]: 77–8)

In our slightly modernised version of the text, we have set out the first
syllogism with a separate line for each constituent part, and highlighted
the technical words. Speght – despite not having read the standard logical textbooks (including Ramus) to which she refers – handles these
terms with consummate confidence. *Ergo* ('therefore') is the once-
familiar Latin word used triumphantly to conclude an argument. The
proposition (now called the Major Premise) is the statement on which
the argument rests; the *assumption* is the Minor Premise through which
the conclusion is drawn. Speght backs up her first syllogism with two
further ones to show what Swetnam deserves to suffer, according to the
scriptures whose authority he pretends so perversely to rely on, and
which are cited by Speght to clinch her counter-argument.

(b) 'Proving' probabilities: enthymeme

The distinction between analytic certainties and the probabilities with
which dialectic and rhetoric are concerned is echoed in the contrast
between *persuasion* and *conviction*, so strongly emphasised by Perelman
and Olbrechts-Tyteca in *The New Rhetoric* (see pp. 14–15 above). If we
paraphrase and develop the implications of this distinction, we can
make the following assumptions. Conviction signifies the assent of the
intellect to a proposition, and involves the belief that any other rational being, anywhere, would reach the same conclusion. Conviction
alone does not necessarily involve the emotions or the will, or produce
committed action, however. Persuasion involves both of these. Though
valid only for a specific audience at a particular time, it produces a
transformation of attitude and action.

Everyone must exercise rhetorical judgement, assessing the validity of
arguments in terms both of their persuasive force and of their logical

probability. In an everyday context, such argument is more informally structured than Rachel Speght's syllogisms. Some elements will remain implicit; but this does not mean that they are not fully connected in the minds of persuadees. When convinced that the Major and Minor Premises (explicit or not) are probable, validly connected and at one with their own emotional and moral judgement, they will be completely persuaded. For example, after a satisfactory interview with a potential baby-sitter, parents are persuaded that the chosen person meets all their criteria and can therefore be trusted to look after their child. The level of commitment in this decision is total, though the purely logical grounds for it amount to no more than strong probability.

To maintain such commitment in the longer term, the persuadee must continue to believe that his or her judgement is substantially more probable than alternative possibilities and as circumstances change, this commitment may need reviewing. In any such review, a less formalised method of implicit syllogistic argument will continue to be used. Aristotle used the term *enthymeme* primarily to refer to the probability of the premises in rhetorical syllogisms. He also indicated that this might involve leaving part of the argument implicit (1926: 24–5). From Aristotle onwards, this characteristic has been understood as the primary reference in the term *enthymeme*. Enthymeme is one of two customary forms of argument used in all kinds of public and private discussion, the other being induction. The use of such argument to assess probability is seen in Catherine Bennett's article on UK Supreme Court proposals (*Guardian G2*, 12 February 2004). Her *kairotic* stance assumes that her readers will share her own distrust of Tony Blair's government and its assurances, subsequent to UK involvement in the 2003 Iraq war. How likely is it, she asks, that the government is telling the truth about its motivation in setting up a Supreme Court?

> Of course, Lord Falconer might remind us that candidates for his supreme court will be selected by a new, unimpeachable appointments commission. It will put forward between two and five candidates for each place on the court, the victorious judge to be selected by – surprise! – the secretary of state for constitutional affairs.
>
> In more punkish, foulmouthed times such a proposal might have led some people to conclude that Lord Falconer's unilaterally imposed programme of 'reform' is not merely a clumsy, ill-conceived insult to the meanest intelligence, whose enormous cost has yet to be revealed, but a calculated attempt to weaken the independence of the judiciary, even as he claims to be doing the exact opposite.

Nowadays, things are different. Today the need to protect the fabric of public life from the whingeing of mandate-free journalists requires that we abandon what Andrew Gowers, the *Financial Times* editor, recently called 'the easy, superficial certainties of *parti pris* opinion', and embrace, instead, the more positive philosophy propounded by Dr Pangloss: 'Observe for instance, the nose is formed for spectacles, therefore we wear spectacles. The legs are visibly designed for stockings, accordingly we wear stockings.' Or as Lord Falconer himself puts it: 'The time has come to make a clear and transparent separation between the judiciary and the legislature.' Accordingly: 'By creating a supreme court, we will separate fully the final court of appeal from parliament'. And all will be for the best in this best and most modern of all possible governments.

This last part of Bennett's article has a rhetorical completeness in itself. The writer is reacting to recently published comments accusing the media of sapping public trust in government and the courts, through an all-pervasive cynicism. Rejecting this charge, Bennett adopts an ironically optimistic, compliant tone purporting to credit the minister concerned with the best possible motives. She thinks it highly unlikely that an up-and-coming minister would be strictly impartial in the choice of Supreme Court judges; this proposal is not only ruinously expensive but innately inimical to justice. Letting the ironic mask slip, she employs the oppositional model of argument, clearly implying that 'the independence of the judiciary' would be against the government's interests and cannot be intended, despite Lord Falconer's claim to the contrary.

We set out Bennett's argument in full syllogistic form to make explicit what was left implicit, and to bring to the surface the cynical assumptions of 'punkish journalists' like herself:

Major premise: Nothing limiting this government's power is likely to be intended by its ministers;

Minor premise: Strengthening the independence of the judiciary would limit the government's power;

Conclusion: Strengthening the independence of the judiciary is not likely to be intended by this government's ministers.

Lord Falconer's incredible claim to be strengthening the judiciary is juxtaposed with a far stronger probability that he is, *de facto*, 'weakening' it. The reader works back from this conclusion through the unstated premises of the enthymeme, and activates the logical deduction set out above.

In her concluding paragraph, Bennett demonstrates the folly of applying a naïve 'positive philosophy' to something so inherently improbable as Lord Falconer's assurances. She compares this with the optimistic belief expressed by the hero's tutor, Dr Pangloss, that 'all is for the best in the best of all possible worlds', in Voltaire's satirical novel *Candide* (1758). Basing his view on an extreme version of the 'argument from design' (i.e. that God made everything to suit humanity) Pangloss claims that noses are designed for spectacles and not spectacles for noses. Using the final cause and similarity models of argument, Bennett suggests similar gullibility in those trusting the government's claim that that the Supreme Court proposals are designed to serve the interests of the judiciary. In her view it is far more likely that they are redesigning the judiciary to serve their own interests. In a final rhetorical flourish, Bennett argues that Lord Falconer's 'explanation' seems not only unconvincing but also disingenuous.

Rhetorical Reasoning

We shall next examine the means of judging types of argument. Here we are not attempting a full treatment either of the technicalities of modern logic, or of reasoning as embodied in everyday language. For further guidance on both these areas of interest (including a modern approach to Aristotelian enthymemes), see the end of this chapter and A. A. Luce's clear introduction (1958) to the older kind of formal logic. Returning to Demosthenes's speech discussed in Chapter 1, we have chosen a different extract to demonstrate the orator's handling of *logos*. This will enable us to look at syllogistic reasoning and induction, in the context of an extended persuasive argument. Four major methods of argument can be demonstrated from the Demosthenes extract: firstly, the rhetorical enthymeme (implicit premise argument); secondly, the method of *induction*; thirdly, the *hypothetical syllogism* ('If . . . then' argument); and, fourthly, the *dilemma*, which is a form of syllogism. A fifth method of argument, the *disjunctive syllogism* ('Either . . . or' argument) will be demonstrated using a different example.

(a)   The extended enthymeme

if you are awake, you have nothing to fear, if you close your eyes, nothing to hope for. To prove this I point to two things, the past power of

Sparta, which we defeated by sheer attention to business, and the present aggression of Macedon, which alarms us because our attitude is wrong. If the belief is held that Philip is an enemy hard to face in view of the extent of his present strength and the loss to Athens of strategic points, it is a correct belief. But it must be remembered that at one time we had Pydna, Potidnea, Methone . . . on friendly terms, and that a number of communities now on his side were then autonomous and unfettered, and would have preferred our friendship to his. If Philip had then adopted this belief in the invincibility of Athens . . . he could not have achieved any of his present successes. . . . As it was, he observed with insight that these strategic points were . . . open to the contestants, and that it is a natural law that ownership passes . . . from the negligent to the energetic and enterprising.

Demosthenes's argument proceeds in two stages. Firstly, he proves the negligence of the Athenians and, secondly, he points to its consequences. His first *implicit major premise*, which employs the oppositional model of argument, is that to disregard the proven effects of 'sheer attention to business' is to display a wilfully negligent attitude. The present lethargy of Athens is both a reversal of its former energies and directly contrary to Philip's vigorous opportunism. This in its turn amounts to a minor premise, i.e. that Athens is disregarding the lesson it should have learnt from past experience and from Philip's current example. Demosthenes draws the conclusion that the Athenians' 'attitude is wrong'; they are wilfully negligent.

This is followed by a second enthymeme, in which only the major premise (the 'natural law that ownership passes . . . from the negligent') is stated. For Demosthenes's audience, the conclusion of the first enthymeme immediately functions as the minor premise of this second one. The Athenians draw a further depressing conclusion: their perverse *inactivity* is as much the cause of Philip's current advance, as his own determined *activity*. This point is proved by Demosthenes's reference to the enemy, who has succeeded not because of his initial strength but simply because of his attitude. Here Demosthenes makes a brilliant fusion of logical and rhetorical judgement, and unexpectedly turns his argument around. What has hitherto demoralised his audience becomes a way of boosting their confidence. Change your attitude, and you change everything.

(b) Rhetorical induction

Aristotle distinguishes (*Rhetoric*, I.ii.8) between two methods of induction, scientific and rhetorical (1926: 18–21). Both processes derive general laws from particular observations, but the latter is founded on the use of *example*. Demosthenes can even be compared to Machiavelli, who wrote nearly two thousand years later. The topic of Chapter 7 of *The Prince* is 'New principalities acquired with the help of fortune and foreign arms'. In it this arch-exponent of political realism draws general conclusions from Cesare Borgia's successful ruthlessness. Similarly, Demosthenes enunciates a 'natural [i.e. generalised] law' of political science derived from particular examples. As we have seen, he refers to the earlier example of Athens and Sparta and the current example of Macedon and Athens. Demosthenes takes two sets of data as adequate to prove the general rule that mind prevails over matter. He makes that into a principle for the guidance of Athens; if Philip can succeed against the odds in opposition to Athens, Athens can do the same in opposition to him.

(c) The hypothetical syllogism

Putting it positively in relation to these historical examples, Demosthenes states that 'alliance and universal attention are the rewards to be won by obvious preparedness and the will to take action'. This becomes the foundation of a new argumentative structure, the hypothetical syllogism (see, for example, Luce, 1958: 145–9; Corbett, 1990: 55–7). In full syllogistic and categorical form, the argument would read:

> **Major**:   'All well-prepared active states are successful';
> **Minor**:   'Athens will be well prepared and active';
> **Conclusion**:   'Athens will be successful'.

Demosthenes, however, does something different. He is making a strong emotional appeal by building up suspense. To do this he puts his argument, in which one premise remains implicit, into hypothetical 'If . . . then' form, using it to spell out how far his Athenian audience must commit themselves to resolute activity regardless of human cost:

> If then, this country is prepared to adopt a similar outlook . . . , if every man is ready to take the post which his duty and his abilities demand . . . , if financial contribution is forthcoming . . . and personal service . . . in a word, if we are prepared to be ourselves . . . we shall recover what is our own . . . and we shall inflict retribution upon Philip.

In formal logic, the major premise of a hypothetical syllogism takes this form: 'If A is B, it is also C.' If we sum up the argument above, it amounts to the following: 'If the Athenians are resolute, they will be successful'. This is what the repeated 'ifs' add up to, indicating as they do the required contribution of each part of the body politic. Rhetoric and logic work together through a highly persuasive and suspenseful ordering of sentence elements. In order to complete the argument we need a premise telling us whether the ultimate condition (the big 'IF') will be fulfilled. This premise hangs in the balance, hinging on the audience's response. Two valid forms of the hypothetical argument face them: (i) 'The Athenians will prove to be resolute' (leading to the conclusion 'They will be successful'); or (ii) 'The Athenians will not be successful' (leading to the conclusion 'They will not have been resolute'). The shadow of this negative conclusion overlays Demosthenes's later appeal to his audience's sense of shame (see the full extract in Chapter 1). If they fail, they will have only themselves to blame for refusing to act like 'free men'.

(d) The dilemma

Demosthenes then remarks of Philip: 'He does not offer us a choice between action and inaction. He utters threats, according to my information, in overbearing terms.' If a choice of action or inaction *had* been offered to the lethargic Athenians, they would have been faced with these unavoidable alternatives: 'If we act, we risk immediate defeat; if we remain inactive we will continue to lose power and influence.' This is the familiar form of the dilemma, where both choices lead to unpleasant consequences.

If we were to develop the implicit Demosthenean dilemma, it would become what logicians call a *complex constructive dilemma* (see Luce, 1958: 155). The minor premise would take the form of a *disjunction* or statement of alternatives: 'But we must either act or remain inactive.' The implied conclusion would be: 'We face either immediate or ultimate defeat.' Demosthenes chooses not to develop the idea, perhaps because he has no wish to offer the Athenians the option of doing nothing! Whether they act or not, the threat to Athens is immediate (though they retain the option of concerted action, promising a successful outcome).

(e)   The disjunctive syllogism

The Either/or explicit premise argument, or hypothetical syllogism, works through a process of elimination: 'A is either B or C; it is not B, therefore it must be C' (see Luce, 1958: 149–54). In *The Law of Freedom* (1652), the early communist Gerrard Winstanley produces a powerful rhetorical persuasion by anticipating arguments that use this process, and dismissing the premises on which they are based. In this instance he concludes (in effect) that A is neither B nor C! In his prefatory letter to Oliver Cromwell, Winstanley imagines himself replying to Cromwell's defence of 'the elder brother' (i.e. the landowning class, of which Cromwell himself was a member):

> But you will say, 'Is not the land your brother's? And you cannot take away another man's right by claiming a share therein with him.'
> I answer, it is his either by creation right, or by right of conquest. If by creation right he call the earth his and not mine, then it is mine as well as his . . .
> And if by conquest he call the earth his and not mine, it must be either by the conquest of kings over the commoners, or by the conquest of the commoners over the kings.
> If he claim the earth to be his from the kings' conquest, the kings are beaten and cast out, and that title is undone.
> If he claim title to the earth to be his from the conquest of the commoners over the the kings, then I have right to the land as well as my brother, for [neither] my brother without me, nor I without my brother, . . . cast out the kings; but both together assisting . . . we prevailed, so that I have by this victory as equal a share in the earth which is now redeemed as my brother . . .   (Winstanley, 1983 [1652]: 283–4)

Winstanley uses *disjunctive* argument to prove, inexorably, that this kind of reasoning affords no advantage whatever to his opponents. He anticipates the landowners' arguments, limiting their possible justification of private ownership to two alternative pleas. Either land was created by 'the spirit' for private ownership or it was conquered for that purpose. He adds two further alternative pleas to support the 'conquest' idea because his opponent has already lost the 'creation right' argument. This either/or process is repeated, uniting powerful *pathos* and *ethos* in its masterly *logos*. Twice he eliminates both alternatives that he imagines Cromwell posing against his case, as spokesman for the landlords. Thus any temporary relief felt by the 'elder brothers' landlords' (in turning to the 'conquest' plea) becomes a logical trap from which there is no escape.

This anticipation and dismissal of the opponent's case is highly effective rhetorically. It is enhanced by Winstanley's tight logical structure, and by his curt 'switch-around' of terms (see p. 182 below), reversing the polarity of cause and effect ('by the conquest of the kings over the commoners, or by the conquest of the commoners over the kings'). From this firm stance, Winstanley projects an image of his opponent's desperate twists and turns through the branching structure of the either/or argument. Logic provides him with a brilliantly persuasive ordering of his material, to create an insoluble dilemma for his opponents.

Spotting the False Argument

We have seen how logically valid reasoning can be attacked on the basis of its false premises. We shall now examine some major errors in the process of *inference* itself. We base our treatment on Luce (1958: 160–71) and Corbett (1990: 73–80), providing short colloquial examples to demonstrate the processes of false inference as succinctly as possible. It should then be possible for the reader to scrutinise any one persuasive text, and either be satisfied of its logical validity or find it faulty.

(a) Undistributed middle

'All great poets are ignored in their lifetimes. I'm ignored; so I must be a great poet.' If the terms of the major premise here are transposed or 'converted'(see, for example, Luce, 1958: 75–8), the reader will recognise that the category of those who are 'ignored in their lifetimes' is far broader than the category of 'great poets'! Logically speaking, we can't 'distribute' the state of being ignored entirely to the category of poetic greatness. Since 'ignored' is the middle term between the two premises, the inference is false.

(b) Accidental connection

'I spent ages over this: how can you say it's no good?' The time someone spends on a task has no logical connection with the quality of the performance. Marlowe's Faustus makes this error in thinking his 'magic' words called up the fiend Mephostophilis (*Doctor Faustus*, I.iii.45–9):

> *Faustus*:   Did not my conjuring speeches raise thee? Speak.
> *Mephostophilis*:   That was the cause, but yet *per accidens*;
>   For when we hear one rack the name of God,
>   Abjure the scriptures and his saviour Christ,
>   We fly in hope to get his glorious soul.
>
>   (Marlowe, 1969: 274)

Faustus's incantations happen to involve serious blasphemy. This, rather than any intrinsic power in the words, summoned the devil. The accidental connection between conjuring and blasphemy misleads Faustus into thinking he has power over evil.

(c)   Ignored qualification

'You said everyone should see this film. I took my son to see it and he was terrified.' In any review of a film known to contain scary scenes (e.g. the Harry Potter series, which has a PG certificate), 'Everyone should see this' carries the unspoken qualification 'provided they're not too young or overly sensitive'. Ignoring the qualification leads to a false inference about the benefit to be derived from seeing the film.

(d)   Missing the point

This fallacy takes two characteristic forms, the *argumentum ad hominem* (i.e. argument directed at a person, not an issue) and the *argumentum ad populum* (playing on emotion or prejudice to distract attention from the issue). The following are examples of the *ad hominem* argument in positive or negative versions: 'Why should we listen to what he has to say? He's such an objectionable man – look at the way he treats his constituents.' 'She gets on so well with people, I'm sure she'd be a good school governor.' Positive and negative versions of the *ad populum* argument follow: 'Take in more asylum seekers? Don't we already have enough pressure on housing and the Health Service?' 'Of course we'll win the war; we're the bravest people in the world!' Here, the first two arguments illustrate the error of directing one's argument at the good or bad qualities of an individual, rather than the overall merits or demerits of their case. The emotional loading of the second pair of arguments distorts the qualitative issues of justice and compassion in the first instance, and in the second the definitive issue of what constitutes readiness for war. Both these fallacies are particular forms of the more general logical error of 'arguing off the point'; it is probably one of the most familiar and tedious of logical errors.

(e) Begging the question

'There are no spots in the Sun,' said the Inquisitor, allegedly refusing to look through Galileo's telescope and verify his discovery of sunspots. Question-begging (*petitio principi*) occurs whenever a proposition or hypothesis, founded on disputable evidence, is not only treated as an established truth but also used to debar further investigation. Thus the Inquisitor believes in a perfect and unchanging universe centred on a flawless and unchanging sun. Dogmatic belief denies the legitimacy of Galileo's scientific evidence.

(f) False cause

'Oh why did I insist that he caught that train?' This kind of exclamation following a tragic rail accident is a natural response but a logical error. Taking the train did not *cause* the subsequent pain or grief. It had no connection with the variable elements whose chance interaction led to the accident. If the individual affected had not taken the train that day, it might well not have crashed in any case. Such a common logical error is conventionally labelled *post hoc, propter hoc* (i.e. 'subsequent to, and therefore caused by'). To distinguish between actual causes and mere coincidences requires scientific rigour, which J. S. Mill embodies in his three 'canons' of experimental observation. Mill's first 'canon' is particularly helpful in the context of this kind of logical error. It directs us to look for a *common* circumstance in any phenomenon which recurs in varying conditions, because that common circumstance *must* be either cause or effect of the phenomenon in question.

(g) Many questions

'Aren't we offering you free elections in April? How can you say we're not supporting democracy?' This fallacy consists of combining two separate issues in a single question and demanding a single answer. 'Are you in favour of free elections?' and 'Do you think an April election would leave enough time for parties to organise?' should be separate questions and may evoke contrary answers. The unanswerable question 'Have you stopped cheating in exams?' (or doing something equally unacceptable) is a comparable example.

Conclusion

We have shown the processes of judgement employed in the construction of arguments, have observed their integration with the principles of *ethos* and *pathos*, and have provided examples demonstrating the destructive or sceptical analysis of erroneous argument. As the examples show, rigorous reasoning contributes powerfully to persuasion. Moreover, logic can in its own right be a major source of emotion, when the reader or audience is struck by the sheer force, elegance and purity of the reasoning.

Further Exploration: the Theory and Practice of Judgement

Readers who wish to learn more about reasoning in the context of rhetoric might usefully start with Luce (1958) who provides a clear re-statement of traditional Aristotelian logic. For logic as embodied in everyday language see: Alec Fisher, *The Logic of Real Argument* (1988), Jeanne Fahnestock and Marie Secor, *A Rhetoric of Argument* (1990), and Deborah Tannen's bid to 'change the way we argue and debate' in *The Argument Culture* (1998). For a technical study of the varieties of Aristotelian enthymeme based on the *topoi*, see T/Ed Dyck (2002).

Readers wishing to practise enthymemic or syllogistic argument, using the models introduced in Chapter 3, will find examples in Appendix A. They will also find Corbett (1990) helpful in this area.

---

5 The Persuasive Process

Introduction: Ideas of Order

In earlier chapters we have analysed and illustrated the structural principles governing persuasive techniques in English, arguing throughout that persuasion consists of an interaction or dialectic between persuader and audience, and that within every persuasive interaction exists the possibility of disagreement and counter-statement.

In Chapter 4 we examined ways of judging persuasive argument in spoken and written language, looking at both sides of the persuasive interaction. In this chapter we shall look at the persuasive ordering of argument and, in the next chapter, at the stylistic choices made by the persuader. In the last four chapters we have explained how *ethos, pathos* and *logos* all help to 'prove' the persuader's position over a point at issue; the next task is to show how all three structural principles become ordered elements in a *persuasive process*. Indeed, the second stage of rhetorical composition has always included not only the judgement of argument but also the arrangement of material. Clearly, the more the persuader understands the audience and anticipates their response, the more this will influence any decision about persuasive ordering.

Writing an essay or report is a familiar task to most people today; similarly, 'giving a presentation' has become an increasingly frequent requirement for anyone with something new to impart in a public context, whether in the worlds of community affairs, business, education, fashion and the media or – and especially if – you are being interviewed for a job! In both spoken and written 'presentations', there is an implicit assumption that certain scripts and schemata will be followed, including the appropriate ordering of the text. Even in a seemingly fluid situation such as a school drama lesson, there will be a closely followed structuring lesson plan (schema/script). Studying the order or arrangement of arguments was a major concern of formal rhetoric as conceived by the Greeks and elaborated by the Roman rhetoricians and their successors. The range of treatments of persuasive ordering is wide and contentious. A very early example of this is Plato's mocking reference to the technical terminology taught by the Byzantine *logodaedalos,* Theodorus (see Plato, 1973: 83); Quintilian presents a lengthy and acute discussion of *dispositio* in three books (1920–2: II); and the acrimonious Renaissance controversies on this matter are surveyed in modern histories of rhetoric (e.g. Howell, 1961). This structuring of arguments (*dispositio*) resulted in a sequence of up to seven stages or parts. These were:

(i)   *Introduction*
(ii)   *Narrative or Statement of Facts*
(iii)   *Proposition, or Determination of the Point at Issue*
(iv)   *Division, or Enumeration and Summary of Points*
(v)   *Proof of the Case*
(vi)   *Refutation of Opponent's Case*
(vii)   *Conclusion*

(Some authorities, for example, Lanham [1991] include *Proposition* and *Enumeration* under the single heading of *Division.*)

This ordering was substantially influenced by the demands of the structuring principles *ethos, pathos* and *logos. Ethos* required that at the outset of a persuasive discourse, time should be devoted to establishing the right kind of rapport with the audience – a major function of the Introduction. Similarly, if the orator wished to benefit from the power of *pathos,* it made sense to develop this in the Conclusion (or peroration), thereby leaving a powerful impression in the audience's memory and a strong stimulus to their wills. A Narrative of salient facts, presented in the clearest light and from the most favourable angle, was also a likely preliminary to any statement of Points at Issue, and to the processes of Proof or Refutation which embodied *logos.* It is important to note, however, that any one of these stages could be omitted, or moved out of order, should the persuader wish. A current example might be an irritable response to someone's over-lengthy exposition 'Oh let's cut the cackle and get down to it!' A much earlier example can be found in *Paradise Lost* (IX.675–6) when the Serpent 'brooks no prologue' in his haste to denounce God's unfair ban on apple-eating. Similarly, marked variations in ordering can be seen in both spoken and written persuasion.

Ordering in the context of persuasion has interesting parallels with oral and written narrative and its associated patterns and structures. The American linguist William Labov in his major study *Language in the Inner City* (1972) developed a narrative structure theory based on the oral narratives of black vernacular speakers in New York. It consists of (a) *Abstract* (what it's all about?), (b) *Orientation* (who did what, when and where), (c) *Complicating Action* (then what happened), (d) *Evaluation* (so what's the point of the story), (e) *Result or Resolution* (what finally happened and how was it all resolved), (f) *Coda* (overview and returning to real time, not narrative time). This structure has fascinating parallels with the Roman rhetoricians' ordering of persuasion, and raises questions about the nature of the link between 'persuasion' and text structure (see Figure 3 for details), which we shall explore further in the next section.

Roman rhetoricians	Labov
Introduction	Abstract
Narrative	Orientation
Determination of point at issue	Orientation
Enumeration and summary of points	Complicating action
Proof or refutation of case	Complicating action
Conclusion (case proven)	Evaluation
Conclusion (response to points proved)	Result or resolution
Conclusion (call to action)	Coda

Figure 3   Parallels between persuasion in ancient Rome and oral narrative in New York

There are slightly different weightings here, and certainly the overt function of each set of structural principles differs (i.e. a speech in court aims to persuade, a comic anecdote 'A funny thing happened to me on the way to . . .' aims to amuse and entertain). As we shall see later, these functions may not be as far apart as they seem.

The need to follow established patterns of ordering in a variety of functional contexts is readily exemplified. The pattern of ordering a scientific report is as follows: *abstract, introduction, method, results, discussion, conclusion*. An academic essay, on the other hand, will balance thesis (arguments for a proposal) with antithesis (counter-arguments and disadvantages), leading to synthesis (elements of both extremes providing a workable solution). In literary contexts the narrative ordering of 'fairy tales' (i.e. oral/written narratives aimed at children) was analysed by Vladimir Propp (1975); he examined a hundred fairy tales and suggested that at an abstract level they 'contained the same underlying story structure' (see Graddol *et al.*, 1994: 230–4). Propp identified eight basic 'character roles' (e.g. villain, hero, heroine, helper) as well as 32 'fixed elements of narrative functions'. He boiled them down to six stages or sections always appearing in the same order: preparation, complication, transference, struggle, return and recognition. Interestingly, these stages can also be parallelled with Labov's categories. In looking at the structure of newspaper stories, Alan Bell has found that 'the most striking characteristics of newspaper discourse come from the non-chronological order of its elements' (see Graddol and Boyd-Barrett, 1994: 115). Many of the Labovian elements are there, but re-ordered and interpreted to match the readers' needs. For example, the story is encapsulated in the headline (e.g. 'Man Bites Dog' or 'Gun Grab Wife Freed'). This is what the story grammarians such as Pollard-Gott (et al., 1979) would describe as the 'minimal well-formed narrative' (see Graddol and Boyd-Barrett, 1994: 117).

Story grammar represents another way of describing narrative structure (story > setting + event structure). Following Propp, Mandler and Johnson (1977) identified these three basic 'units' as the building bricks of any narrative, which are linked together by 'and' (signifying number, relationship), 'then' (signifying temporality) and 'cause' (signifying cause/effect). What is particularly interesting for us is that these narrative structure units are similar to the scripts, scenes and other schemata that are now recognised as integral aspects of the cognitive dimension of persuasion, and which we have already discussed.

In our analysis of persuasive ordering, we started with Roman rhetorical principles, moved to the structure of contemporary oral narrative, and noted how narrative structure theory applies to genres seemingly as divergent as fairy tales and news stories. We have suggested how story grammar might assist our understanding of narrative structure, and have established links with cognitive script, scene and role as defined by schema theory. We have seen how all these theories corroborate and shed light on each other in relation to narrative structure theory.

How can we exemplify this? Perhaps the easiest thing to do is to look at a simple narrative which has a moral (i.e. there is an element of persuasion). The following poem by Hilaire Belloc may serve our purpose. It is taken from *Cautionary Tales* (1907), a collection of comic–gruesome poems describing (with tongue in cheek) the Awful Fate awaiting children who are Naughty, and the Rewards for those who are Good (e.g. Matilda who would play with matches and burnt up herself and her house, or Jim who ran away from his Nurse and was eaten by a Lion). This lighthearted attitude to the grisly fate visited on misbehaviour is reflected in this narrative (see Figure 4).

HENRY KING

WHO CHEWED BITS OF STRING, AND WAS EARLY CUT OFF IN DREADFUL AGONIES

Preparation	The Chief Defect of Henry King	Story/setting/Abstract/Introduction
Complication	Was chewing little bits of String	Orientation/Narrat./Deter.PoV
Transference	At last he swallowed some which tied	Complic. action/Narrat/Det.PoV
Struggle	Itself in ugly Knots inside.	Complic. action/narratio/Det.PoV
event 1	Physicians of the Utmost Fame	Complic. action/Narrat./Det.PoV
Struggle	Were called at once; but when they came	Complic. action/Narrat.
event 2	They answered, as they took their Fees	Complic. action/Narrat.
Return	'There is no Cure for this Disease.	Result/Resolution/Proof/Refutation
Return	Henry will very soon be dead.'	Result/Resolution/Proof/Refutation
event 3	His parents stood around his Bed	Result/Resolution/Proof/Refutation
Recognition	Lamenting his Untimely Death,	Result/Resolution/Conclusion
	When Henry, with his Latest Breath,	Result/Resolution/Conclusion
Recognition	Cried – 'Oh, my Friends, be warned by me,	Evaluation/Conclusion
	That Breakfast, Dinner, Lunch, and Tea	Coda/Conclusion
	Are all the Human Frame requires . . .'	Coda/Conclusion
Recognition/ event	With that, the Wretched Child expires	Coda/Conclusion

Figure 4   Hilaire Belloc's Cautionary Tale, 'Henry King', with 'rhetorical' comments (adapted from Belloc, 1970: 32)

It is clear from the above that there are some interesting parallels between persuasive ordering and narrative structure. Having touched a little on generic variation (science report, academic essay, political speech, fairy tale, news story, comic verse) we need to look much more closely at genre and its contexts, because the structuring of any discourse must be affected by its genre and the expectations thereby aroused. Selecting an appropriate genre for a particular persuasive purpose is as important as assessing audience and context.

Persuasion and the Question of Genre

'Genre' is a concept that most of us feel quite familiar with – until we try to define exactly what it means. Its denoted meaning is 'kind, sort', but its etymology leads us back through French to Latin *generare* ('to beget'). The term *genus* has one particular meaning in logic (see the genus/species model of argument detailed in Chapter 4) and a different one in science. In logic it denotes 'a general concept'; in biological classification it represents the next stage down after 'family', meaning 'a group with general attributes in common, often divisible again into species and sub-species'. This description could equally be applied to genre in literature. People readily identify the major genres of drama, prose fiction and poetry, but each genre has its own 'sub-species' (or sub-genres). Drama, for example, includes tragedy, comedy, farce, epic, history play; fiction includes the novel as well as the short story and novella; and poetry includes everything from sonnet to epic, lyric, ode, ballad or satire.

'Genre' in its broader sense can refer to any specific range of activities with features in common, such as music, dance, film, sculpture, architecture or even historical texts. It includes spoken as well as written texts. New genres evolve as new media develop; today the genre of 'film' includes television programmes, video and advertising, as well as commercial, experimental and 'special effects' cinema, not to mention computer and video games. . . . Within the context of functional persuasion, genres range widely from parliamentary language to advertising copy and journalism. A useful term that can be applied to any genre, spoken or written, and the whole range of 'species and sub-species' is *text type*, and we shall make use of this throughout the chapter.

Further relevant (and more theorised) aspects of genre emerge if we look at Fredric Jameson's definition of literary genres in his book *The Political Unconscious*. He described genres as 'institutions or *social contracts* (our italics) between a writer and a specific public' (Jameson, 1983: 106). This is a different way of expressing the point made earlier, that the selection of one particular genre will arouse mutual expectations in both author and audience about mode, structure and likely content. Again, this links back to schema theory that should now be a familiar concept. For example, in the genre of tragedy the audience does not expect a happy ending; they may also anticipate certain structural patterns of events, and even character types. Jameson would go on from this to argue that the form and structure of any literary genre is socially engendered – since our very ideas of a happy or unhappy ending will be moulded by ideology. He would argue that as a result creative writing becomes 'commodified . . . and institutionalised'. It is, however, just as possible for any 'institutionalised' or established genre to overturn deliberately the socially constructed expectations of writer and public and become a new genre. James Joyce did exactly this in *Ulysses,* by turning upside down traditional expectations of fiction, and producing the ultimate modernist novel. As we saw in relation to film, new literary genres are constantly evolving (the 'slave narrative' and 'Indian captivity') or metamorphosing ('science fiction' now includes 'utopia' and 'dystopia'. Transformations of older genres such as the epic have produced a dramatic rise in 'fantasy fiction', myth and epic (for example, the trilogies *The Lord of the Rings* and *His Dark Materials* by J. R. R. Tolkien and Philip Pullman, respectively).

Another relevant aspect of Jameson's 'social contract' theory is that every text expresses its 'idealogeme' (or world-view) within the actual form, structure and mode. An interesting implication of this for our purposes is that a persuasive text (literary or functional) may itself be a texture or interweaving of several such idealogemes. For instance, a romantic appeal to honour (derived from the feudal model of society) might be interwoven with utilitarian considerations of more recent origin. For example, in Patrick O'Brien's naval novels, patriotism and group solidarity go hand in hand with the material motivation of prize money. This modal or functional description of genre (where form communicates ideology) will be highly relevant to our discussion of the relationship of genre to persuasion and persuasive ordering – since, on this view, genre *itself* may have a persuasive function (if only at an unconscious level).

But the next question to ask must be whether persuasion can be regarded as a genre in its own right. It is likely that no hard and fast answer will emerge. Earlier in the book we described persuasion as an interaction that effectively constitutes a social and ideological contract between persuader and persuadee. This sounds remarkably like Jameson's description of literary genre as social contract. Yet if Jameson is right that all literary genres are ideologically structured, many will include a persuasive element independent of the writer's conscious purpose. Dickens's novels, for example, whilst frequently focusing on current social issues, yet reveal a broader and deeper response to the human predicament beyond their overt or implicit ideology. Similarly a functional genre such as legal language may or may not involve a direct persuasive function – a deed of conveyance will not involve persuasion whereas a counsel's plea certainly will. Yet on the other hand another functional genre (or text-type) like advertising is overtly persuasive in both function and purpose, as is most parliamentary language.

We see here a range of possibilities associated with genre and persuasion. There appears to be a kind of *persuasive continuum* ranging through literary and functional genres or text-types, in that some genres will have a primary persuasive purpose (sermon, political speech, advertising); others will include the persuasive function along with others (literary genres with or without a didactic element) and some will be expected to involve no persuasion at all (dictionary definition, instruction booklet, shopping list). Each genre will have its own characteristic structure and form (or mode), reflecting the expectations of author/reader, speaker/listener in appropriate language. The persuasive function seems, therefore, to be an extra element in any genre (except for overtly persuasive genres).

As we have already suggested, persuasive ordering is a vital part of persuasive function in any genre. It would now appear that this function may well be additional to the primary purpose of any genre or text-type. Therefore to understand the persuasive process – to see how it might be integrated with the other generic characteristics of a text – we need to consider recent theory about discourse structure and ordering.

H. P. Grice's theory of conversational 'maxims', noted in the Introduction, provides some valuable insights into the criteria governing interactional structures. As we saw earlier, he argues that effective exchange depends on: (i) truthfulness (*'quality'*); (ii) proportionality (*'quantity'*); (iii) relevance; (iv) clarity (*'manner'*). These maxims can also be said to reflect many characteristic features of the persuasive genre. If we are to be persuasive in the fullest sense, we must measure our use of *logos* (argument) in proportion to the distance existing between the audience's views and our own. We must argue relevantly, establishing a convincing ethos by our truthfulness and clarity of manner, as well as matching *pathos* fully to the audience and the occasion. This will have substantial implications for the selection and ordering of the persuasive text.

Ruqaiya Hasan, in her seminal essay 'The Nursery Tale as a Genre' (1984: 71–102) theorises a relationship between genre and ordering, which focuses on the basic and irreducible structural elements (rather than the more 'idealised' Gricean maxims of interactional co-operation). Hasan starts by confirming, like Jameson, that genre is socially constructed. She argues that every genre or text-type has its own 'pragmatic' purpose, with language functioning in either an ancillary or a *constitutive* role within any given genre. The *ancillary* role of language is when its use is secondary to the pragmatic purpose of the interaction, such as making a purchase, visiting the doctor or advertising a product. The constitutive role is when, despite its social context, the actual language becomes 'the primary source of its definition' (i.e. a literary text). Language in literary genres is therefore constitutive, and in non-literary genres it is ancillary. In both roles, the emphasis is on function.

We come now to the most relevant part of Hasan's discussion for our purposes, where she proposes a theoretical framework for the structure and ordering of any text-type or genre. This may provide a crucial model for our own study of persuasive ordering. Hasan proposes a GSP

(Generic Structure Potential) that is 'an abstract category . . . descriptive of the total range of textual structures available within a genre . . . designed to highlight the variant and invariant properties of textual structures within the limit of one genre'. The GSP must be capable of specifying in any text structure: (i) the obligatory elements required to define the genre; (ii) the optional elements which may or may not appear; and (iii) the 'obligatory and optional ordering of these elements'. Hasan goes on to emphasise that every element of the GSP will have semantic attributes and lexico-grammatical realisation.

Every genre, therefore, has its own GSP and its own pragmatic purpose. We know that some genres include an overt persuasive function, others do not. The interesting question is whether the persuasive ordering in a genre can be modelled on the GSP. In other words, is there what we might call a GPP (Generic Persuasive Potential) in addition to the GSP, within any given genre? Can we similarly isolate certain obligatory elements, certain optional elements and a particular ordering of them? Another question will be whether these 'obligatory and optional elements' could reflect the traditional stages of persuasive ordering mentioned earlier in the chapter? We can look for some possible answers in the following analyses.

Persuasive Ordering: Variations and Examples

We shall explore a range of genres (both functional and literary) in order to observe the interplay of persuasive elements, and to assess which elements are obligatory and which optional. We have chosen six text-types for detailed consideration, of which three use persuasive ordering in a non-literary or functional context, and three are examples of literary persuasion.

We must now try to identify which obligatory and optional elements might constitute the GPP of a text. As we know, a persuasive interaction will include three basic constituents – the persuader, the text/message and the audience. How can these be linked with the GPP? First of all, in whatever genre the persuasion appears, there will be an Opening/Initiating Statement which will be a lexico-grammatical realisation of the persuasive purpose of the text. This purpose may be expressed either as a question, a statement or a command, in ancillary (functional) language or constitutive (literary) language. It will not necessarily follow a linear sequence or ordering, but may start *in medias res,* and neither the persuader's point of view, nor the point at issue necessarily appear. Just as Hasan identifies the Initiating Event in the nursery tale as obligatory and fixed, so we can assert that in persuasion some sort of Opening is equally obligatory. This Opening element differs from Hasan's GSP in that it remains an aspect of function rather than fact or event. Similarly, the conclusion of any persuasive process is not a fixed 'Final Event' as in Hasan, but a function. Like the Opening, the Conclusion will be expressed either as a question, a statement or a command, in ancillary or constitutive language depending on the literary or non-literary nature of the text. How this position is arrived at will depend on the persuader's choices of argument, and his or her methods of utilising proofs and disproofs. From this we can deduce a third obligatory element in the persuasive ordering and function, namely Proof/Disproof. This element will remain obligatory, whatever form the persuasion takes, and whether it is overt or not.

We have established three obligatory elements as part of the GPP (Opening, Conclusion, Proof/Disproof). Now we can consider what *optional* elements may be involved in the persuasive process. We suggest that the following rhetorical elements are significant optional elements within the persuasive process: sub-divided argument; factual statement or narrative; repetition of argument; deliberate omission; variation in ordering and sequence; and opening or closing appeals to the audience's emotions/goodwill. We would also suggest that another significant function in persuasive ordering, and hence a further dimension of the GPP, is *evaluation.*

According to Hunston and Thompson (2000: 1), evaluation has three functions; 'to express the speaker or writer's opinion, and in doing so reflect the value system of that person and their community'; 'to construct and maintain relations between the speaker or writer and hearer or reader'; and 'to *organise the discourse*' (our italics). The links with rhetorical function are clear: the first function ('expressing opinion') is associated with *ethos*, ideation and stance; the second (maintaining relations between speaker/hearer, writer/reader . . .) with *pathos*, interpersonal relations and emotional engagement; and the third with textual structure and ordering. (We should also recall at this point that Evaluation is an important part of Labov's narrative structure theory discussed earlier in this chapter). The next question must be how are these evaluative functions realised linguistically? It's obvious that lexical choice, syntactic variation, grammatical features and sound patterning will be variously used, but there will be much cross-over between them. For example, Hunston and Thompson cite an unpublished paper by J. H. Sinclair suggesting that discourse markers are one way of monitoring and hence evaluating spoken or written language; they note Labov's comment that: 'departures from the basic narrative syntax have a marked evaluative effect'; they quote Stubbs (1986): 'modal grammar' or 'point of view' as highly relevant to evaluation; and cite Biber and Finegan (1989) and their list of 'stance markers' as 'the lexical and grammatical expression of attitudes, feelings, judgements' (Hunston and Thompson, 2000: 11, 18–19). Their conclusion, however, is that 'it seems possible to group the linguistic features . . . signalling evaluation into three, each of which prioritises a different inherent characteristic of evaluation' (2000: 21). We summarise Hunston and Thompson's conclusions below:

(a) *evaluation involves comparison*: realised in comparative adjectives and adverbs; adverbs of degree; comparators 'just, only, at least'; negativity (not, never, dis-, un-); lexis such as 'fail';
(b) *evaluation is subjective*: markers of subjectivity include modal verbs and modality; deixis; pronominalisation; attitudinal adjuncts (grammatical, not rhetorical adjuncts); metadiscourse; sentence structure;
(c) *evaluation is value-laden*: markers of value include lexical items used in an evaluative environment and indications of goals (achieved or otherwise).

Hunston and Thompson conclude that (a) and (b) are more grammatical in nature and (c) more lexical. The point we can draw from their analysis is that evaluation is integral to the persuasive process and to persuasive ordering; we need to be aware of its functioning within every aspect of the persuasive texts.

It would appear that although our proposed GPP is analogous to Hasan's GSP, there is a fundamental difference. In the persuasive process/persuasion, the 'elements' are closer to being functions rather than actual textual structures realised in linguistic form. Moreover, these rhetorical functions can be found in any genre, text or discourse type that includes a persuasive component. It seems to follow that any given genre, functional or literary, will have not only a Generic Structure Potential (GSP) but also a Generic Persuasive Potential (GPP). Furthermore, we hypothesise that any persuasive text (whether written or spoken), will utilise both optional and obligatory elements of the GPP in its persuasive ordering, and will be positioned along the persuasive cline or continuum. At one extreme are texts with primary or secondary persuasive purposes (hard-sell advertising, tabloid news reports, address to the jury, political speech, poetry, romance or tragedy) in which the GPP is fully realised in terms of lexis, grammar, syntax and ordering. At the other extreme are those texts which have only referential and/or phatic purpose (dictionary definition, insurance policy, science text book, *Gray's Anatomy*, financial report, shopping list, phatic exchange). Their GPP is not lexico-grammatically realised. Yet even these texts have the potential to *affect* the listener or reader, for whom these texts have some personal meaning (the politics of the lexicographer are recognisable; the science text threatens long-held religious views; the shopping list reveals personal tastes that we will share or dislike!). In other words, the GPP remains even in these texts as a potential inviting subjective response in the reader or audience (this recalls our earlier mention of subjectivity within evaluation). The interpersonal metafunction is present in language however impersonal it seems to be – and it is here that we may locate the central role that persuasion (or the GPP) takes in every act of human communication.

We shall now look at the six selected examples of text-types and analyse the persuasive ordering involved, noting in each genre the range of obligatory and optional GSP and GPP elements, as well as determining the degree of persuasive purpose involved, and the way evaluation is realised.

(a) Unscripted discussion

We can find many examples of unscripted discussion on radio and television today, but the most extensive and searching discussions tend to be associated with current affairs programmes such as *Any Questions* (radio) and *Question Time* (television). In *Any Questions* a panel of public figures discusses questions put forward by members of the audience; in *Question Time* the formula is similar, except that after the panel discussion, members of the audience (including the questioner) are invited to comment. Each programme is chaired by a highly skilled presenter. Both are formulaic (panellists are asked in turn for their views) but spontaneous debate also occurs, particularly with the audience in *Question Time*.

Analysing the persuasive structure of one of these discussions presents difficulties; their formulaic quality means that each panellist has an individual schema that is part of the overall schemata of the programme, and will certainly utilise all the obligatory elements of *opening proof/disproof/conclusion* that we identify as the GPP. In order to demonstrate that the GPP is present in less elevated private discussion, we have chosen to analyse an extract from a transcribed conversation between three female sixth-form college students (aged 17–18) on the topic of euthanasia. (The speech overlaps have not been marked since they are not germane to our purposes.) The students (A, B and C) are close friends.

A: I think it's wrong.

B: So you think that somebody, even if they think . . . if they appear to be completely brain-dead, should be left on a machine that . . . for evermore . . .

A: Wasting valuable resources for people who could make it . . .

B: While somebody else's life could be saved if they'd been able to use that equipment.

A: I reckon that everybody should have the chance to live; I mean, if they're on that machine they're still alive, aren't they? There still must be some life in it for that person to breathe.

C: They're still technically alive; but they're not really alive. They don't think; they're just a cabbage.

B: They're just a breathing corpse; that's not living.

A: Yeah, but there still must be some life in it for that person to breathe.

B: I mean, that's all to do with what's more important, life or the quality of life. I mean, that goes back to the abortion argument; that, you know, should they kill off . . .

C: Should you take life as its own thing?

B: Er, no, should you kill off handicapped children before birth, abort them? Is that the right thing to do; I mean, that's the argument between life and quality of life.

A: It's all concerned with . . .

B: That's the same thing with euthanasia, isn't it; should somebody who's just breathing, totally brain inactive, be allowed to stay alive?

C: It all comes down to if you're going to enjoy your life or not; I mean people who're on a life-support machine aren't probably having a great time, a great party in there, are they?   (laughter)

B: You see; the thing is, the thing is, you never know – you can't tell, even if you . . . the machine . . .

A: You know, they said they could still be aware, of what's going on round them . . .

C: Imagine: they can hear people talking and saying, 'Well, they're obviously not thinking; why don't we just turn off the machine?'

A: Switch them off . . .

C: Just imagine that!

B: Oh, that's a horrible thought; that's a nightmare.

In this text-type the exchanges are all focused on a specific issue. The three participants are exploring a question together, and A initiates the discussion with the opening statement 1, 'I think it's wrong', which she reiterates and rephrases: 'I reckon that everyone should have the chance to live': C introduces the implied opening statement 2, which is redefined and exemplified by B '. . . that's all to do with what's more important, life or the quality of life'. This also constitutes a point at issue, and it is repeatedly explored, with proofs and disproofs being presented. The third opening statement is introduced by B: 'You see; the thing is, the thing is you, never know – you can't tell, even if you – the machine'. A and C support this with proofs, and B makes the concluding statement, which is an assessment and comment on the discussion but not a conclusion in logical terms.

Thus although the participants exchange views on three related issues, and adduce some syllogistically varied proofs for each argument, there is no substantial use of disproof because they are in basic agreement. The main issue is certainly redefined and elaborated at each turn in the argument, but as you might expect in spoken discourse, characteristic modal attributes of the genre (incomplete sentences, repetition, fillers, monitoring devices, hedges and overlapping) tend to blur the persuasive ordering. What we can confidently identify, however, are the opening and closing statements, as well as some use of the optional elements such as sub-divided arguments, repetition and appeals to audience. We also see evaluation processes at work, from the use of modals ('should be left', 'should have the chance') to verbs of mental process ('I think', 'I reckon') and hedges ('I mean', 'You see . . . the thing is') and the comparator adverb 'just', as well as expressions of comparison ('more important') and negative lexis ('horrible thought', 'nightmare').

(b) The set speech

When Queen Elizabeth I made the following speech to her troops waiting at Tilbury, the Spanish Armada consisting of 130 ships with 17,000 troops, and intent on invasion, was approaching English shores. The previous day, when the queen reviewed the troops, a contemporary account notes that 'full of princely resolution and more than feminine courage, she passed like some Amazonian Empress through all her army'.

Queen Elizabeth I: 9 August 1588

My loving people, we have been persuaded by some that are careful of our safety, to take heed how we commit ourselves to armed multitudes, for fear of treachery. But I assure you, I do not desire to live to distrust my faithful and loving people. Let tyrants fear . . . I have always so behaved myself that, under God, I have placed my chiefest strength and safeguard, in the loyal hearts and goodwill of my subjects, and therefore I am come amongst you at this time, not for my recreation and disport, but being resolved, in the midst and heat of the battle, to live or die amongst you all, to lay down for my God, and for my kingdom, and for my people, my honour and my blood, even in the dust. I know I have the body of a weak and feeble woman, but I have the heart and stomach of a king, and of a king of England too, and think foul scorn that Parma or Spain or any Prince of Europe should dare to invade the borders of my realm, to which, rather than any dishonour shall grow by me, I myself will take up arms, I myself will be your general, judge and rewarder of every one of your virtues in the field. I know already for your forwardness you have deserved rewards and crowns, and we do assure you, in the word of a Prince, they shall be duly paid to you. . . . By your valour in the field, we shall shortly have a famous victory over these enemies of my God, of my kingdom and of my people.

The queen adopts the voice of both queen and king in this address to the soldiers preparing to meet the daunting force of the expected Spanish invasion. Our source, *The Penguin Book of Historic Speeches* (MacArthur, 1996: 41), quotes the historian Carole Levin's comment that the only way a woman 'could assume leadership without contradiction was by combining in herself the attributes of King and Queen'. It appears that on 9 August the queen rode out 'mounted on a fine white horse and carrying a small silver staff' before addressing her soldiers 'with the words read out to the companies by their officers'.

The address before battle by a leader to the people is a well-established English genre, ranging from Shakespeare's imagined account of Henry V's exhortation 'We few, we happy few' to Churchill's 'finest hour' speech. Indeed, the tradition goes back much further, to classical times and beyond. The usual purpose is to rally and encourage the soldiers, to persuade them of the validity of the cause, and to describe the rewards of victory and the unpleasant consequences of defeat. It aims to increase the adrenalin, fire the imagination, and inspire hope (however difficult the odds).

In the case of Elizabeth I's speech, her aim is to convince the armies that being led by a queen rather than a king is not a disaster. Her military credibility is paramount, and the need to establish this explains her two-day review of the troops at Tilbury. On both days she is 'presenting herself' to the soldiers (no doubt magnificently clad to support the powerful icon of royalty being created). It is only on the second day, when everyone has actually seen her, does she speak. Her opening statement also includes a vital optional element (i.e. securing the soldiers' goodwill) by unexpectedly focusing on their relationship to the queen, and not *vice versa.* Elizabeth also includes a very brief but important narrative of facts. She says she 'has been persuaded' (passive voice – she is not party to this view) that she may be in personal danger of 'treachery' – an idea no sooner raised than forthrightly dismissed (she is no tyrant, and therefore is safe with her own 'faithful and loving people'). She tells them she trusts them, and is assured of their trust of her. The first task is completed – the soldiers support her as head of state. Her next task is to remove their doubts about having a woman as their military leader. Again she describes herself as having 'the body of a weak and feeble woman', admitting with seeming ingenuousness to what is undeniable. However, the forceful conjunction '*but* . . .' turns her admission of weakness into a source of strength, as she asserts 'I have the heart and stomach of a king'. Here we see *proof and disproof* at work. The body metaphor is maintained and turned to her advantage, as the general term is replaced by the more specific 'heart and stomach' symbolising her potential courage and resolution.

The queen has succeeded in her first two aims – to acquire the soldiers' trust and loyalty, and to assert her joining of kingly strength with her queenly status. Now, in the concluding statement (with its powerful emotional appeal), she must assume their shared indignation ('foul scorn') at Philip of Spain's arrogant plans, promise them reward for their loyalty and service, and promise 'a famous victory'. (This of course did happen, though at sea, away from the land armies, when Francis Drake and Howard of Effingham attacked the Armada, and a storm scattered it, ending the Spanish threat to England.)

The speech shows skilful ordering in terms of logic: the validity of the persuader must be agreed, then the validity of the persuasion, and finally a shared resolution. The queen's pronominal usage signifies the persuasive development; 'we' at first is the Royal plural; then she returns to the personal 'I' to signify her total personal commitment to 'my people, my honour and my blood', returning in the final lines to 'we' but this time signalling shared commitment with the soldiers, her people. The powerful contrasts between 'people'/'honour'/'blood' and 'dust'/'weak'/'feeble' convey the queen's confident self-evaluation, and the repetition of 'I assure you', 'we do assure you' confirm this.

(c)   Written argument: commercial persuasion

May we suggest you tell the board you are choosing a five-seater family saloon

So you've spent the last few months diplomatically 'losing' at golf. You've laughed at the MD's jokes (some were even funny) and you kept schtum when the Chairman's wife deliberately forgot your name.

Yesterday it paid off. Your back was patted (not stabbed) and you've just been told to invest some company money in some brand new metal.

Allow us to make a suggestion. Test drive the stunning new CD Carlsson from Saab. Of course, you'll be hooked from the moment you sit in the driving seat, but then there's a problem. People may think you're getting ideas above your already lofty station. And you didn't get where you are today by people thinking you're getting ideas above your already lofty station.

So here's what you tell the Financial Director:

Firstly, the new Saab is a four-door, five-seater, family saloon. Don't mention the integrated aerodynamic skirts, alloy wheels, or exclusive badging.

Secondly, inform him there is 23.8 cu. feet of luggage space in the boot, but omit there's 195 b.h.p. 16-valves, and an all new turbo-charged power unit under the bonnet.

Say that it's quite nippy, and jolly safe when overtaking. But please leave out the 0–60 in 7.5 seconds, forget that it's faster than a Ferrari Mondial from 50 to 70 m.p.h.

Oh, and mention the 38.1 m.p.g. Not the 140 m.p.h.

And finally, whatever you do, don't say the new CD was partly developed by Erik Carlsson, the legendary rally driver. Just explain that it's wholly favoured by Harry Dobson, the frugal company car manager.

If all goes well, you'll soon be driving the new Saab Carlsson CD into the company car park. Obviously, you'll be hiding it in a corner until it's time to make your move. That day, in the not-too-distant future when you 'accidentally' park it in the Chairman's space.

Or have we been addressing the Chairman all along?

(advertisement in *The Independent* magazine, 21 October 1989)

Although this advertisement is over 15 years old, we are retaining it for this second edition because of the timelessness of its manipulative skills, by kind permission of Saab (Great Britain). Using deliberately unsubtle but nevertheless powerful flattery, this advertisement is persuading the prospective buyer (whose identity is cunningly disguised at first) to choose a Saab Carlsson CD for his next company car. The overall tone dominates actual content at first; it is conspiratorial and cynical, yet flatteringly polite. The potential buyer (assumed to be male) is implicitly complimented on his ambition-led tactics of manipulation and deceit. The colloquially styled invitation seems framed to invite collusion between customer and salesman, whilst the advertisement seeks at the same time to present the car as powerfully 'macho' and eminently practical. The target audience consists of the businessman himself – and also the company finance director!

The persuasive ordering of this advertisement opens with two paragraphs of *narrative/statement of facts*, used with cynical humour to characterise the go-getting behaviour of the 'typical' customer, and to speculate (with overt flattery and covert mockery) on the cunning way he engineered this opportunity. It also successfully establishes the *point at issue* – which car to buy? – in the context of company politics. The ordering is unusual in that it's not until paragraph three that the *initiating statement/command* is spelt out – choose a Carlsson CD. Subsequent paragraphs offer *proofs* that this car is simultaneously a family saloon and an excitingly sporty car. The ordering alternates one set of arguments (turning on the qualitative issue of practical utility and economy) with another (relating to the issues of pleasure and ambition). Just as there was no obvious *opening statement*, there is no overt *concluding statement*; the real conclusion lies in the flattering revelation of the addressee's actual identity. The ideal customer for the Carlsson CD is not, after all, one who merely aspires to be chairman of the company – but the Chairman himself! By choosing this car, he'll be showing what has got him to the top and what keeps him there; he'll have the double satisfaction of thwarting any upstarts and cornering the pleasure for himself.

This advertisement demonstrates clearly that the familiar persuasive ordering of initial statement, narrative, proofs and (implicit) concluding statement is subject to adjustment. Interwoven with it is a further range of structural and lexical variations specific to the copywriter's ingenious rhetorical strategy. There is significant use of evaluative comparison at text level ('patted [not stabbed]', 'it's faster') as well as the implicit comparison throughout between the Saab and any other cars.

Turning to persuasive ordering in literary genres, we shall find some rather different and less predictable patterning. The GPP still applies, in that there are always elements that can be described in terms of 'opening' and 'closing statements' but the role of *argument/proof* is much less significant. The way most writers persuade depends as much on lexical choice (and connotations) and the patternings created by sound, syntax and sentence structure as on 'proofs' in any specific sense. In the following extracts we shall see how persuasive ordering nevertheless does have a crucial function within literary genres. We may also see how story grammar structure can be applied to literary persuasion.

(d) Dramatic dialogue

This example is taken from Samuel Beckett's, *Waiting for Godot*, Act II. This two-act play for the most part is a grimly comic dialogue between Vladimir and Estragon, two strange tramp-like figures vainly waiting for Godot, the 'man of power' to solve their problems.

> *They resume their watch. Silence.*
> Vladimir
> Estragon } *turning simultaneously.*) Do you –
> *Vladimir.*   Oh, pardon!
> *Estragon:*   Carry on.
> *Vladimir.*   No no, after you.
> *Estragon:*   No no, you first.
> *Vladimir.*   I interrupted you.
> *Estragon:*   On the contrary.
> *They glare at each other angrily.*
> *Vladimir.*   Ceremonious ape!
> *Estragon:*   Punctilious pig!
> *Vladimir.*   Finish your phrase, I tell you!
> *Estragon:*   Finish your own!
> *Silence. They draw closer, halt.*
> *Vladimir.*   Moron!
> *Estragon:*   That's the idea, let's abuse each other.
> *They turn, move apart, turn again and face each other.*
> *Vladimir.*   Moron!
> *Estragon:*   Vermin!
> *Vladimir.*   Abortion!
> *Estragon:*   Morpion!
> *Vladimir.*   Sewer-rat!
> *Estragon:*   Curate!
> *Vladimir.*   Cretin!
> *Estragon:*   (*with finality*): Crritic!
> *Vladimir.*   Oh!
> *He wilts, vanquished, and turns away.*
> *Estragon:*   Now let's make it up.

Vladimir: Gogo!
Estragon: Didi!
Vladimir: Your hand!
Estragon: Take it!
Vladimir: Come to my arms!
Estragon: Your arms?
Vladimir: My breast!
Estragon: Off we go!
   They embrace. They separate. Silence.
Vladimir: How time flies when one has fun!
   Silence.
Estragon: What do we do now?
Vladimir: While waiting.
Estragon: While waiting.
   Silence.
Vladimir: We could do our exercises.
Estragon: Our movements.
Vladimir: Our elevations.
Estragon: Our relaxations.
Vladimir: Our elongations.
Estragon: Our relaxations.
Vladimir: To warm us up.
Estragon: To calm us down.
Vladimir: Off we go.
   Vladimir hops from one foot to the other.
   Estragon imitates him.

(Beckett, 1956: 75–7)

This extract is not persuasive in any conventional sense of the word; what Beckett is doing, however, is persuading us of the tragic futility of his protagonists' existence through their patterned, ordered but ultimately meaningless discourse. All they can do is talk and wait, quarrel and wait, make up their quarrel and wait. These smaller structures hint at linear narrative, only to fizzle out. Each of these exchanges is introduced by a variant of the opening statement – 'Now let's make it up' – balanced by a variant of the concluding statement – 'Off we go' (used twice), to initiate meaningless action. Clearly the ordering of the passage is in itself a persuasive device to make Beckett's point – this rhetoric, far from being persuasive, achieves precisely nothing because nothing is being attempted. Vladimir and Estragon have given up; they are simply 'waiting' for somebody else to act for them.

The exchanges are also interesting in that each has its internal phonetic and semantic patterns and a climactic structure. For example:

'Moron!', 'Vermin!', 'Abortion!', 'Morpion!' (i.e. scorpion/moron), 'Sewer-rat!', 'Curate!', 'Cretin!', 'Crritic!', Through this grimly punning humour Beckett further persuades us of his nihilistic view of humanity. The role of evaluation here ranges from the ironic courtesy of 'No, no, after you' and 'Let's make it up' or even 'Come to my arms!' contrasted with the astonishing range of insults. All this is couched in a linear narrative of minuscule stops and starts, an imperfect variation on the Propp-derived story > setting + event structure, where the 'then' element is desperately foregrounded by Vladimir and Estragon's waiting situation.

(e) Poetry

We contrast two short poems here, one by Philip Larkin, one by Ann R. Parker:

'A Study of Reading Habits'

When getting my nose in a book
Cured most things short of school,
   It was worth ruining my eyes
To know I could still keep cool,
And deal out the old right hook
   To dirty dogs twice my size.

Later, with inch-thick specs,
Evil was just my lark:
   Me and my cloak and fangs
Had ripping times in the dark.
The women I clubbed with sex!
   I broke them up like meringues.

Don't read much now: the dude
Who lets the girl down before
   The hero arrives, the chap
Who's yellow and keeps the store,
Seem far too familiar. Get stewed:
   Books are a load of crap.
                    (Larkin, 1988: 131)

The poem describes the state of mind of its 'hero' in boyhood, adolescence and early maturity, reflecting these stages in his changing attitude to books. The title is at once serious and ironic. Larkin seems to have a dual purpose in the poem: to show his 'hero' as unappealing but vulnerable, and to challenge any easy assumptions about the 'value of reading'. To achieve this, Larkin persuades us of the authenticity of the boy's changing response to books, as imagination and fantasy are gradually replaced by the disillusionment of reality. The carefully differentiated ordering of the stanzas reflects the stages of his life. The contrast of lexis in stanza 1 produces a form of Narrative, and we have adult cliché ('ruining my eyes', 'getting my nose in a book') balanced by the language of heroic fantasy ('keep cool', 'the old right hook', 'dirty dogs twice my size'). In stanza 2 the pattern is different – the schoolboy language ('inch-thick specs', 'lark', 'ripping times') is contrasted with the absurd but gross sexual fantasies of the adolescent, linked by the ambiguous use of 'ripping'. In the final stanza there is a different pattern of ordering (this time a linear one) as the narrator gradually reveals his currently unhappy and embittered state of mind.

By this unconventional use of persuasive ordering, Larkin convinces us of the ambivalent nature of his central figure, and of the tragic way that books have lent themselves to his self-deception. At the end of the poem we become persuaded of the ambivalent nature of books themselves, having been taken stage by stage through the 'hero's' disillusioning experience. The deliberate crassness of the final line 'Books are a load of crap' is in many ways both a closing statement and an opening statement for the next argument.

Copyrighting the Dormouse

Copyright practice states on every form:
This document is not licensed for resale.
Add title, journal, volume, date,
   Title, journal, volume, date,
    Vitle, dournal, diurnal, nocturnal . . .
Somnolence is slinking in.

A student now returns a book; *The
Common Dormouse.*
This dormouse is not licensed for resale.
It is nocturnal. Add diurnal, title, tittle-tattle,
Tale. Long-tailed dormouse, best seen
In evenings. Note the time and date.
Copyright the details.

The Common Dormouse has been returned.
You may not make one further copy.
Please sign the appropriate dormouse and
Consult your tutor before licensing
Another document. Do not return any
Further diurnals or nocturnals – The
Librarian is asleep, still copyrighting dormice.

Parker's poem 'Copyrighting the Dormouse', published privately (2003) and reproduced here by kind permission of the poet, contrasts with Larkin's poem in almost every respect. Its faintly surreal but 'somnolent' quality persuades us of the comic absurdity of rules and regulations by providing variations on the theme of the opening statement ('This document is not licensed for resale'), leading us via the narrative ('A student now returns a book; *The / Common Dormouse*') to a bizarre and gently disruptive closing statement ('. . . The / Librarian is asleep, still copyrighting dormice'). Both poets use irony (and both are librarians) but Parker's irony is playful and self-mocking ('vitle, dournal, diurnal, nocturnal . . .', 'Please sign the appropriate dormouse') instead of the black, visceral gloom of Larkin's version. Story, setting, event, temporality and cause are all fused in this wry poem.

(f)   Prose narrative (fiction)

This example is taken from *The History Man* by Malcolm Bradbury. Here, Bradbury presents a satiric picture of the university world of the sixties, its pretentiousness, cold-blooded ambition and obsession with style. This passage reveals the protagonist, sociology lecturer Howard Kirk, preparing for a beginning of term party.

> After a while, Howard leaves the kitchen and begins to go around the house. He is a solemn party-giver, the creator of a serious social theatre. Now he goes about, putting out ashtrays and dishes, cushions and chairs. He moves furniture, to produce good conversation areas, open significant action spaces, create corners of privacy. The children run around with him. 'Who's coming, Howard?' asks Martin. 'A whole crowd of people,' says Howard. 'Who?' asks Martin. 'He doesn't know,' says Celia. Now he goes upstairs, to pull beds against the walls, adjust lights, shade shades, pull blinds, open doors. It is an important rule to have as little forbidden ground as possible, to make the house itself the total

stage. . . . Chairs and cushions and beds suggest multiple forms of companionship. Thresholds are abolished; room leads into room. There are speakers for music, special angles for lighting, rooms for dancing and talking and smoking and sexualizing. The aim is to let the party happen rather than make it happen, so that what takes place occurs apparently without hostly intervention, or rather with the intervention of that higher sociological host who governs the transactions of human encounter. (Bradbury, 1975: 71)

Bradbury's purpose in this extract seems to be two-fold. First, in structural terms this party plays a crucial role in establishing character, attitudes and relationships (balanced by another party at the end of the novel, in which a kind of resolution is reached). Secondly, the way in which Howard 'sets the scene', closely replicates the fictional construction and ordering of a text. The structural pattern here is interesting because it changes from linear narrative (including dialogue) to authorial comment and descriptive detail. Bradbury uses the present tense and simple (not continuous) aspect to emphasise the step-by-step nature of the 'scene-setting' narrative. From a persuasive perspective the ordering is significant, as the extract starts with the opening statement: 'He is a solemn party-giver, the creator of a serious social theatre'. The subsequent passage confirms this description, as Howard arranges furniture and props like a stage manager preparing for a play, the only difference being that many scenes will take place simultaneously on this sophisticated and complex stage: 'It is an important rule to have as little forbidden ground as possible, to make the house itself the total stage'. Having designed the set, and established the code ('one of possibility, not denial'), the final statement is made: 'the aim is to let the party happen rather than make it happen . . . without hostly intervention . . . rather with the intervention of that higher sociological host who governs the transactions of human encounter.' This pattern of stage management, interrupted by assessment, will continue as the novel (and the character of Howard) unfolds. We are to be persuaded that he is a ruthless and theatrical manipulator of other people's lives, and by presenting this detailed account of the party preparations, Bradbury convinces us. Persuasive ordering is of value here in that it provides a rhetorical framework in which Howard 'moves . . . pulls . . . produces . . . adjusts . . . opens . . . designs . . . shades' in preparation for 'dancing and talking and smoking and sexualising'. This verbal detail together with the high degree of nominalisation ('ashtrays, dishes, cushions, chairs . . . beds . . . lights . . . shades . . . blinds. . . doors') enhances the persuasiveness. In terms of evaluation, the lexis is mainly neutral, with the exception of terms used to describe Howard ('solemn', 'serious') and the underlying message that good parties are those where things 'happen' unplanned. The irony is that Howard's party preparations are entirely manipulative and restrictive. The evaluative giveaway is the adjunct 'apparently'.

Conclusion

Having inspected a wide variety of persuasive ordering in functional and literary texts, we can with more confidence leave our readers to their own experimental devices. We have sought to develop a sense of the persuasive process in relation to genre and its Generic Structural Potential, as well as demonstrating our own Generic Persuasive Potential. We have shown how persuasive intentions are structurally signalled within texts, so that it should be possible for the reader to assess the ordering appropriate to topic, audience and occasion. We have noted the structural variations offered from other theoretical perspectives such as story grammar, and we have drawn attention to the complex way in which evaluation functions in relation to the GSP and the GPP within a text. In the final chapter we shall focus on the lexical and stylistic devices available to the persuader – namely, the *persuasive repertoire*.

Further Exploration: the Theory and Practice of Ordering

The traditional theories of persuasive ordering may be of interest to readers, if only to discover what provoked Plato so much in the reports he heard about Theodorus's lectures (see Schiappa, 1999; Plato, 1973: 83). Michael Gagarin in *Rhetorica* (2001) discusses the possibility that Sophistic rhetoric was not only unconcerned with truth, but (more surprisingly) unconcerned to persuade. If its purpose was simply to give pleasure, the way a text was ordered would play a major part in achieving this effect.

Readers may also be interested in the controversies about the Ramistic doctrine of 'method', which began two millennia later and continue today. According to Ramus, 'method' was an

→

→

unchallengeable principle of dialectical ordering, which reflected perfect truth with maximal clarity. Unsurprisingly, this supremely confident approach to persuasive order has been much debated (see Ong, 1958; for a summary statement of the alleged damage done by Ramus to the whole culture of dialogue, see Ong, 1982: 134).

A stronger and more confident understanding of the complexities of persuasive ordering can be developed by applying cognitive analysis to persuasive texts (both written and spoken). This critical perspective will provide a clearer picture of the relationship between 'parts' of a text and the 'whole' text. For example, in considering a short story, it may be fruitful to apply cognitive analysis to the opening section; similarly, insight may be gained into any sort of persuasive communication by reflecting on those types of social encounter which are closest to each stage of the traditional rhetorical order.

Further insight into persuasive structure can be gained through scrutinising the most compact forms of communication such as 'soundbites', or literary forms such as the epigram or haiku (see the dog collar couplet below, p. 174).

Finally, readers may like to consider the varieties of persuasive structure devised for particular purposes, as surveyed by Nash (1989: 23–8).

6 The Persuasive Repertoire

Introduction: Persuasive Style

In Chapter 5 we considered the ways in which ordering functions in the persuasive process. We shall now turn to an examination of the actual language of persuasion. This will mean looking at the range of lexical choices, syntactic structures and sound patterning. We should emphasise that in this analysis of the persuasive repertoire, our aim is not to propose restrictive models but to encourage stylistic experimentation. Such experimentation will almost certainly yield better results if it is supported by wide reading with an eye to persuasive effects of all kinds and in all sorts of texts. Readers may wish to try out the persuasive repertoire for themselves, though how they use the figures will be very much determined by individual ways of writing or speaking. Our prime focus will be on the *stylistic repertoire* available to the persuader.

To define style is a task that can seem either utterly simple or alarmingly complex, depending on your linguistic perspective. Although few people would accept the extreme position of the Sapir–Whorf hypothesis, that language determines the way we think, it nevertheless 'influences the way we perceive and remember, and . . . the ease with which we perform mental tasks' (Crystal, 1997: 15). It does this in symbolic terms, through a system of graphemes (written language) or phonemes (spoken language). A writer or speaker will adopt whatever style seems appropriate to the situation, audience and message. If the context is familiar and the message routine, these choices will be as instinctive as swimming or riding a bicycle. But if the audience is less familiar and the message delicate or urgent, conscious persuasive choices will have to be made.

The broad concept of three levels of rhetorical style, high, middle and low persisted through Greek and Roman antiquity into Renaissance and Enlightenment culture, though these were sometimes refined or elaborated. The *high style* combined figurative language and ornament with complex syntactic structures. Besides being a major resource of oratory, this style was associated with elevated genres such as the ode and the epic. The *middle style,* characterised by wit, urbanity and incisiveness, was associated with satire and epigram and especially with rhetorical proof and disproof. *Low* or *plain style* meant simpler forms of lexis and sentence structure and was used in comedy, fables and familiar letters. Moreover, there was an implicit link between these 'levels' of language and social hierarchy. As the *Rhetorica ad Herennium* puts it:

> The Grand type consists of a smooth and ornate arrangement of impressive words. The Middle type consists of a lower, yet not of the lowest and most colloquial, class of words (*ex humiliore neque tamen ex infima et pervulgatissima verborum dignitate*). The Simple type is brought down (*demissa*) even to the most current idiom of standard speech.   (1954: 252–3)

High, middle and low style were all incorporated in both literary and non-literary genres. Comic characters are viewed by Aristotle in the *Poetics* as representing 'the ridiculous, which is a species of the ugly' (1963: 10–11). Hence the low style is particularly appropriate to comedy.

Texts were not always written throughout in one single style, but a blend of high, low and/or middle styles could occur within the same text, as we see in John Milton's *Areopagitica* (1644), a pamphlet arguing for 'the liberty of unlicenc'd printing' (Milton, 1974: 196–248), which switches between plain speaking, wit, and elevated figurative language as appropriate. Thus high, middle and low became accepted stylistic conventions open to individual variation. A persuader might opt for the high style in a formal speech or prefer to use the plain or familiar style, depending on the audience.

Today these categories of high, middle and low style seem inadequate to describe current variations in spoken and written discourse. Hermogenes, 'Longinus' and others (AD 1st–3rd centuries) identified seven qualities or 'ideas' of style; clarity, grandeur, beauty, speed, character, truth and gravity. One of these qualities, gravity, may have contributed to the later development of 'metaphysical' style in Donne and his contemporaries (see Shuger, 1988: 259–60; Biester, 1996). Modern linguists prefer the broader term *register* to signify the enormous range of style available to the speaker or writer. However, this scale of progression (from 'plain' colloquial language via 'middling' styles conveying intellectual agility and wit, to 'higher' styles associated with profound feeling and expanded imagination) still provides useful points of stylistic reference.

After these preliminaries, we can turn to the central purpose of this chapter – to demonstrate the resources of the persuasive repertoire, including lexical choice, sound patterning, figurative language and schematic devices. We shall look at a wide range of examples from functional and literary contexts, concentrating on how more localised stylistic effects are achieved. In the final chapter we suggest how some of these might be put to experimental and practical use. Limitations of space led us to opt for this focused approach; we refer readers to Nash (1980) for a more detailed and discriminating study of prose structure.

Lexical Choice

The key importance of lexis is evident, though impossible to treat adequately here (see Carter, 1987, for more detail). We shall use *ethos, pathos* and *logos* to provide specific focus and examine some important aspects of persuasive lexis. Choosing the 'right' word in a given context will be influenced by stance and situation (*ethos*). For example, lexical choice in conversation may or may not take into account political correctness: is the person referred to 'an actress' or 'an actor', 'a yachtswoman' or 'a sailor', 'the doctor' or 'the lady doctor'? The usage is significant whether it reflects a conscious decision or force of habit. Age group and gender can also affect the decision. Similarly, positive or negative emotion (*pathos*) will be conveyed by lexical choice. Are they field-sports or blood-sports? Is he a know-it-all TV junkie or a couch potato? Was it youthful high-spiritedness or drunken yobbishness? In yet another context, that of science and technology, *logos* will be the dominant influence, as in this statement of Newton's Law: 'Every body continues in a state of rest or uniform motion in a straight line unless acted upon by a force.' It is, however, worth noting that purely scientific lexis can take on a positive or negative emotional charge in accordance with prevailing social attitudes (e.g. cloning, IVF, genome engineering, GM crops).

(a)   Lexical choice in literary persuasion

In Chapter 7, we shall look in more detail at the opening passage from

Charles Dickens's *Hard Times*. However, the following brief quotation (Dickens, 1955 [1854]: 5) illustrates one of the central themes of the book, namely the damaging effect of the utilitarian educational philosophy, with its absolute insistence on 'Facts'. Bitzer, the model pupil, gives his (utilitarian) definition of a horse: 'Quadruped. Graminivorous. Forty teeth, namely twenty-four grinders, four eye-teeth, and twelve incisive. . . .' This coldly *logos*-oriented language reflects the power of this philosophy to wither the human spirit.

In the eighteenth-century comedy *The School for Scandal*, by Richard Sheridan, there is an amusing instance of *ethos* affecting lexis. Mrs Candour (who affects to despise ill-natured gossip) enters the salon of Lady Sneerwell with the very latest salacious news, adding:

> I confess, Mr Surface, I cannot bear to hear people attacked behind their backs; and when ugly circumstances come out against our acquaintance I own I always love to think the best. By-the-by, I hope 'tis not true that your brother is absolutely ruined?   (Sheridan, 1979 [1777]: 20)

The malicious relish of 'attacked', 'ugly', 'ruined' contrasts amusingly with Mrs Candour's pious insincerity ('I confess', 'I love to think the best', 'I hope 'tis not true') and conveys her character to the audience.

In Sylvia Plath's poem 'Metaphors', her lexical choice reveals the emotional complexity (*pathos*) of her state of mind as a pregnant woman:

> I'm a riddle in nine syllables,
> An elephant, a ponderous house,
> A melon strolling on two tendrils.
> O red fruit, ivory, fine timbers!
> This loaf's big with its yeasty rising.
> Money's new-minted in this fat purse.
> I'm a means, a stage, a cow in calf.
> I've eaten a bag of green apples,
> Boarded the train there's no getting off.
> (Plath, 1981: 116)

First the reader feels a sense of mystery and excitement (the 'riddle' of a nine-month pregnancy posed in nine nine-syllable lines); then amusement and irony ('elephant', 'house', 'melon', 'cow in calf'); pleasure ('red fruit', 'ivory', 'fine timbers'); pride ('yeasty rising', 'new-minted', 'fat purse'); and finally apprehension ('bag of green apples', 'Boarded the train there's no getting off').

(b)   Lexical choice in functional persuasion

There are many examples of functional language (scientific texts, legal documents etc.) where *logos* determines lexical choice. News reporting, however, is interestingly different, because although the journalist's prime responsibility is to report facts (*logos*), political and emotional bias (*ethos* and *pathos*) will inevitably occur. Typical tabloid headlines ('Tug of Love Drama', 'Migrant Mayhem', 'Cop Sex Rap KO'd') reflect this in their lexical choice. Such choices – though formulaic – work well with their audience; in contrast, misjudged lexical choice will confound the persuader's intentions, and generate the wrong kind of *pathos*. An amusing example of this was the placard carried by a member of the Association of University Teachers when lobbying Parliament in the eighties about pay discrepancies. The legend on the placard included the ringing phrase 'RECTIFY THE ANOMALY!'. This lexis came from the semantic field of formal salary negotiation, and was entirely inappropriate to a political 'demo'. The message triggered a very different emotional response from the one hoped for by the organisers. Instead of evoking public sympathy, it prompted ridicule, creating an image of stuffy, pedantic academics out of touch with reality!

Sound Patterning

Spoken and written language in general, and persuasive language in particular, make substantial use of *sound patterning* to create and enhance meaning. This may be conveyed by using particular syntactic structures or intonation patterns, and by familiar devices such as alliteration, assonance, consonance, dissonance, onomatopoeia, rhyme, half-rhyme, and internal rhyme. We shall look at a range of examples here; later in the chapter we shall also consider other schematic devices that make use of sound components, such as puns and word-play.

(a) *Alliteration* (repetition of initial consonant): 'Simple, stylish, solid wood' (New Heights furniture, *Guardian Weekend,* 6 March 2004). Functional persuasion, urging audience to buy.

(b) *Assonance* (repetition of medial vowel): 'Am*a*zing gr*a*ce! H*ow* sweet the s*ou*nd . . .' (hymn). Religious persuasion (emotive use of theological concept).

(c)   *Consonance* (repetition of consonant in medial or final position): 'Cut is the branch that might have grown full straight' (Epilogue to Marlowe's play *Dr Faustus* [1969: 339]). Repetition of final dental stop 't' stresses finality of Faustus's damnation. Moralising persuasion.

(d)   *Dissonance* (mingling of deliberately discordant sounds), as in Pope's *Dunciad* (1742), ll.228–31:

> 'Twas chatt'ring, grinning, mouthing, jabb'ring all,
> And Noise, and Norton, Brangling, and Breval,
> Dennis and Dissonance; and captious Art,
> And Snip-snap short, and Interruption smart.
>   (Pope, 1968: 744)

Pope is attacking bad writers, the dissonance reflecting their dullness. Satirical persuasion.

(e)   *Onomatopoeia* (the sound suggests the actual meaning of a word):

> The sleepy sound of a tea-time tide,
> Slaps at the rocks the sun has dried, . . .
> And filling in, brimming in, sparkling and free,
> The sweet susurration of incoming sea.
>   (Betjeman, 1978: 109)

In these opening and closing lines from 'A Bay in Anglesey' (ll. 1–2, 19–20), John Betjeman seeks to convey the harmonious mood of the sea shore. Lyrical persuasion.

(f)   *Rhyme, half-rhyme, internal rhyme* (exact or partial repetition of sound, usually in final position; repetition of a group of sounds within the same line), as in British Airways' proclamation of a new competitively priced service (*The Observer*, 7 March 2004): 'Warsaw with added draw'. Here the internal rhyme, the half-rhyme ('add-ed'), and the symmetrical interplay of initial and final '*w*' *enact* the appeal of a journey with in-flight comforts (unlike 'no-frills' rival airlines). Commercial persuasion.

Figurative Language or Trope

Trope (Greek 'turn') is a traditional rhetorical term, still used by critical

theorists, denoting the whole range of figurative language. Its deriva-
tion implies its function – to turn meanings in words via a less direct
mode of expression. Meaning is thus conveyed through the perception
of similitude, association or opposition. In recent years it has been
more emphasised by linguists such as R. W. Gibbs (1994) that the
conventional distinction between a literal and a figurative understanding of words is highly problematic. All users of language spontaneously
resort to figurative expressions based on perceived similarity, opposition
etc., to explore ideas and to communicate them. This is confirmed by
analysis of the corpora of spoken language, most recently in Ronald
Carter's important book *Language and Creativity* (2004), based on the
CANCODE corpus. This is a development of his earlier report (1999)
on the same corpus. Carter demonstrates the remarkable extent to
which 'ordinary conversation' is richly creative, making use of figurative
and innovative language of all kinds. Besides symmetrical structure and
repetitive patterning, this typically involves word-play and metaphor.

To maximise persuasiveness, however, it will be necessary to intensify and focus figurative effects. The traditional concept of trope retains
its usefulness for this purpose, and we shall examine four basic kinds of
trope, together with one less common, but interesting variant, *catachresis*. *Metaphor, metonymy, synecdoche* and *irony* are all key elements in the
persuasive repertoire.

(a)   Metaphor

In its simplest form, metaphor replaces one word with another, resulting in one concept representing another. Jakobson's theory (conve-
niently paraphrased and developed by David Lodge in *The Modes of
Modern Writing* [1977: 73–81]) argues that this process takes place on
the paradigmatic axis of language, when we select one word from an
associated series or semantic field. Our first example, 'The Sergeant-
Major was *barking* orders', is chosen from the semantic field of loud
aggressive utterances (human and animal). The metaphor 'barking'
represents a kind of short, sharp shout, and is selected because of the
common ground between *source* domain (dog's bark) and target
domain (sergeant's orders).

Moving on from this single-word example, metaphors are also
embodied in single phrases or paragraphs, or in more complex forms
like personification and in extended allegories such as *Animal Farm*.
The more metaphors are foregrounded in a persuasive text, the more

important their originality and aptness becomes. At best, metaphors need to have the force and memorable quality that the most insightful proverbs still retain today. Once a metaphorical collocation has turned into a cliché, its power is lost. Not only must the persuader seek aptness, but he or she must also carefully control the orientation of metaphor during the persuasive process. At successive stages a well-chosen metaphor might illuminate stance, referential content and textual function, besides anticipating the audience's response.

(i)   Ordinary conversation

'Isn't she a live wire?'
'Yes, but doesn't she wear you out!'

Each speaker employs a stock metaphor/cliché to express an individual viewpoint. The first speaker's metaphor is oriented primarily towards the subject of the exchange, and the second speaker's towards herself. A more joky response, which is both *ironic* and metaphoric, would be 'Yes – I'm electrified!'

(ii)   Oratory

In Churchill's 'Finest Hour' speech (18 June 1940) we see a notable example of what cognitive linguists call schema refreshment. Using the terminology applied by Peter Stockwell in his *Cognitive Poetics* (2002) the conceptual metaphor LIFE IS A JOURNEY is enriched, as Churchill draws more material from the source domain of journeying and almost literally maps it on to his target domain, 'the life of the world'. Not only is there a contrast of high sunlit ground and dark abyss, but also an implied parting of the ways, where the British people must act as examples to the world. By refreshing the thematic linkage of 'life' and 'journey', Churchill engages the audience ethically, emotionally and logically. *They* are to make the essential difference:

I expect that the battle of Britain is about to begin. Upon this battle depends the survival of Christian civilisation. . . . Hitler knows that he will have to break us in this island or lose the war. If we can stand up to him, all Europe may be free and the life of the world may move forward into broad, sunlit uplands. But if we fail, then the whole world . . . will sink into the abyss of a new Dark Age made more sinister . . . by the lights of perverted science. Let us therefore . . . so bear ourselves that, if the British Empire and its Commonwealth last for a thousand years, men will still say, 'This was their finest hour.'   (Churchill, 1941: 234)

The famous last sentence derives much of its emotive power from the accumulated charge of the contrasted metaphors preceding it: 'broad, sunlit uplands' (the pastoral ideal, prosperity, health, peace and freedom), and the looming 'abyss' (Nazi rule and the hell of 'perverted science').

(iii)   Literary persuasion

The Octopus is both title and centrally structuring metaphor for Frank Norris's fictional exposé of unscrupulous monopoly capitalism in nineteenth-century America. The railroad system becomes an octopus in the reader's imagination, despite the matter-of-fact tone of the description. We can't see this as refreshment, since the metaphor is highly original; but it's certainly enriched. The railroad map pulses, simultaneously, with life, movement, intelligence and menace:

> The whole map was gridironed by a vast, complicated network of red lines. . . . These centralized at San Francisco and thence ramified and spread north, east, and south. . . . From Coles, in the topmost corner of the map, to Yuma in the lowest, from Reno on one side to San Francisco on the other, ran the plexus of red, a veritable system of blood circulation, complicated, dividing and reuniting, branching, splitting, extending, throwing out feelers . . . laying hold upon some forgotten village or town, involving it in one of a myriad branching coils, one of a hundred tentacles, drawing it, as it were, towards that centre from which all this system sprang.   (Norris, 1964 [1901]: 204–5)

(b)   Metonymy

Metonymy is a difficult term to define, and is thought to reflect a process fundamentally different from that involved in metaphor. Lodge (1977: 73–7) argues that metonymy is combinative (working on the syntagmatic axis), whereas metaphor is selective (working on the paradigmatic axis). Thus metonymy employs a principle of structural association and metaphor functions on a principle of semantic association. In metonymy one part of a syntactic structure is used to express another part of that structure. We are familiar with the statement: 'The White House (or '10 Downing Street') issued a denial'. This is an example of the *container/content* metonymy, where the residence of the President (or Prime Minister) represents the staff working there who issued the denial. (See also the variant (ii) below.)

Metonymy has close links with the associational model of argument (discussed in Chapter 3). Through a common association, or 'compact reference' (Nash, 1980: 55) within the minds of author and audience, an idea put into words metonymically represents unexpressed or implicit ideas and associations. This will have obvious implications for persuasion in general, and advertising in particular. In the Business Section of the *Guardian* (10 March 2004) an advertisement for 'InFocus' projectors uses the image of a small gesturing figure throwing an enormous trumpet-playing shadow which, metonymically, represents the enhanced impact of a presentation given with this equipment. Visual trope thus reinforces the degree-based *logos* of the slogan 'We make big ideas bigger.'

Metonymy has also been a major resource of modern fiction. It can reveal, through the realistic description of an environment, those intangible human qualities that characterise an individual or social group Although cognitive theory has not so far extended its investigations into metonymy, it seems likely that (as in metaphor) schema refreshment also occurs when new areas of association are introduced.

Just as the association model of argument had some important variations, metonymy can also be divided into several categories (see below). A general proviso about metonymy is that all variations are susceptible to oversimplification and stereotyping, as our first example shows.

(i)   Subject/adjunct metonymy

'None but the Brave deserves the Fair' (Dryden). This association of bravery with men, beauty with women, persuades the modern reader of nothing more than the gender stereotyping of the age, endorsed by the poet ('Alexander's Feast' [1697], ll. 12–19: see Dryden, 1987: 545). A different example is provided in Oscar Wilde's much-quoted and now proverbial epigram on fox-hunters: 'The unspeakable in pursuit of the uneatable' (with assonance further reinforcing the metonymy).

(ii)   Container/content metonymy

Here we quote part of the description of a fenland abortionist's cottage from *Waterland* by Graham Swift:

> Hanging from the ceiling beam, like amputated, mummified legs, a pair of long leather waders. But take a look at that ceiling! Look what else it's hung with. It's hung with dead birds. . . . It's hung with strips of fur and eel-skin,

a bloody-mouthed water rat dangling by its hairy tail. It's hung with unname-
able bunches of leaves, grasses, roots, seed-pods, in every stage of freshness and desiccation. With misshapen things blackened with smoke that
you don't like to ask what they are. With all manner of bags and pouches
that you don't like to ask what's inside.   (Swift, 1984: 262–3)

Reflecting the occupations of both husband and wife, Swift's description conveys a sense of menace. Death, whether procured by abortion
or by destruction of animal life, is their only means of stunted survival.
Close to raw nature, they are remote from civilised ideals of humanity.
All this suggests the impending fate of the protagonist and his pregnant
girl friend. The figurative effect here works primarily through the
container/content association, the grotesquely burdened ceiling representing their life style.

(iii)   Cause/effect metonymy

A short example of this is the disapproving remark 'That's the drink
talking' (i.e. inappropriate speech caused by drunkenness). A comparable example is the way in which Roman poets such as Ovid used the
name of 'Venus' (i.e. the goddess of sexual love and personified source
of sexual feeling) when they meant sexual activity itself. This usage was
also commonplace among classically educated English libertines across
the centuries.

(iv)   Clothes/wearer metonymy

Here again, a simple example is the comment, 'It's a case of the blue
jeans versus the blue rinse' (representing antagonism between youth
and age). This kind of metonymy is infinitely extendable and changes
in response to fashion, group behaviour and the direction of journalistic interest. Thus, within the broader category of weather-proof clothing, 'anorak' has tended to denote the obsessive pursuer of an
unfashionable minority interest; and 'Barbour' represents a typical
wearer of the kind of coat or jacket worn at open-air activities with a
higher social *cachet*, such as point-to-points or polo matches.

(v)   Inventor/invention metonymy

'Sandwich', 'kleenex', 'wellingtons', 'hoover', 'xerox' are all words in
common use which were originally metonymical (i.e. inventions or
innovations named after their creator or original manufacturer).

(c)   Synecdoche

Synecdoche is a combinative device involving a relationship between an expressed idea and an unexpressed one. It works on the mathematical principle of dividing a whole into its parts (whereas metonymy works on the associational principles of *relation* or inherence). Thus in synecdoche the part represents the whole, as in American movie slang 'Get your ass outa here', meaning 'Get yourself out of here'. Just as part represents whole, species represents genus, singular represents plural (and *vice versa*). Synecdoche can be an important ideological weapon through which people, issues or ideas can be effectively marginalised by omitting to mention them. For example, the unmarked form 'man' is still sometimes used to represent humanity; similarly, the stereotype upper-class Englishman (in bowler hat or tweeds) was once taken to represent 'the English national character', completely marginalising the rest of British society.

(i)   Part–whole/whole–part synecdoche

Here a *part* of something is used to signify the *whole* ('The cattle rancher owned one thousand head more than his neighbour'). In reverse, the whole signifies the part: an amusing example of this reverse structure appears in the film script of *Lucky Jim* (1954) where the pompous Professor of History identifies himself to a telephone caller as 'History speaking'. The humour depends on the audience appreciating the absurdity of his remark, subsuming in one person the totality of history!

(ii)   Genus–species/species–genus synecdoche

Though less common than the part–whole variety, this form of synecdoche does occur. An example would be the kind of remark made by a sentimental parent to a young child: 'Mummy has to go to work to earn the pennies to pay for our tea.' The *genus–species* variant is used to sinister effect in T. S. Eliot's poem 'Sweeney Among the Nightingales' (1963: 59–60). The theme of this poem is suggested by its title that refers primarily to the nineteenth-century slang meaning of 'nightingales' (i.e. prostitutes – see Green, 1998: 839), not birds. Amongst a group of low-life figures including Sweeney (the jocular but menacing sensualist) is a stranger who seems to have an 'interest' in the two seemingly drunken women present. Whereas Sweeney is metaphorically linked with animals (see Stanza 1), the mystery man is referred to as 'The silent vertebrate in brown' (l. 21), thus reducing him to a common biological feature shared not only with mammals and birds, but also with reptiles. This instance of synecdoche contributes to the threatening mood created by Eliot, reflecting what he perceived to be the catastrophic loss of human identity and of religious tradition (Jewish, Christian and pagan), as well as the devaluing of symbolic meaning. The nightingale, once a poetic symbol of consolation, now represents corruption and lust.

(iii) Plural–singular/singular–plural synecdoche

The *plural–singular* structure is seen in the disapproving phrase 'Some people!' (which actually refers to one obnoxious person rather than a number). A familiar example of *singular–plural* synecdoche is the phrase 'the man in the street', meaning 'people in general'. In 'The Mask of Anarchy' (1819), a poem written in the style of a popular broadside ballad following the Peterloo massacre at Manchester, Shelley makes powerful use of this form of synecdoche in stanza LIV, as he describes the beneficent effects of Liberty. These are being spelt out at length by a single maternal figure who personifies England and her blood-soaked earth:

> 'For the labourer thou art bread
> And a comely table spread
> From his daily labour come
> To a neat and happy home.
>   (Shelley,1934: 342)

Although this image represents how life ought to be for working-class people in general, Shelley's use of singular for plural personalises his portrayal. Each man, woman and child (by implication) is of equal importance and should be able to enjoy the benefits of peace and prosperity, conferred by liberty.

(d) Irony

Unlike the other three kinds of trope so far discussed, *irony* is essentially oppositional. A word, phrase or paragraph is turned from its usual meaning to a sense that is either directly or indirectly opposed to this meaning. Although irony can be employed in many ways, its oppositional nature makes it especially useful in dialectic. We are all familiar with the commonplace irony of everyday conversation (e.g. 'How kind of you!' meaning the reverse); nevertheless, it is worth teasing out this trope to show its flexibility for persuasive purposes.

Irony can be conveyed by intonation in speech, and by tone in writing, thereby communicating the persuader's *ethos, pathos* and *logos*. Earlier rhetoricians, such as George Puttenham in his *Arte of English Poesie* (1589), delight in distinguishing several types of ironic figures, on the basis of difference in tone. These types are quite recognisable today, and include the cutting 'bitter taunt' of sarcasm (in Greek this meant 'a tearing of flesh'), the 'merry scoff' of light mockery, and the 'fleering frump' (delivered with a sneer) (see Puttenham, 1968: 157–9). The main point to note is the sheer range and variety of shading between the two extremes of bitterness and humour .

(i)   Single word irony (antiphrasis)

Here the ironic sense is the exact opposite of the word's usual meaning; the tone is not necessarily sarcastic, but can be affectionate or admiring. For example, tall men are often addressed as 'Tiny', and traditionally Robin Hood's stout henchman was called 'Little John'. In political persuasion we might encounter a critical comment like this: 'A prudent budget? It's given us a balance of payments crisis!' Mark Antony's speech to the Roman mob, cited earlier (see pp. 69–70 above) is an excellent example of irony in literary persuasion, his purpose being to demolish the principled stance of Brutus's previous speech. The refrain-like word 'honourable' is steadily undermined, until it eventually signifies the direct opposite of what it first meant.

(ii)   Epigrammatic irony

This occurs in a variety of forms, including the ironic one-off comment and the more formal poetic epigram. In the 1970s, the Chancellor of the Exchequer, Dennis Healey, compared Sir Geoffrey Howe's onslaught on his Budget statement to the experience of 'being savaged by a dead sheep'. This quip was remembered for years afterwards. The irony of the poetic epigram is usually expressed in punning or word-play, as we see in Pope's *Epigram: Engraved on the Collar of a Dog which I gave to His Royal Highness* (1968: 826):

I am his Highness' Dog at *Kew*;
Pray tell me Sir, whose Dog are you?

In a society dependent on patronage (an earlier form of 'networking'), this ironic play on the literal and metaphoric senses of 'Dog' would sting anyone who stooped to read the collar.

(iii)   Sustained irony

Sustained irony is a major resource of the satirist, and appears everywhere from political journalism to letters to the press. Sometimes an entire discourse sustains and conveys a meaning quite opposite to its real sense and purport – though the mask does occasionally slip. The most famous literary example in English is probably Jonathan Swift's *A Modest Proposal* (1729) , in which a fictional enthusiast for public improvement sets out his scheme for fattening up the children of the Irish poor, to serve as food for the gentry (see Swift, 1932: 19–31). As these landlords 'have already devoured most of the Parents [they] seem to have the best Title to the Children' (1932: 24).

(e)   Mislabelling (catachresis)

We conclude our discussion of trope with a distinct sub-variety, which capitalises on a sense of incongruity, and may involve metaphor – or any other of the main tropes. *Catachresis* means the deliberate misapplication of a word. It involves a form of figurative language (most often metaphor). Typically, a word relating to one sense may be used to describe another. In John Donne's *Elegy 6: The Perfume*, line 41, the poet recalls how his use of 'A loud perfume, / which at my entrance cried' betrayed his love affair to the lady's family. This brings the moment alive for the reader (Donne, 1990 [1633]): 21). Sometimes the choice of word may be *ironic*, as in 'He threatens to raise my salary!' where the mislabelling lies in the word 'threaten'. This device invites us to use language inventively!

Schematic Language

So far we have dealt with three of the four major categories in the persuasive repertoire – lexis, sound patterning and trope. We shall now turn to the fourth category, a broad class of devices traditionally referred to as *schemes*. This will immediately recall the word schema, a key concept in our applications of schema theory elsewhere. Although both words derive from the same Greek source, there is an important difference. 'Scheme' is a classical rhetorical term applied to an 'arrangement' or 'structure'; 'schema' is a recent and much broader theoretical concept which, as we have already seen, is applicable to much longer stretches of written or spoken discourse. We will continue to use the classical term scheme in this section, since it precisely describes the general characteristics of these figures. We must also clarify another area of potential confusion, by distinguishing between the term 'figurative language' and the phrase 'figures of rhetoric'. The latter traditionally embraced both tropes *and* schemes. As we have already shown in this chapter, the narrower term 'figurative language' applies only to trope. The remaining 'figures of rhetoric' fall within the category of schematic language in this sense.

It would be impossible to examine the whole range of schematic devices in this chapter. As a result, we have selected some of the most frequently encountered and most useful for discussion, such as antithesis, puns and word-play, syntactic devices, amplification and diminution, and tricks and ploys. (A further selection may be found in Appendix B.)

The traditional terminology for these schematic devices can present problems for the modern reader. There are advantages, however, in using just the Greek and Latin terms since quite a few (e.g. *antithesis, hyperbole*) have gained general currency. Moreover since scholars still dispute the exact meanings of the traditional terms, and use them differently, it would be virtually impossible to establish an internationally agreed English terminology. We shall continue to use the Greek and Latin 'labels', but use them selectively. In order to make the schemes more immediately accessible, we have in most cases prefaced the Greek or Latin with our own English equivalent.

(a)   Antithesis

This important schematic device (recognised by both Classical and Renaissance rhetoricians) occurs in its simplest form when two words are opposed in a contrary relationship. This may be deliberate or accidental; in either case the lexical opposition of contrary meanings will be of prime importance. In this exchange (*Macbeth*, v.i.23–4) between the Gentlewoman and the Doctor, observing the sleepwalking Lady Macbeth, the opposition is subtler than it seems:

Doct.:   You see her eyes are open.
Gent.:   Ay, but their sense is shut.
          (Shakespeare, 1997: 2609)

Antithesis will appear again in the chapter as an integral part of more complex structures.

(b)   Puns and word-play

These schematic devices involve playing or punning on sound, sense and the structure of individual words, and we shall be looking at four types. It's worth noting that these devices can be used for serious ends (to convey *ethos, pathos* and *logos*) as well as for comic and trivial purposes. Many involve 'double-takes', as a second or third sense strikes the reader or listener; these senses may be linked by similarity or opposition, thus creating a condensed cognitive *thematic organisation point* (see Appendix A).

(i)   Deliberate distortion (rhetorical mispronunciation)

This can be an effective way of conveying negative attitudes, ranging from bewilderment to mockery or contempt. Churchill was said to have pronounced 'Gestapo' as 'Just a *po*' ('po' being the Victorian schoolboy slang for chamber pot).

(ii)   Same-sound pun (antanaclasis)

This familiar device has several variants: when we have 'same sound/same spelling/different meaning', it is called a *homonym*; when it is 'same sound/different spelling/different meaning it is a *homophone.* Both variants are included under the term *antanaclasis* (our same-sound pun) and are frequently found in persuasive contexts. Uses range from advertising ('Sheer Delight' as the slogan for a brand of tights), to Milton's Samson denouncing Dalila's treacherous attempts '. . . to win from me / My capital secret' (Milton, 1968: 360). Samson's use of 'capital' has at least three meanings, as the *Oxford English Dictionary* will confirm. The word 'capital' relates firstly to the hair on his head (where his strength lies). Secondly this is a secret of overwhelming importance; and thirdly it will be literally fatal ('capital' as in 'capital punishment') for Samson to betray it.

(iii)　Similar-sound pun (paronomasia)

Here Shakespeare provides a useful illustration, again from *Macbeth*. Lady Macbeth's 'what thou wouldst highly / That thou wouldst holily' (I.v.17–18) attacks her husband's scruples about murdering his king. There is a similarity of sound between 'highly' and 'holily', but a significant contrast of meaning (also involving the trope of irony). In contrast we have the joky catchiness of the advertising slogan 'Beans means Heinz', tempting us to mispronounce both ways.

(c)　Syntactic devices

When considering this category of schematic devices, we might profitably recall Halliday's description of language functions as ideational, interpersonal and textual. The main function of syntax is textual – to make a text cohere and be comprehensible. As we might expect, persuasive language subsumes textual function to interpersonal (*ethos* and *pathos*) and ideational function (*logos*). Nevertheless, skilfully chosen syntactic structures will enhance these functions, and add persuasive strength. Far from being merely ornaments, such figures can be instruments of thought and feeling, according to the most recent rhetorical theory. (For further varieties and examples, see Appendix B below: Lanham, 1991; Nash, 1980.)

There are multiple possibilities for syntactic variation in extended discourse, paragraphs, sentences, phrases and even in individual words as they change their grammatical function. We shall look at a varied selection, including some devices that involve other resources of the persuasive repertoire.

(i)　Word-class variation (traductio)

This is commonly used to surprise an audience accustomed to a certain word having one grammatical function only. An instance occurs in *Billy Budd* by Herman Melville, when the hero (a strangely innocent young sailor) is challenged by the Satanic master-at-arms for accidentally spilling soup on the mess deck: 'Handsomely done, my lad! And handsome is as handsome did it, too!' (Melville, 1967: 350). Claggart's malign obsession with Billy (leading to both their deaths) makes powerful and ironic use of this word-class variation.

(ii) Verb-based variations

These variations are somewhat difficult to disentangle, since they depend on differing permutations of the subject/verb/object structure. For example, a verb with one or more subjects may govern a *variety* of phrase structures (including object complement, infinitive phrases, participial phrases and adverbial phrases). *Zeugma* is the name for this structure. It has several sub-varieties including *syllepsis,* which occurs when a verb with one subject governs two object-nouns, one abstract and one concrete – 'He put on his business sense with his business suit.' Another variant of the subject/verb/object structure is hyperactive subject (*diazeugma* or *colon*). Here a single subject is followed by one or more verbs, each with its own object complement.

For economy of explication, we have selected examples of zeugma from literary persuasion, and hyperactive subject from functional persuasion.

The lines quoted in Chapter 3 from Andrew Marvell's love poem 'To his Coy Mistress' (see p. 102 above), employ zeugma to add to the impression of single-minded and infinitely extended 'adoration' of the love-object. Going back to that passage, the reader will find that Marvell wittily links what interests him – the expanding time-scale of this sexual and philosophical fantasy – to an unusual syntactic structure. A single modal verb ('should go') governs a series of infinitive phrases, and this use of zeugma highlights its odd semantic disproportions. Thus the figure itself becomes a means for the imaginative exploration of time and its duration as experienced by a lover. In the last line, almost as an afterthought, a new verb governs a new object, 'your heart' – the key to all.

By contrast, the copywriter for Neutrogena Moisture Cream (*Vogue,* March 1991) contrived to convey a much more threatening sense of time (and since age has not withered his or her eloquence, we retain this example from the first edition):

> . . . Your skin is fighting a constant battle against dehydration, struggling to maintain moisture in the face of an onslaught from sun, wind, natural evaporation and central heating. A moisturiser can help by both adding moisture directly to your skin and by attracting already present moisture from within to the surface.

Both of the single hyperactive subjects, 'skin' and 'moisturiser', are linked through an auxiliary to chains of active verb-forms.

(iii)   *Syntactic parallelism (isocolon)*

The persuasive effects of syntactical structures can be developed by using various kinds of parallelism to add emphasis, clarity, balance, and cumulative weight. At best they convey the spontaneous energy of deep feeling or conviction; over-use produces banal and trivialising effects. With this in mind, development should normally be limited to three phrases or clauses (*tricolon* or triple structure) or at most four. Listed below are some examples that can be used separately or in combination.

1.   identical syntactic structure in each clause;
2.   identical or similar length in each clause;
3.   a similar rhythm in each clause;
4.   an antithetical balance within or between clauses.

Within these options substantial variation is possible, and can be extended beyond the single sentence to the paragraph as a whole. A literary example of syntactic parallelism is found in this account of the Happy Valley in Samuel Johnson's *Rasselas* (1759), in which the balanced clauses poise the physical characteristics of the animals contributing to the general life and richness of the scene, against their correspondent activities and settings. The lack of variation points to the monotony of Rasselas's life in the valley:

> On one part were flocks and herds feeding in the pastures, on another all the beasts of chase frisking in the lawns. The sprightly kid was bounding on the rocks, the subtle monkey frolicking in the trees, and the solemn elephant reposing in the shade.   (Johnson, 1957: 392)

(iv)   *Left- and right-branching sentences*

Walter Nash has usefully identified these syntactic structures (1980: 112–16). To summarise, a *left-branching or suspended sentence* keeps you waiting for the main verb (one or more subordinate clauses preceding it); a *right-branching sentence* comes in quickly with the main clause, followed by one or more subordinate clauses or extended participial phrases. Left-branching sentences are tenser, more dramatic and potentially more emotive. Right-branching sentences offer a more 'relaxed' structure, suggesting a confident exposition or argument. In literary persuasion the alternation of left and right branch can help the flow of narrative from paragraph to paragraph, as well as helping to set up emotional and imaginative cross-currents. This is seen near the opening of Virginia Woolf's *Mrs Dalloway:*

> . . . In people's eyes, in the swing, tramp and trudge; in the bellow and uproar; the carriages, motor cars, omnibuses, vans, sandwich men shuffling and swinging; barrel organs; in the triumph and the jingle and the strange high singing of some aeroplane overhead *was* what she loved; life; London; this moment of June.   (*left-branching*)

> For it was the middle of June. The War *was* over, except for someone like Mrs Foxcroft at the Embassy last night eating her heart out because that nice boy was killed and now the Manor House must go to a cousin; or Lady Bexborough who opened a bazaar, they said, with a telegram in her hand, John, her favourite, killed; but it was over; thank Heaven – over.   (*right-branching*)

> (Woolf, 1964 [1925]: 6–7)

The discordant elements (1st sentence), and the pressure of the immediate past on bereaved women (2nd sentence) work against any easy confirmation of the statements made in both sentences. The italicised stative verbs are differently positioned; in the first sentence delayed to heighten drama, and in the second placed early to make the reader anticipate a further confirmation that 'the war was over'. For many people, as the novel will show, this isn't true.

(v)   Listings or 'heapings-up' (synathroesmus)

The effect of piling nouns or verbs within a sentence can be highly persuasive, replicating a sense of emotional, intellectual or sensory pressure in the audience. Woolf uses it to convey the confusion of London in the passage above. A further powerful instance is seen in John Donne's comprehensive listing (*Holy Sonnets*, 4:)

> All whom the flood did, and fire shall o'erthrow,
> All whom war, dearth, age, agues, tyrannies,
> Despaire, law, chance, hath slaine . . .
> (Donne, 1990: 175)

Here Donne uses metonymy *as* well as 'heapings-up' in his account of all the different ways of dying. The pounding, staccato emphasis of the death-list also draws power from the use of antithesis ('flood' and 'fire'). An effect of overwhelming accumulation is achieved through a sense of weight as well as number.

Puttenham also describes this term in his *Arte* (1968 [1589]: 197) and calls it 'the heaping figure'. There are four ways of doing this: (a) using single 'staccato' words; (b) using short phrases of differing structure; (c) using multiple conjunctions ('and . . . and'); (d) creating an abrupt effect by omitting all conjunctions (see Appendix B).

(d) Repetition

This is probably the major resource of schematic rhetoric and the one with closest affinity to the spontaneous expression of emotion. The pattern created by a repeated word, or the rhythm created by a repeated phrase, validate Coleridge's remarkable insight about rhythm 'striv(ing) to hold in check the workings of passion' (Coleridge, 1956: 206). Seven types of repetition are summarised below, followed by an example each from functional and literary persuasion.

(i)   *Initial repetition* (*anaphora*): word or phrase repeated at the beginning of each one of a series of sentences or clauses.

(ii)   *Terminal repetition* (*antistrophe*): word or phrase repeated at the end of each one of a series of sentences or clauses.

(iii)   *Random repetition* (*ploche*): piecemeal repetition of important word or phrase at points of emphasis in a sentence or paragraph.

(iv)   *Instant repetition* (*epizeuxis*): a word or phrase immediately repeated one or more times.

(v)   *Refrain* (*epimone*): self-explanatory, but note that refrains may be varied.

(vi)   *Stop-and-start* (*anadiplosis*): repetition at the beginning of a sentence of the word or phrase that closed the previous sentence.

(vii)   *Switch-around* (*antimetabole*). Words or phrases repeated, often with variation, in transposed or inverse order (A becomes B, B becomes A). Further kinds of repetition will be found in Appendix B.

(i)   Functional persuasion

'You can't get social security to pay your rent without a fixed address, and you can't get a fixed address without social security to pay your rent!' Here the switch-around (*antimetabole*) actually presents an urgent and disturbing process of thought – a 'Catch-22'. Interestingly, this figure is one of those singled out by Jeanne Fahnestock (1999) as a stimulant to scientific insight.

(ii) Literary persuasion

In this extract from Ben Jonson's *Celebration of Charis*, 4 ('Her Triumph', ll. 21–30), Shakespeare's contemporary describes his imaginary beloved, using initial repetition (as well as syntactic parallelism and other devices) with power and delicacy:

> Have you seen but a bright lily grow,
>   Before rude hands have touched it?
> Have you marked but the fall o'the snow
>   Before the soil hath smutched it?
> Have you felt the wool o' the beaver?
>   Or swan's down ever?
> Or have smelled o'the bud o'the briar,
>   Or the nard i' the fire?
>   Or have tasted the bag o' the bee?
> O so white! O so soft! O so sweet is she!
>   (Jonson, 1985: 313)

(e) Amplification and diminution

This category of apparently opposed schematic devices is probably the most large-scale we have yet encountered. It is important because it provides the persuader with specific frameworks for structuring discourse, offering the opportunity to *amplify* and *diminish* in two closely related senses. Amplification and diminution can be used both to develop an argument in detail, and to shorten it; to enhance the importance of the subject, and to denigrate it. Either can produce powerful persuasive effects, often involving the use of trope.

The first devices to be examined are rather different from the rest, in that they are ways of making a statement (i.e. overstating or understating). They can equally apply to single words, or be extended to whole discourses according to need.

(i) Hype or exaggeration (hyperbole)

Persuasive exaggeration, or overstatement, is familiar to us all. It is a stock feature of tabloid headlines; any reported disagreement has to be a 'row', and any hint of an emotional response to some unwelcome decision is amplified into 'fury'. Hyperbole can be used literally, although the trope of metaphor is often introduced. In the following groupings of words, denoted meaning contrasts with non-figurative hype and then with a figurative version: 'shocked'/'appalled'/'poleaxed'; 'disagreement'/'row'/'punch-up'; 'pleased'/'thrilled'/'over the moon'.

The effects of hype can range from crude exaggeration to sublime poetry (as in Marlowe's Faustus addressing his 'Helen': 'Oh, thou art fairer than the evening's air, / Clad in the beauty of a thousand stars' [1969 [1681]: 331]). They may include ironic self-mockery ('I'm totally exhausted by doing nothing all day').

(ii)   Understatement (litotes)

In this device (the opposite of hype) the audience is left to deduce that the speaker could put the point much more strongly. This amplifies the persuasive effect by conveying powerfully understated confidence. Again, understatement may be expressed literally or figuratively ('he wasn't short of money'/'he wasn't short of two pennies to rub together'). Another version of litotes uses the double negative, as in 'he was not uninterested', meaning he very definitely was interested.

(iii)   Categories of description (enargeia)

In traditional rhetoric there were several devices for developing graphic description of real or imaginary people, places, actions, times and seasons, in order to actualise emotion (readers may recall Quintilian's evocative example, quoted in Chapter 2). For example, rhetoricians distinguished topographia (description of a real place) and topothesia (description of an imaginary place). This distinction still has some value, suggesting as it does the legitimate differences between faithful reportage and the symbolic evocation of imaginary places. (The same point will apply to the other categories to be found in Appendix B.) Metonymy and metaphor can also be seen in this context.

We have chosen two passages of description to demonstrate topographia and topothesia. One is by the social historian Henry Mayhew, which appeared in the Morning Chronicle on 9 November 1849, and describes the room of a poor seamstress (Mayhew, 1984: 166); the other appears in Dickens's account of Satis House in Great Expectations (Dickens, 1965 [1861]: 89–90):

(Mayhew)   There was no table in the room; but on a chair without a back there was an old tin tray, in which stood a cup of hot, milkless tea, and a broken saucer, with some half dozen small potatoes in it. It was the poor soul's dinner. Some tea leaves had been given her, and she had boiled them up again to make something like a meal. She had not even a morsel of bread. In one corner of the room was a hay mattress rolled up. With this she slept on the floor.

(Dickens)   It was then that I began to understand that everything in the room had stopped, like the watch and the clock, a long time ago. I noticed that Miss Havisham put down the jewel exactly on the spot from which she had taken it up. . . . Without this arrest of everything, this standing still of all the pale decayed objects, not even the withered bridal dress on the collapsed form could have looked like grave-clothes, or the long veil so like a shroud.

Mayhew's stark detail metonymically reflects the tenant's wretched poverty, while in Dickens the objects in the room metaphorically share the 'arrest' of Miss Havisham's life – indeed, 'standing still' almost suggests that the room has a perverse volition like that of its owner.

(iv)   Amplificatory frameworks

Types of framework include:

- *build-up* or *incrementum* (an artful device achieving impact through a mounting series of 'increments' e.g. from 'bad' to 'worse' to 'worst' or from A to B to C);
- antithetical structures;
- summary statements preceding or following a set of graphic details, in order to focus their effect.

In the following extract from an unpublished letter in a private collection, written in 1859 by a young Yorkshirewoman, Sarah Ellen Gaukroger, to the man who later became her husband, she uses this device in vehement protest at his apparent inconstancy:

. . . if it had been a youth in his teens one would never have thought anything more off it, but a man of your years and I ought to be able to say *sense*, I could never have expected it, or if it had been a mere act of gallantry I should never have thought off it again, but if you recall all or a small part of what you said & tried to make me believe of those occasions, you will I am sure be led to think you behaved very wrong.

She uses build-up twice, first to amplify her incredulity at his behaviour ('teens' to 'years' to 'sense'); and secondly to increase the recipient's sense of shame after his protestations ('gallantry' to 'all' to 'small').

(f)   Tricks and ploys

We have selected seven of these for consideration, all of which have substantial persuasive potential. It's worth noting that syntax often plays an important part in achieving these effects, as well as lexis. This is especially true of the first two devices, which have a strong lexical element. They are nevertheless highly charged psychologically, for or against the subjects to which they refer. We will comment on the cognitive processes which may be involved in each case.

(i)   *Whitewash* (paradiastole)

This is the most potentially corrupting of all schematic devices in the persuasive repertoire, unless used ironically. It shifts between life themes characterised by debased goals, to better ones more reflective of the persuadee's values, flattering vice or error by the application of a neutral or even a positive term. Examples might be: 'severe' (for 'cruel'); 'tired and emotional' (for 'drunk and disorderly'); 'a free spirit' (for an irresponsible person).

(ii)   *Doing-down* (meiosis)

The opposite of whitewash, this involves hostile or reductive word-choice: as in 'tarted up' (i.e. redecorated), or 'fiddling' (i.e. rearranging). The life-theme-shift works the other way, towards cynicism and disgust.

(iii)   *Self-correction* (epanorthosis)

Like whitewash and doing-down, this entails a life theme-shift, but an overt one. A word is expressed, then queried and replaced: 'We have a very clever man as Sales Director. . . . Did I say "clever"? *Plausible* might be nearer the mark.'

(iv)   *Breaking off* (aposiopesis)

This device imitates the emotional, exasperated or insinuating *breaking off* of a sentence. Cognitively it's a kind of broken script, in that it thwarts expectation of a complete message. The effect ranges from the comic '. . . say no more: nudge, nudge, wink, wink' to the speechlessness of extreme rage or grief. It may arouse the audience's curiosity, prompt their collusion, or impress them with a painful sense of stress or suffering.

(v)   Doubting (aporia)

Still a current critical term, this is used to amusing effect by the academic and critical theorist David Lodge in his 'condition of England' novel, *Nice Work* (1988). His young female academic, following deconstructive methodology, explains the instability of a line in Tennyson to her students (including her 'shadow', the besotted industrialist, Vic Wilcox). 'It's an aporia. . . . A kind of accidental aporia, a figure of undecidable ambiguity, irresolvable contradiction.' She continues: 'In classical rhetoric it means real or pretended uncertainty about the subject under discussion' (Lodge, 1988: 337–8). Emotionally *aporia* conveys an inability to respond to a topic because of its momentousness. We might call it cognitive overload.

(vi)   Passing over (occultatio)

Although this is very much a ploy, it is also notable for its amplificatory and emotive effect. Persuasively it switches goals from something avowedly instrumental to resolution of the issue, to something aimed at a different though related goal. The ploy is to pretend not to mention what *is* being mentioned. (A twentieth-century example is the famous episode from *Fawlty Towers*, 'Don't mention the War!' where the unfortunate Basil Fawlty finds himself doing just this all the time, and creating predictable chaos.) The device is used repeatedly in Cicero's face-to-face denunciation of Catilina in the Roman Senate:

> I shall say nothing, either, about the financial ruin into which you will be plunged upon the thirteenth of this month.
>   Instead, I shall turn to matters which relate not to the squalor of your personal depravities, not to the sordid tangle of your personal affairs, but to the supreme interests of our commonwealth. . . .   (Cicero, 1969: 83)

(vii)   The question

Probably the most familiar of all rhetorical devices, this need only be treated briefly here. There are various ways in which the question can be used for particular persuasive effect. We may use one question, or a series of questions, which may be authentic or inauthentic (i.e. the questioner may really want to know the answers, or he or she may only be using the form of the question for dramatic effect, or to pressure the audience). For further discussion see Appendix B.

Conclusion

We started our examination of rhetoric as a compositional process with the concept of *inventio* (creation of content) and moved on through *dispositio* (arrangement of content) to *elocutio* (expression of content). It is also true, however, that individual 'figures' from the persuasive repertoire may, in their own right, become a source of inspiration. According to Jeanne Fahnestock (see above) the more structural figures have also acted as stimuli to scientific thought. We end with a familiar quotation. Is it possible that in creating Mark Antony's speech, Shakespeare was inspired by the rhetorical and dramatic potential of the refrain itself ('For Brutus is an honourable man'), rather than working doggedly through the processes of invention and arrangement? We shall never know.

Further Exploration: the Theory and Practice of Persuasive Repertoire

Insights gained from linguistic theory can also benefit stylistic practice. A good example of this is Jan Firbas's theory of *communicative dynamism* and *sentence perspective* (1992). Firbas calls attention to the apt ordering of sentences, so as to give maximum impact to 'context independent' lexis; this will help writers to control their style, guiding decisions about appropriate use of figures. Too much use of repetition, for example, reduces the persuasive impact.

Harold Bloom offers a very interesting and idiosyncratic account of the way in which poetic originality enforces a progression through the major tropes. Even if readers are unconvinced by Bloom's epic presentation of the 'strong poet's struggle', using the

→

→

tropes as weapons against the 'anxiety of influence', it is worth reading him to gain a sense of how tropes form part of a larger rhetorical or poetic structure (see Bloom, 1973, 1975).

Readers will find it useful to go deeper into the nature of metaphor, in order to improve their understanding of how it can unite the persuasive functions of *ethos* and *pathos*. It might be useful to follow the progression of thinking on this topic, beginning with Richards's discussion (1965), going on to look at Paul Ricoeur's acute and scholarly treatment (Ricoeur, 1979, 1996), and ending with the most recent treatments of innovative metaphor (in which schema and 'possible worlds' theory are applied – see Semino, 1997; Stockwell, 2002).

7 Practising Persuasion

Introduction

The difference between understanding the theory and being able to apply it effectively is substantial, whatever the skill. We have spent the preceding chapters examining the elements of the art of persuasion. In this chapter we offer our readers opportunities to practise and develop their own rhetorical skills. Despite its ancient origins, the art of persuasion has not dated, but is being practised today as a discipline in its own right, and in numerous special applications (e.g. giving a presentation, writing advertising copy, briefing a group of colleagues). Being able to argue persuasively seems to be a valued skill in a wide range of working environments

'To exercise' and 'to practise' have similar but not quite the same meaning. Both words can refer to preliminary work on acquiring a skill or to its employment once acquired; but 'practise' also implies regular employment in a variety of situations. This has implications both for the way rhetoric is learned and how it is used. Throughout the book we have seen how the persuader uses rhetoric to address real and imaginary audiences and situations, to adopt appropriate stances, to invoke emotional responses and to exploit the resources of logic. As we have shown, the functional applications of persuasive skill range from the mundane to matters of national emergency; in literary persuasion, the range is almost as wide. The exercises in this chapter provide an opportunity (through awareness of *kairos*) to engage the creative imagination of both persuader and audience.

We suggest that a good way to practise rhetorical skills is to follow our version of the classical *progymnasmata* or 'elementary' exercises, which deal one by one with the elements of a speech. These exercises were attributed to Aphthonius who wrote around AD 400, and would be familiar in Rudolph Agricola's Latin translation to every Elizabethan and Jacobean schoolboy (and to a few privately educated young women). This translation carried a full commentary by the German schoolmaster Reinhard Lorich, of which there were numerous editions.

These exercises have been comprehensively described and adapted for modern use by Crowley and Hawhee (1999: 320–66, Chapter 16), and are now being taught successfully in European and American universities and colleges by rhetoricians such as Professor Alan Church at the University of Texas, Brownsville, and Dr Anders Sigrell at Umeå University in Sweden. Incidentally, these scholars have also worked on these exercises collaboratively and compared the benefits accruing to their students (see Church, 2004).

From our perspective, it is significant that the original exercises did involve separate practice with the three 'proofs' of *ethos*, *pathos* and *logos*, besides working on different types of persuasive process as well as some features of rhetorical style. Readers will immediately recognise that this pattern is close to the chapter sequence in this book. Indeed, six of our chapters follow this structure.

Starting with a selection of the *progymnasmata* exercises, we shall focus on particular features linking back to each chapter, and offering varied opportunities for rhetorical 'bending and stretching'. In each example we shall briefly describe the exercise and sketch out some typical scenarios or situations for its application. A theoretical perspective showing the concept being applied in the exercise will be outlined and the exercise concluded with some alternative activities.

In the last part of the chapter we make suggestions for collaborative work, noting some contemporary contexts in which rhetorical skills might be developed further. This 'building block' approach should help the rhetorical apprentice to keep his or her feet on the ground. We shall alert readers to instances where particular models of argument and cognitive perspectives might apply in either literary or functional cases.

Practising expression as well as reasoning is important when 'taking [rhetorical] exercise', and we shall provide many opportunities for varying persuasive structure and drawing on the persuasive repertoire.

Practising the *Progymnasmata*

(a)   Ethos: *character and situation*

The focus of *ethos* is on the persuader and their personal stance. The best way to understand stance is to stretch the imagination and powers of empathy by trying to write or speak in such a way that a potential audience is convinced. (In traditional rhetoric, this exercise was called *ethopoeia moralis* or representation of character.)

(i)   Possible situations

- Recalling how it felt to start a new job abroad (travel or business journalism);
- Live radio commentary on the experience of parachute jumping;
- Re-living a key childhood experience from an adult perspective;
- Recounting characteristic 'anxiety' dream to a friend (missing train/plane/exam//medical appointment/interview; giving public speech dressed in underwear or pyjamas; having tea with the Queen and spilling it)

(ii)   Theoretical perspectives

In this situation, someone is placed outside their usual cognitive framework (schema) for interpreting experience, as in Aphthonius's example of the backwoodsman seeing the sea for the first time. The traditional structure of this exercise contrasts present with past experience and looks forward to the future, using flashback as well as flash forward.

(iii)   Example

'The Idiot Boy' by William Wordsworth (*Lyrical Ballads*, 1798) is a poem on a radical topic for its time. The eponymous hero, Johnny, is sent on an errand one moonlight night and gets lost in the woods. Wordsworth imagines the boy's account of his experience with striking empathy:

> 'The cocks did crow to-whoo, to-whoo,
> And the sun did shine so cold.'
> – Thus answered Johnny in his glory,
> And that was all his travel's story.
> (Wordsworth and Coleridge, 1963 [1798]: 101)

(iv)   Suggested activity and plan of action

- Choose one of the situations described above, or produce a comparable one. Choose the mode and identify the audience.
- Select a suitable style to match the character being portrayed (e.g. simple, flamboyant, pompous, hesitant) and check the persuasive repertoire. Note that Aphthonius's original advice on creating a vivid impression was to use a kind of speech 'which is clear, brief, descriptive and distinct, without rhetorical turns or figures'. Write

or record your example, inviting comment from friends or colleagues on the degree of empathy achieved.

(b)   Ethos: character and choice

The persuader imagines himself or herself in a situation of emotional stress in which a decision has to be made. (Aphthonius's example was the Greek hero Achilles, whose grief at his friend Patroclos's death made him abandon his previous isolation and take revenge on the Trojan prince Hector.) A more recent example might be the peace-loving hero in a Wild West movie strapping on his six-shooter to confront the ranchers' hired guns. This persuasive stance is often linked with social issues (e.g. in political journalism, including broadcast news interviews with people under the stress of events).

(i)   Possible situations

- Director announces closure of longstanding manufacturing business to workers, board, shareholders or press;
- head teacher addresses colleagues in school going into 'special measures' after OFSTED visit;
- old people having to sell their family home to pay for care (interview on radio 'social issue' style programme);
- lottery winner giving interview to media on future plans (staying in same job/setting up charitable foundation/determining to splurge the lot);
- personal letter explaining writer's decision to join religious or political group that involves absolute separation from close family contact;
- political speech defending unpopular political or painful economic or foreign policy initiative.

(ii)   Theoretical perspective

In any of the above contexts, a writer or speaker acting as persuader will need to be aware of – and make appropriate adjustments to – his or her stance. This must reflect not only the direct addressee, but anyone else with a general or personal interest in the situation (e.g. television audience watching extract from ministerial statement in Parliament). Stephen Levinson's essay on production and reception roles may be useful in this context (1998).

(iii)   Example

In his elegy *In Memoriam* (1850), Alfred Tennyson writes of the pain of leaving the Lincolnshire home of his childhood where his dead friend Arthur Hallam had often visited. He chooses to leave the now desolate house and landscape for others to enjoy:

> Till from the garden and the wild
>   A fresh association blow,
>   And year by year the landscape grow
> Familiar to the stranger's child;
>
> As year by year the labourer tills
>   His wonted glebe, or lops the glades;
>   And year by year our memory fades
> From all the circle of the hills.
> (Tennyson, 1969 [1850]: 954 [Section C1, 17–24])

Even in this brief extract, we see Tennyson contrasting another child's future with his own constantly receding past, as the perennially present agricultural work in the fields (i.e. the 'glebe') continues.

(iv)   Theoretical perspective

The writer or speaker will need to use not only contrast but also narrative structure as part of the necessary explanation of the 'choice'. Models of argument such as cause/effect and definition could be used. The style should reflect the character of the persuader in a clear and convincing way for the audience.

(v)   Suggested activities and strategies

- Choose one of the situations above (or a comparable one) and write the text to be spoken or read, using appropriate style to convey character and stance to envisaged audience;
- using a dialogue format, produce a scripted text of one of the above situations.

(c)   Ethos: *Attitude and exposition*

This exercise was traditionally known as *chreia*. Its objective was to use a well-known saying/famous action to stimulate a writer/speaker to endorse it. Today, more questioning attitudes are acceptable, and a famous saying or action may be handled in a negative or satirical way.

(i)   Sayings or actions: examples

Sayings: 'History is bunk' (Henry Ford); 'There is no such thing as society' (Margaret Thatcher); 'I have a dream' (Martin Luther King); 'Think not what your country can do for you, but what you can do for your country' (John F. Kennedy'); 'Education; education; education' (Tony Blair); 'This House would not fight for King and Country' (1933 Oxford Union motion).

Actions: going to join International Brigade in Spanish Civil War (1930s); burning Draft Papers for service in Vietnam (1970s); joining anti-war demonstration or countryside march; joining any valued or undervalued profession; acting on any 'call' or vocation.

(ii)   Theoretical perspective

It is important that the persuader knows *why* the saying/action possesses the power to impress or provoke an intended audience. An invaluable study of the way language mediates power can be found in Norman Fairclough's book *Language and Power* (2001).

(iii)   Example

In *Brave New World* (1932), Huxley suggests the full implications of Henry Ford's saying, as the World Controller addresses his awe-struck listeners:

'You all remember,' said the Controller, in his strong deep voice, 'you all remember, I suppose, that beautiful and inspired saying of Our Ford's: History is bunk. History,' he repeated slowly, 'is bunk.'

He waved his hand; and it was as though, with an invisible feather whisk, he had brushed away a little dust, and the dust was Harappa, was Ur of the Chaldees; some spider-webs, and they were Thebes and Babylon and Cnossos and Mycenae. Whisk, whisk – and where was Odysseus, where was Job, where were Jupiter and Gotama and Jesus? Whisk – and those specks of antique dirt called Athens and Rome, Jerusalem and the Middle Kingdom – all were gone. Whisk – the place where Italy had been was empty. Whisk, the cathedrals; whisk, whisk, King Lear and the Thoughts of Pascal. Whisk, Passion; whisk, Requiem; whisk, Symphony; whisk . . .   (Huxley, 1994 [1932]: 30)

(iv)   Suggested activities and strategies

- Look at the way in which the narrative voice 'comments' via the Controller's words on the saying 'History is bunk'. How does Huxley convey negative attitudes to the reader? Is it through *ethos, pathos* or *logos*?
- Choose one of the sayings or actions above and draft a speech in which the speaker conveys strongly positive or negative attitudes towards the saying or action by unfolding its implications (just as Huxley does with Henry Ford's comment).

(d)   Ethos: praise or blame

The aim here is to celebrate or denounce the characteristics of people, places or things. This activity is endemic and worldwide; for example, in some southern African cultures *praise poetry* is a living tradition (see Gunner, 1994: 251–63).

(i)   Possible situations

- *praise*:   best man's speech; farewell to work colleague; eulogy or tribute; successful school or business; triumphant sports team;
- *blame*:   satirical broadcast sketch; denunciatory newspaper editorial or article.

(ii)   Theoretical perspectives

What can be achieved with praise when the subject is controversial, was famously illustrated by the sophist Gorgias's *Encomium to Helen* written in the late 5th century BC (see Shaffner, 1998: 243–57).

(iv)   Example

In this unconventional eulogy to his Newfoundland dog, Boatswain, Lord Byron subverts the conventions of praise, as lavished on aristocratic tombs:

> When all is done, upon the tomb is seen,
> Not what he was, but what he should have been:
> But the poor dog, in life the firmest friend,
> The first to welcome, foremost to defend,

Whose honest heart is still his master's own
Who labours, fights, lives, breathes for him alone.
Unhonour'd falls, unnoticed all his worth,
Denied in heaven the soul he held on earth,
While man, vain insect! hopes to be forgiven,
And claims himself a sole exclusive heaven.

(Byron, 1945: 54)

(v) Suggested activities and strategies

- The standard order of formal praise included ancestry, parents, place of birth and education culminating in a celebration of achievement, honours, good fortune and friendships. (Dispraise followed a corresponding sequence.) Choose your subject for blame or praise from the categories above, and identify the genre. Experiment with the traditional order to produce your own celebratory or denunciatory piece. As an alternative the 'praise or blame' sequence could be adapted to a place, institution or group achievement. It may also be possible to research African praise poetry and to use its conventions as a creative model.
- Write from the standpoint of a manager to produce a 'praise sandwich' (praise/constructive criticism/praise) on an imaginary employee.

(e) Pathos: character and passion

This exercise (*ethopoeia passiva*) invites speakers or writers to imagine extreme states of emotion so that, whenever necessary, they can engage empathetically with an audience's feelings. In order to do this, they script a speech or monologue in the voice of a real individual, or in the voice of an imagined or representative character, relating their present state of feeling to their immediate past and likely future.

(i) Possible situations

- an existing 'soap' character reacts to death, betrayal, rivalry, envy-inducing success etc.;
- someone who has just been through a strongly emotional experience – pleasant or unpleasant – is overheard on his/her mobile telling a friend about it;

- a major historical figure responds emotionally to some event in which he/she is known to have been involved.

(ii)   Theoretical perspective

Like other *ethopoeia* exercises, this is often structured on contrasts of past, present and future. The way in which emotions find expression in language is currently being investigated by linguists such as Raymond Gibbs (1994: 124–34).

(iii)   Example

The reported last words of King Priam of Troy, in Marlowe's early tragedy *Dido Queen of Carthage* (*c*.1587), embody the three elements of past, present, and future (the last of these reflected in a helpless plea). With no choices left, he is addressing the man who is about to kill him:

> Achilles' son, remember what I was:
> Father of fifty sons, but they are slain;
> Lord of my fortune, but my fortune's turn'd;
> King of this city, but my Troy is fired;
> And now am neither father, lord, nor king:
> But who so wretched, but desires to live?
> Oh, let me live . . .
> (Marlowe, 1969: 61)

(iv)   Suggested activities and strategies

- Construct an imagined mobile phone conversation in which two people discuss some traumatic or joyful event in which both were involved.
- Script a scene from a play or soap opera in the course of which the main speaker is interrupted by further news, good or bad, as a consequence of which emotion changes or intensifies.
- Construct a letter or diary entry written immediately after a major historical event by one of those principally involved.

(f)   Commonplace

This differs from 'Ethos: Attitude and Exposition' because it articulates the persuader's general values (or their opposites), and links them to entire groups of people, not to individuals. The process of conceiving such values helps the persuader to define his or her stance and to choose appropriate emotive abstractions. Aphthonius, however, uses the exercise to train students in writing emotive denunciatory conclusions to speeches. This involves a brief 'exposition' of facts to 'inflame the hearer', before going on to show their deplorable consequences.

Possible commonplaces

- public statements asserting libertarian values and human rights in various contexts, e.g. emergency legislation relating to terrorism;
- assertion or redefinition of values governing any major aspect of life, e.g. family values, individualism, self-worth, community, cultural richness and diversity, enterprise, public service;
- positive values contrasted with distortion of values, e.g. greed, indifference, mendacity, excessive self-promotion, narcissism, spin etc.

(i)   Theoretical perspective

In its original conception, the exercise dealt with 'things commonly encountered in human affairs and in writing, such as fortune, riches, honours, life, death, courage, prudence, justice, generosity, temperance, and everything contrary to these'. Quintilian describes commonplaces as 'weapons which we should always have stored in our armoury ready for immediate use' (1920–2: I, 208–9). A useful modern perspective on evaluation is provided by Hunston and Thompson (2000) (see Chapter 5).

(ii)   Example

This slightly edited extract is taken from the Prime Minister's speech at the 2003 Labour Party conference (UK) and exemplifies commonplace, in its combination of general principles with strong emotional loading.

New Labour for me was never a departure from belief. It is my belief. The just society in which each person is a full and equal citizen of our land, irrespective of birth, class, wealth, race or sex. Where through solidarity we build a society in which collective strength compensates for individual weakness. Where privilege cannot just be handed down from generation to generation but success has to be earned on merit. Where self-respect and respect for others is the hallmark of our communities, and where the fight against poverty and oppression is Britain's mission in the wider world. These are my values and yours. They are the key. But the door they must unlock is the door to the future.

Because values not put to work in the real world are mere words, lying idle, there to console us but not to change lives for the better. When almost 10 years ago we ditched the old Clause IV, we didn't do it just to ditch nationalization. The new Clause IV was a fundamental restatement of ideology: 'by the strength of our common endeavour we achieve more than we achieve alone . . . a community in which power, wealth and opportunity are in the hands of the many not the few.' From now on, we said: we stand for certain values. The values are unchangeable. But the policies are open to change. We made the ends sacrosanct. We put the means up for discussion so that each time could find the right expression for values that are for all time.

(iii)   Suggested activities and strategies

Today commonplace is most likely to be encountered in journalistic writing aimed at a whole cross-section of society (e.g. readers of a national newspaper) or at special interest or local groups.

- As a speech writer for a politician, draft a section of a major campaigning speech articulating the party's values, giving them full emotional resonance.
- As Leader of the Opposition, draft a conclusion to a parliamentary speech attacking the values of the ruling party and showing what negative consequences result.

(g)   Logos: analysing rhetorical logic

In this exercise (without equivalent in the *progymnasmata*) we demonstrate how models of argument are used in fictional writing. The following extracts from Dickens's 'condition of England' novel, *Hard Times* (1854), use a variety of models and forms of argument to support his hostile view of utilitarian philosophy. Interested readers will find the whole text of Chapter 1, followed by an analysis of topical logic within the chapter, together with associated stylistic features in Appendix A, Section 4. In the first extract Mr Gradgrind sets out the educational philosophy governing his school. The chapter continues with a long emphatically repetitive description of Mr Gradgrind – 'square coat, square legs, square shoulders' – and ends with our second extract.

Extract 1

'NOW, what I want is, Facts. Teach these boys and girls nothing but Facts. Facts alone are wanted in life. Plant nothing else, and root out everything else. You can only form the minds of reasoning animals upon Facts: nothing else will ever be of any service to them. This is the principle on which I bring up my own children, and this is the principle on which I bring up these children. Stick to Facts, Sir!'

Extract 2

The speaker, and the schoolmaster, and the third grown person present, all backed a little, and swept with their eyes the inclined plane of little vessels then and there arranged in order, ready to have imperial gallons of facts poured into them until they were full to the brim. (Dickens, 1955 [1854]: 1–2)

The 'little vessels' are the children sitting on the raked seating in the 'plain, bare, monotonous vault of a schoolroom'.

(i)   Suggested activity

Having noted the models of argument and rhetorical figures used in both extracts, construct a contemporary scenario in which educational philosophies are satirised (e.g. part of an episode from the television situation comedy *Teachers*)

(h)   Logos: *proof and disproof*

The purpose in this *progymnasmata* exercise is to prove the persuader's position on any point at issue, or to refute an opponent's case on the same issue.

(i)   Possible situations

- any issue in an imaginary trial or historic case;
- some political issue of national or international importance;

- a local controversy;
- something controversial within a special interest group well known to the persuader (e.g. music, football, rock-climbing etc.).

(ii)   Theoretical perspective

Crowley and Hawhee (1999: 333–4), following Aphthonius, provide the order and the topics for the *refutation* of a false assertion (see below). *Confirmation* begins by strongly affirming the proposition, and then progresses through a series of positive arguments. In assessing an audience's likely response to persuasive proof, writers or speakers need to be aware of the changing role of argument in contemporary culture (see Tannen, 1998).

(iii)   Example

In this extract from his article (the *Guardian*, 13 March 2004) on the Madrid bombings, Timothy Garton Ash refutes an American assertion regarding the 'War on Terror' and how to conduct it. Note the adept use of an oppositional model as a way into argument:

> If you want to know where it's going wrong, you should read a clever, foolish book by David Frum and Richard Perle, entitled *An End to Evil: How to Win the War on Terror*. (People cannot be wise and foolish at the same time; but clever and foolish, yes.) As part of its strategy to win the war on terror, Frum and Perle argue, the United States should stop supporting 'a more closely integrated Europe' and 'force European governments to choose between Paris and Washington'. European governments like the Spanish one, that is, currently among Washington's closest allies.
>
> But now consider, in the light of the Madrid bombings, what is really needed for Europeans to be effective partners in the war on terror. Whether al-Qaida or Eta were responsible, the answer is: closer cooperation inside Europe and, specifically, with France. It's France that has the largest Muslim population in the European Union and, since the Basques live on both sides of the Franco-Spanish frontier, it's France that is Spain's most important European partner in dealing with the threat of Basque terrorism. Yet here are those clever men in Washington trying to drive a wedge between Spain and France, in the name of the war on terror. In the face of what is unquestionably evil, let's drop these silly transatlantic polemics and get serious.

(iv)   Suggested activities and strategies

- Choose an assertion to refute (any national newspaper should provide a suitable issue), and follow the traditional structure of disproof. Begin by stating the assertion to be refuted; then put it into context. Next argue that the assertion is (a) uncertain, (b) incredible, (c) impossible, (d) inconsistent, (e) improper, (f) inconvenient.
- To *confirm* an assertion, follow the same order expressing initial approval, contextualising the assertion and showing that it's certain, credible, possible etc.
- Starting from the chosen assertion, the persuader might adopt a less formulaic way of refuting or confirming it by using the cause/effect model of argument, supported by other models of argument such as definition.
- Literary treatment could take the form of a fictional dialogue or a monologue.

(i) Logos: *thesis*

In the order of difficulty followed by Crowley and Hawhee, this exercise is the second most advanced of all the *progymnasmata*. It relates to an issue of wide general importance, without referring to particulars. Aphthonius's example (a highly politically incorrect view) addresses the question 'Should a wife be taken in marriage?' His argument confirms that she should, but gives her little choice in the matter. It is appropriate to group this exercise under *logos* despite its strong ethical and emotional overtones, because it is essentially an exercise in generalities, and draws on definition, genus/species, cause/effect, and association (especially *indicative quality*) models of argument. Placing the subject on a moral scale in the course of recommending it or dissuading from it, the exercise sets a challenging test in expressive style.

(i)   Possible situations or topics

- arguing for or against any important life-choice;
- arguing for or against any radical change in the ideologies governing society;
- global warming and environmental strategies (e.g. renewable energy and its sources).

(ii)   Theoretical perspectives

In his example, Aphthonius begins by setting out the general benefits of marriage from the male viewpoint, and then goes on to provide detailed answers to a series of briefly phrased objections (see Crowley and Hawhee, 1999: 360–2). Whatever case is being put forward today, the persuader needs to be similarly prepared to meet counter-arguments.

(iii)   Example

Milton's celebration of marriage (*Paradise Lost*, IV, 750–70). Here the poet answers two implicit 'objections': (a) that married sexuality is inconsistent with the purity of Paradise; and (b) that married love isn't (in the modern sense) 'romantic':

> Hail wedded love, mysterious law, true source
> Of human offspring, sole propriety
> In Paradise of all things common else.
> By thee adulterous lust was driven from men
> Among the bestial herds to range, by thee
> Founded in reason, loyal, just, and pure,
> Relations dear, and all the charities
> Of father, son, and brother first were known.
> Far be it, that I should write thee sin or blame,
> Or think thee unbefitting holiest place,
> Perpetual fountain of domestic sweets,
> Whose bed is undefiled and chaste pronounced,
> Present, or past, as saints and patriarchs used.
> Here Love his golden shafts employs, here lights
> His constant lamp, and waves his purple wings,
> Reigns here and revels; not in the bought smile
> Of harlots, loveless, joyless, unendeared,
> Casual fruition, nor in court amours
> Mixed dance, or wanton masque, or midnight ball,
> Or serenade, which the starved lover sings
> To his proud fair, best quitted with disdain.
>   (Milton, 1968: 658–9)

(iv)   Suggested activities and strategies

- Choose a situation or topic listed above (or some comparable issue); argue the case for or against in a short speech, dealing with any possible objections.
- Develop a similar argument more briefly in verse.

(j) Practising narrative

In the original *Progymnasmata*, narrative was treated as the second easiest exercise of all. Today linguists, anthropologists and literary critics regard narrative and its processes as something far more complex. We are using one exercise only to practise narrative: *text transformation*. This involves the transformation of a text from one genre into another, by changing the appropriate generic characteristics (including narrative structure etc.). Examples of this include Robert Browning's transformation of one narrative statement in *King Lear* ('Childe Roland to the dark tower came') into a sinister Gothic ballad; the American writer, Jane Smiley's retelling of Lear's story as fiction in *A Thousand Acres* (1992); and James Joyce's updating of Homer's epic poem *The Odyssey* into the modernist novel, *Ulysses* (1922), set in Dublin.

For our purposes text transformation is useful because it shows how narrative works. For example a nursery rhyme like 'Jack and Jill went up the hill' can be transformed into a police report of the accident, a sensational/human interest newspaper version of the same, Jack or Jill's personal narrative, or an allegory of the triumph of good (brown paper and vinegar) over evil (Wicked Witch of the Well). In each instance, questions of narrative structure, text organisation, point of view, time management and other generic characteristics need to be considered in the course of the transformation.

(i) Suggested activity and strategies

- transform a literary genre into a functional genre (e.g. short story, episode in novel, scene in play, fairy tale, ballad, dramatic monologue, nursery rhyme). Suggested examples might include writing extracts from Mrs Fairfax's diary (housekeeper in *Jane Eyre*); newspaper accounts (tabloid and broadsheet) of the tomb scene and its consequences in *Romeo and Juliet*;
- transform news story (local, national or international) into a short story, scene from a play, narrative poem, or extract from a novel;
- suggested strategies include changing the order of narrative including management of time (e.g. flashback, flash forward, *in medias res*); changing tense, mood, aspect of verbs; changing narrative voice; using omniscient narrator; changing point of view, context and social distance; changing audience and style.

(k) Practising style: vivid description (ekphrasis)

'The road of excess leads to the palace of wisdom' is one of Blake's *Proverbs of Heaven and Hell*, and this is good advice for anyone practising persuasive style. In the effort to achieve clarity, economy, and vividness of expression, it helps to explore the rich variety of rhetorical choices, since simple reliance on direct sensory description can be limiting. The secret is to acquire the skill of discrimination by learning how to concentrate effects in the right places.

(i) Suggested contexts for 'vivid description'

- describing a 'celebrity' (present day), or an impressive individual well known to the writer, or a famous historical figure (using any available sources of information, including pictures);
- personifying an abstraction is a traditional mode of *ekphrasis*, and is much used in television advertising (e.g. 'Mr Kipling', or any cartoon-style visualisation of the need for or benefits of a particular consumer product such as household cleaners or snack food);
- describing a public event or situation (e.g. an international emergency) using figures from the persuasive repertoire to increase the impact of vivid description.

(ii) Theoretical perspective

Quintilian's formula for raising feeling through mental visualisation is not straightforward to put into practice, because it has so many varieties and applications (see Appendix B). The Greek word *ekphrasis*, translated as 'vivid description', often signifies a description in words of the visual effect of a picture or other artefact.

(iii) Example

In *Jane Eyre* (1847) Charlotte Brontë uses *ekphrasis* to reveal both to the reader and to Mr Rochester the intensity and peculiarity of the heroine's imaginative life. The picture described is the second of three water-colours Jane has been asked to show him. The reader is free to make his or her own interpretation:

The second picture contained for foreground only the dim peak of a hill, with grass and some leaves slanting as if by a breeze. Beyond and above spread an expanse of sky, dark-blue as at twilight: rising into the sky was a woman's shape to the bust, portrayed in tints as dusk and soft as I could combine. The dim forehead was crowned with a star; the lineaments below were seen as through the suffusion of vapour; the eyes shone dark and wild; the hair streamed shadowy, like a beamless cloud torn by storm. or by electric travail. On the neck lay a pale reflection like moonlight; the same faint lustre touched the train of thin clouds from which rose and bowed this image of the Evening Star.   (Brontë 1996 [1847]: 139–40)

(iv)   *Suggested activities and strategies*

- Create an evocative description of a real place or person experimenting with one or more figures from Chapter 6 or Appendix A.
- Describe from your own observation any 'celeb' whom you find particularly irritating or engaging, with close attention to characteristic dress, pose, expression etc.
- Create (in modern dress) a personification of some abstract quality or entity.
- Describe to a friend a portrait (painting or photograph) you admire or find unconvincing, taking into account the artist's representation of the subject, and the subject's self-presentation.

(l)   Practising style: using the repertoire

In *Poetria Nova* (late twelfth century) the author demonstrates how thirty-five 'ornaments of words' can be used in quick succession in a single composition. Professor Marjorie Curry Woods of the University of Texas at Austin recommends this task to her students as an effective method of developing their stylistic skills (Woods, 2003).

(i)   *Suggested activity and strategy*

The object of this exercise is to see whether Blake's Proverb (cited above) is valid (i.e. can discrimination in the use of rhetorical figures be gained through excessive use). Having selected a topic of interest to the persuader and the prospective audience, the following stage-by-stage process below can be used:

(i)   Referring to Chapter 6 and Appendix A, select between ten or fifteen figures which seem to have potential for the chosen topic and audience.

(ii)   Consider whether puns and wordplay would be an effective way of introducing the chosen topic and audience.

(iii)   Would syntactical figures be useful to express activity or convey relationships?

(iv)   Consider how the use of parallel phrases or clauses might help the audience to weigh one idea against another.

(v)   Assess the value of using verbal and phrasal repetition, suspense, accumulation, *ekphrasis* and build-up or *incrementum* as means of creating emotional and intellectual engagement.

(vi)   Consider how tricks and ploys might be used to disarm the opposition.

(vii)   Scrutinise the resulting draft, and decide which devices have worked well, which haven't, and which should be pruned. Invite your prospective audience to confirm your judgement and assess the overall success of the draft.

Putting Together a Persuasion

One good way of applying the techniques explored in the exercises above is to work collaboratively. Each member of a group takes responsibility for one of the Aristotelean 'structural principles'; suggested titles for these roles are Ethos-Keeper, Pathos Specialist and Logician. Each specialist has prime responsibility for one principle but works co-operates with the other two in the achievement of individual and shared objectives. One of the co-authors of this book implemented the strategy with University of Nottingham undergraduates, who produced joint projects on topics such as anorexia, police recruitment, human cloning, and the effect of television on children (see R. Cockcroft, 2004). Different methods were adopted in the writing of these projects: for example, three shorter texts might address the same issue from three perspectives, each mainly reliant on one of the 'proofs'; another method was to script a dialogue on their chosen issue, involving distinct voices; a third method was to compose a single extended persuasive text. This collaborative approach helped each of the persuasive partners to appreciate the importance of the other's roles, and hence to understand better the complex nature of effective persuasion.

Practising Persuasion in the Real World

How can we put all this into practice in the world outside the library, study or other formal learning environment? In this final section we shall review the applications of persuasion in creative and professional contexts, in personal and social life, and in the workplace or public domain.

(a)   Persuasion in creative and professional contexts

Whether the reader is interested in professional script or copywriting, or in writing original fiction, drama or poetry, many of the *progymnasmata* techniques will (like the subjects to which they are typically applied), have developed your skills, boosted your confidence, and opened up possibilities. Here you can be left to work out the detailed potential for yourself. We will list a few possibilities.

- *Character and situation*: realising dramatic characters in comic situations or stories about individual growth; soap scripts; certain advertising scenarios.
- *Character and choice*: social issues drama; confessional poetry; reporting.
- *Attitude and exposition*: definition of attitude in fiction (e.g. reaction to established opinion); feature and leader writing.
- *Praise or blame*: profiles of people (journalism); celebratory or satirical poetry.
- *Character and passion*: dramatic writing, soap scripts, public service advertising.
- *Commonplace*: journalism, political speech writing, fiction with a message.
- *Analysing rhetorical logic*: dialogue and monologue of strong fictional characters, argumentative journalism (features and column writing).
- *Proof and disproof*: legal argument, controversial writing.
- *Thesis*: political and journalistic writing, fashion and lifestyle magazines.
- *Practising narrative*: fiction writing, narrative poetry
- *Vivid description*: poetry, satire, travel writing, copy writing
- *Using the repertoire*: general (discriminating) use

(b)   Persuasion in personal and social life

Practice in persuasion, when combined with insight, goodwill and tact should be an asset in all celebration involving family or friends, at which people expect and enjoy something said to the group at large, and also at the major 'rites of passage' whether joyful or solemn. We mention two tests of rhetorical skill: one spoken, one written.

- *Weddings*: empathy with audience will ensure that family and guests are equally comfortable with the speeches and that anecdotes (if any!) are neither embarrassing nor mawkish.
- *Christmas/New Year circular letters*. These letters (much mocked but seemingly unstoppable) require a testing combination of modesty, truthfulness, concision, information, humour, and sensitivity as they report family achievements to appropriately selected recipients. A practical test in *kairos*!

(c)   Persuasion in the work-place

Here we consider one broader and one narrower area where rhetoric (whether or not recognised as such) is now applied in business and the professions. This technical aid, and this procedure, should both be welcomed by people with persuasive skills – who will (on the other hand) be best placed to make really effective use of them.

- *Computerised presentation aids:*   The world of salaried work now features a combination of rhetorical technique and electronic technology which parallels some of the most elaborate, multi-stage processes of classical rhetoric (see Chapter 5). At university or earlier, students will almost certainly have become familiar with computer-based presentation systems for projecting the main points and illustrative content of lectures; and once established in a profession or business firm they are likely to employ these systems for their own presentations. As typified by the Microsoft PowerPoint system (Version 97), the formulaic material provided for presentations not only provides complete templates for every stage of a communication, as adapted to a specific purpose such as 'Business Plan', 'Company Meeting', 'Project Overview' or 'Motivating a Team', but also ranges between objective, analytical *logos*, and arrangements plainly designed to involve what we have identified as *ethos* and *pathos*. For instance, the outline for 'Motivating a Team' clearly begins with an *ethos*-based introduction, proceeds to a narrative designed to evoke a highly positive emotional response, and then raises an issue for discussion, namely an identification of the team's next 'motivating' goal. The suggested movement through the stages of Introduction and Narrative, though it does not use those terms, irresistibly recalls the topic-sequence of an Aphthonian exercise: 'Deliver an Inspirational Opening/Relate an example of teamwork/Tell a personal story/Read a testimonial/Hear Reports on Achievements/Congratulate award winners/Note areas of growth/Have impromptu reports on success/Address the Sales Challenge/etc., etc.' Skilled persuaders will know *how* to make best use of all these cues, and *when* to omit the suggested sections, and *what* to substitute for them as occasion demands.

• *The SWOT analysis*: This analytical procedure, familiar in business and other contexts, involves a sequential analysis of each point indicated by the acronym: Strengths > Weaknesses > Opportunities > Threats. It is typical of the many methods of organising material which have evolved for the purposes of management, sales, public relations etc., and which are essentially rhetorical in conception. In the SWOT procedure, the aim is to take a purely logical view of the points named, before considering how conclusions might impact on people. The exercise seems likely to progress through conjectural, definitive and qualitative questions, e.g. What are our material resources (money, buildings, hours of work)? What is distinctive about our experience and approach? What makes our method of work, our philosophy or our motivation qualitatively better than the opposition? Or (typifying use of another model in the assessment of Threats), are 'they' reaching parts of the market, or the curriculum, or the concerns of the public, or the international sphere of influence, that 'we' can't reach – or encroaching on our particular 'niche'?

(d)   Persuasion in the public domain

Here there is nothing to be said, except to remind readers of what has been emphasised more than once before in this book: observe the principles of *kairos*, and build confidence through your evidently intimate knowledge of the subject-area within which the issue has arisen, and about which you are persuading your audience.

8 Conclusion: Fast Forward

The purpose of this book has been to demonstrate conclusively that the ancient science or art of rhetoric is not dead, outmoded or merely a subject for disengaged admiration in the museum of history. It is very much alive and kicking, more than relevant, and inextricably part of every act of human communication, written or spoken, within our global village. We have shown how close are the links between Aristotle (and other classical rhetoricians and orators) and modern-day theorists or practitioners in linguistics and the media. In our examples, we have ranged widely over the centuries, and drawn on increasingly diverse and dynamic applications of persuasive language, as our complex, media-driven society evolves. Rhetoric has never been so important, and the genres and sub-genres of persuasion have never been so thoroughly utilised (or many claim, so widely misused and trivialised). Our overall aim has been to rebut, where appropriate, such charges, and to persuade our readers that rhetoric, like power, retains its potential for 'corruption' but that in responsible hands its force and subtlety can only be constructive.

Our hope and expectation is that readers of this book will be able to use rhetoric with newly acquired insight and confidence for their own purposes, and be able to judge and assess the ways in which it is used by others. They should be more alert to deceitful and manipulative uses of language, and be able to demonstrate to others where and how 'truth' has been adulterated. In personal terms readers may find it easier to make clear and tactful critiques of others' persuasive efforts, and to be equally and constructively self-critical when appropriate.

A further benefit of the book (deriving in particular from its examples of literary persuasion) will be felt by readers in the contexts of academic, literary and cultural debate. They should be encouraged to explore the persuasive function in texts of all kinds (including critical writing), with greater sophistication and heightened awareness of

213

how the writer or speaker 'works on' the attitudes of a given audience. By taking a balanced and all-round approach to rhetoric, using the three 'structural principles' of *ethos, pathos* and *logos,* our aim has been to combat tunnel vision and thus promote a richer understanding of what is happening in a given text. It should now seem a matter of course to link the topic being treated with the personal or ideological stance in a text, and with the response which it anticipates. Above all, we hope to enable readers to tune in to the infinite range of patterns and structures in language which are available to any persuader, and which can be readily recognised, learnt and applied.

Turning to the practice of rhetoric, users of this book who want to develop their persuasive skills, should be able to recognise what path to follow, founded on the key structural principles, and working from the types of exercise we have recommended towards engagement with real audiences, wherever required. Once interest is awakened, sources of inspiration will be discovered in specialised treatments of rhetoric and in the classic orators, as well as in contemporary good practice. Indeed, though persuasive skills can be engagingly and efficiently used for the most ephemeral purposes, it will be crystal clear that the serious use of rhetoric involves a far deeper and self-transcending involvement on the part of a persuader.

To this end, current research into cognitive linguistics, and especially recent theories about deixis, mental spaces and prototypes (see, e.g., Stockwell, 2002) should prompt new ways of rhetorical thinking and new types of rhetorical engagement; for example, empathy will be refined, conventional ideas on genus/species challenged, and emotion made more vivid and immediate.

So, fast-forwarding to the future, what is the new role of rhetoric in the twenty-first century? Until recently, the intellectual and moral validity of rhetoric has been in question, and it has lacked the high esteem it securely held in the past. Our book seeks to continue this 'rehabilitation' by addressing the orators of the future, and persuading them of its public and private value. The dialogic structure of rhetoric is a natural model for communication in every context, and as educational milestones are passed and higher levels of public education achieved, we anticipate that a new habit of rhetoric could transform the public 'mindset'. In every kind of discussion, from book groups to company meetings, from pressure groups to televised debate, this revitalised understanding of rhetoric should be seen as supporting the democratic struggle, rather than undermining it. The possibility of challenging entrenched positions in any context will be a natural consequence of this new 'habit'. Re-evaluations of rhetoric and what it entails can contribute to a much-needed revitalisation of the democratic process.

Appendix A: More on the Models

In this appendix – for use as required – we provide information and explanation about the deliberate use of 'models of argument', as well as a full and ordered account of the schemata. This includes: (1) a fuller exposition of the terms used in cognitive engagement; (2) a demonstration of the ten models of argument used as the basis of syllogistic and enthymemic argument; (3) a brief account of current theory that implicitly links the intuitive employment of models of argument to their conscious persuasive application; and (4) an analysis of the models of argument used in the passage from Dickens's *Hard Times* featured in Chapter 7.

The Models and Cognition: Schema Theory

To show how schema theory represents the process of cognition, we use the terms devised by R. C. Schank, first in collaboration with R. Abelson (1977), later in *Dynamic Memory* (1982) and later still in *Dynamic Memory Revisited* (1999). Elena Semino also provides a short and accessible account in *Language and World Creation* (1997: 138ff). The phrase 'cognitive engagement' denotes the efforts of a persuader (intuitively or deliberately) to use the whole range of resources represented by these schemata for maximal effect.

The main categories of schemata and their distinctive functions in the organisation of memory and interpretation of experience are as follows:

- **Plans**, which persuaders will often attribute to the persuadee, and then seek to challenge or modify (especially in the context of deliberative rhetoric), 'contain information about the sets of actions that someone may perform in order to accomplish a certain objective' (Semino, 1997: 138). In seeking to facilitate, challenge or modify or the persuadee's Plans, the persuader will inevitably draw in every aspect of cause and effect. The process of causation may at one extreme be more or less thoroughly analysed to engage and excite the persuadee's interest, or at the other, links invoked may amount to little more than association based on what usually happens. Planning is also likely to involve such models as part/whole, as in putting together a 'package' of measures.

- **Goals** are 'schemata that contain knowledge about the aims and objectives that people are likely to have'. Schank and Abelson (summarised by Semino, 1997: 139) propose seven: three representing desired states (Satisfaction, Enjoyment and Achievement), two seeking to avoid undesirable states (Preservation and Crisis), and two types of goal (the Instrumental and the Delta) which help us to achieve the others. (The Delta goal, a much more broadly conceived objective involving the coordination of general plans to achieve an ulterior purpose, appears less frequently.) When engaging with Goals in any of these categories, the persuader is also likely to begin by invoking cause and effect, whether the intention is to invoke the Goal as a desired effect, or to challenge it as an undesirable one. This activates other models, such as opposition, or genus/species (e.g. when the persuadee's recognised goal is recategorised and placed in an unfavourable light).

- **Themes** 'provide background information about the origin of people's goals' (Semino, 1997: 140), i.e. their characteristic preoccupations or 'what makes them tick'. Themes provide an important means for the effective deployment of *ethos* and *pathos*, based on the persuader's positive or negative categorisation of these driving motives. *Role themes* refer to the individual or collective relationship a persuader (such as an employer or a police officer) may have with distinct categories/groups of people. *Interpersonal themes* are characteristic either of close personal relationships or of public reference to private experience (e.g. a politician refers to his youthful misuse of alcohol).

  Life themes relate to values and aspirations (e.g. experiential, moral, social, religious, political) – what Semino (1997: 140) calls 'the general position that a person aspires to in life'. Thus the models of definition, genus and species, association, and witness are most likely to be used in connection with life themes whether the persuader intends to reaffirm the persuadee's values, to challenge them, or to re-orient them.

- **Scenes** are schemata that include familiar environments or contexts, e.g. physical settings, large or small, well known to an audience through daily experience, or familiar fictional scenarios within which certain scripts or situations may unfold, such as the 'sitcom' format. Semino summarises: 'Scenes are general schemata containing information about different types of situations and what happens in them' (1997: 142), and in explanation she quotes Schank (1982: 86): 'As long as there is an identifiable physical setting and a goal being pursued within that setting, we have a scene'. Nevertheless, 'scene' as a term has a broader extension than this would suggest, since individual realisations (or instantiations) may be of three kinds: 'Physical scenes are defined in terms of a particular physical setting. . . . Social scenes . . . in terms of a particular social setting. . . . Personal scenes . . . in terms of the pursuit of a goal that is private and idiosyncratic to a particular person' (Semino, 1997: 143). Persuaders may wish to play on the association between a scene and the activity or script taking place within it.
- **Scripts** are sequences of actions in furtherance of one or more goals, which in any given instance instantiate a particular scene, and which might involve three scripts simultaneously (e.g. a wedding ceremony includes physical, social and personal scripts). Cognitive engagement with scripts will typically involve criticising somebody's performance of a familiar task or a reappraisal of the task in its own right.
- **Memory organisation packets** (MOPs) link scenes and scripts into larger, more flexible sequences of schemata. Semino quotes Schank (1982: 97): 'A MOP consists of a set of scenes directed towards the achievement of a goal.' For example, preparing a familiar recipe involves certain sequences of scripts. However, convenience foods persuade the shopper that time can be saved by discarding one or more scripts, thus applying the part/whole model.
- **Meta-MOPS** are even larger organisations of schemata constructed by the memory, which sequences individual MOPs. Once acquired, this extended schema makes it easier to undertake more complex activities such as buying a house, in which A (meeting the estate agent) is followed by B (viewing a property), which is followed by C (making an offer) and so on (cf. Semino, 1997: 144). Cognitive engagement with meta-MOPs is likely to involve the use of all or most of the models of argument.

- **Thematic organisation points** (TOPs) are 'high-level memory structures' that bridge the gap between diverse schemata on the basis of some perceived similarity. They can either occur spontaneously in the course of lively conversation or as part of a planned approach to an audience, i.e. 'talking their language'. The correlation between TOPs and simile and metaphor is clear; both derive from the similarity model with the 'source domain' being mapped on the 'target domain'.

Any persuader who has developed an awareness of these schemata (and of the way they respond to changing events and contexts) should be able to engage with them, using them to intuit the right stance for each specific audience and situation.

Using the Models

It seems helpful to provide some examples of how the ten models of argument can be combined to produce persuasive deductions. Such combined arguments are not set out formally like old-style academic syllogisms, but in a style appropriate to persuasion, whether they state two premises and a conclusion (thus taking the form of a rhetorical syllogism) or leave part of the argument implicit (thus constituting an enthymeme in the commonest sense of that word). We provide syllogistic and enthymemic variants of each argument based on a particular model. All the examples are 'made-up' ones unless otherwise indicated.

From definition

Enthymeme: 'Human beings can't really be thought of as rational animals till they think rationally about what it means to be an animal'

Syllogism: 'No species can be defined as a rational animal that doesn't reason about what it means to be an animal; as human beings we generally prefer not to think about that. So do we actually deserve to be defined as rational animals?' (NB: *This argument is derived from the classic definition of human kind as a species [genus: animal; differentiating factor: rational].*)

From cause/effect

(a) Efficient, material and final cause/effect

Enthymeme: 'If we want a better health service, we'll have to give it the human and material resources that it needs.' (*hypothetical proposition*)

Syllogism: 'If we really wanted a better health service, we'd give it the human and material resources it needs; but at present we're not providing these, so we can't *really* want it to improve.' (*hypothetical proposition*)

(b) Formal cause

Enthymeme: 'Now we've cracked the genetic code, we can at last know ourselves.'

Syllogism: 'Everyone's nature is determined by genetic coding. Now we know the code, we can know ourselves, and what determines our nature individually.'

(c) Final cause

Enthymeme: 'Just for a handful of silver he left us / Just for a riband to stick in his coat' (*Robert Browning, 'The Lost Leader', 1940: 208*)

Syllogism: 'Leaders who lower their objectives, betray their followers. Wordsworth lowered his objectives from the ideals of liberty to those of wealth and status and thus betrayed his fellow poets.' (NB: *Leadership is linked to the final cause* [*i.e. motivating 'life themes' of political liberty, reward, status*] *in both of the premises.*)

From similarity

Enthymeme: 'And although cruise-junkies and honeymooners may sound like strange company to keep . . . you don't have to worry because the island [Aruba] has a sponge-like ability to soak them up and secrete them away on beaches, on the water, or in the desert-like interior.' (*J. Axworthy,* Guardian, *17 March 2001, Travel supplement*)

Syllogism: 'The island of Aruba absorbs visitors as a sponge absorbs water; water is *secreted* everywhere inside a sponge, without being noticed – and the same is true of Aruba.' (NB: *Axworthy puns clev-*

erly on two senses of 'secrete' [to exude and to hide away]; he thus points back to the word's primary meaning, 'to separate' [cf. root meaning arguments, below].)

From opposition

Enthymeme: 'If you really wanted to give up smoking you'd stop telling me how it helps you to relax!'

Syllogism: 'People who really want to give up smoking can't go on making excuses for carrying on with it; but all this stuff about needing to relax is just an excuse. It shows that you can't really mean it.'

From degree

Enthymeme: 'This car's got more of everything – and it costs a whole lot more!' (*motoring journalist*)

Syllogism: 'So more of everything means better value for money? OK, there's a bit more performance, a bit more gadgetry, and a whole lot more on the price. Where's the value there?' (NB: *Here the greater hike in price negates the other degree-based argument [i.e. that more is always better]. This uses all three parts of the syllogism with the Conclusion in the form of a rhetorical question.*)

From testimony

Enthymeme: 'Was slavery really such a bad thing – in the ancient world at least? After all, Aristotle supported it.'

Syllogism: 'Every institution upheld by Aristotle must have an ethical basis; so if Aristotle supports slavery it must have some ethical basis.' (NB: *Does this example expose a lack of innate logicality in the testimony model, as was commonly claimed?*)

From genus/species

(a)   From genus

Enthymeme: 'All civilisations depend on a planet untouched by asteroid impact, so sooner or later ours is doomed.'

Syllogism: 'No civilisation can exist without a habitable planet; our planet won't be habitable once an asteroid hits it; sooner or later, we'll cease to exist.'

(b)   From species

Enthymeme: 'We're getting some tigers: we'd better provide a water-splash.'

Syllogism: 'The basic needs of all our big cats must be met. Tigers need a water-splash, so we must provide one.' (NB: *As a species, tigers are distinguished from other members of the cat genus by their love of water; hence the safari park owner has to respond to their need.*)

Association

(a)   The adjunct (in the older logical sense, i.e. the attributed quality)

Enthymeme: 'He may be economical with the truth, like all politicians, but basically he's an honest person.'

Syllogism: 'So what's compatible with honesty and what isn't? Surely all politicians distort the truth? If some honest people are politicians, the inescapable logic is that some honest people distort the truth and even tell lies.'

(b)   Clothes/wearer association

Enthymeme: 'You're not wearing that tatty shirt to Mary and John's wedding.'

Syllogism: 'You shouldn't wear clothes that make people think you can't be bothered, and that shirt would. So *don't wear it!*'

(c)   Place/function association

Enthymeme: ' "Theatre magic," I said to the leading lady, raising my glass in salute. "Did you think I was good, then?" "Doesn't 'theatre magic' say it all?" I replied.'

(d)   Time/activity association

Enthymeme: 'Nothing stressful should be discussed over lunch, so don't talk company politics.'

Part/whole

(a)   Argument from part to whole

Enthymeme: 'Just from the carving of the features, we can see how wonderful the complete statue must have been.' (*art historian*)

(b)   Argument from whole to part

Enthymeme: 'Look, the whole company's a mess – do you really think the research department can be any good?' (*head-hunter doubts recommendation of senior manager*)

Syllogism: 'Bad management infects an entire organisation. X company is notoriously badly managed; how likely is it that the Head of R and D will be an exception?'

Root meaning

Enthymeme: 'You should avoid calling anybody 'churlish'; it just reeks of class superiority.' (*This refers to the fact that 'churlish' originally meant 'characteristic of a landless peasant'*).

Syllogism: 'We should avoid all terms of approbation that have their roots in class-based difference; 'generous' means 'characteristic of noble birth', so the logic is we should avoid using it!' (*sociolinguist discussing political correctness*)

The Models: from Intuitive Use to Conscious Application

As the persuader seeks to use *logos* when engaging with an issue, projecting *ethos* or managing *pathos*, s/he presupposes the audience's ability (in whatever context) to follow reasoning. As discussed earlier, theories about cognition entail several different forms of association, further confirmed in clinical psychology research. In the eighteenth-century, David Hume detected mental processes of 'resemblance, contiguity in time or place, and cause and effect'. More recently, as David Lodge notes in *The Modes of Modern Writing* (1977: 77–9), studies of aphasia or language deficiency support the view that the mind links words along the selective and combinative axes (paradigmatic and syntagmatic). Thus, aphasics with a similarity disorder have difficulties in the precise choice of words, and especially at the beginnings of sentences. They could not generalise, were unable to group ideas together on the basis of similarity and thus depended on context and immediate association. Subjects would say 'knife-and-fork' meaning 'knife', or use the metonymy 'smoke' to mean 'pipe'. In contrast, subjects with contiguity disorder were unable to grasp the connective sequence and mental structuring of grammar and syntax, having to rely on perceived similarity and using 'quasi-metaphoric' expressions such as 'fire' for 'gaslight'. The association between 'resemblance and contiguity' that Hume noted seems to underlie the normal operations of language, and makes possible the mental processes of generalisation and specialisation (e.g. the genus/species model of argument).

Interestingly, William Downes observes (see Chapter 2, p.000) that similar mental processes are involved in 'inductive generalisation' (or intuition) that is based on prior experience. People (like animals) intuit and evaluate opportunities and threats in their environment, entailing a sense of cause and effect.

We can conclude that some mental processes closely correspond to key models of argument and are also intrinsic to normal comprehension and use of language. It seems that people can have considerable confidence in their first focused thoughts on any topic, before proceeding to more conscious and fully developed analysis. Persuaders, in order to use the sets of cognitive schemata effectively, need to recognise their own individual thought patterns, before trying to adjust them to the likely cognitive patterns of any prospective persuadee.

Topical Logic and Style in Dickens's *Hard Times*, Chapter 1

(a)   Text

CHAPTER I
The One Thing Needful

Now what I want is, Facts. Teach these boys and girls nothing but Facts. Facts alone are wanted in life. Plant nothing else, and root out everything else. You can only form the minds of reasoning animals upon Facts: nothing else will ever be of any service to them. This is the principle on which I bring up my own children, and this is the principle on which I bring up these children. Stick to Facts, Sir!'

The scene was a plain, bare, monotonous vault of a schoolroom, and the speaker's square forefinger emphasized his observations by underscoring every sentence with a line on the schoolmaster's sleeve. The emphasis was helped by the speaker's square wall of a forehead, which had his eyebrows for its base, while his eyes found commodious cellarage in two dark caves, overshadowed by the wall. The emphasis was helped by the speaker's mouth, which was wide, thin, and hard set. The emphasis was helped by the speaker's voice, which was inflexible, dry, and dictatorial. The emphasis was helped by the speaker's hair, which bristled on the skirts of his bald head, a plantation of firs to keep the wind from its shining surface, all covered with knobs, like the crust of a plum pie as if the head had scarcely warehouse-room for the hard facts stored inside. The speaker's obstinate carriage, square coat, square legs, square shoulders – nay, his very neckcloth, trained to take him by the throat with an unaccommodating grasp, like a stubborn fact, as it was, – all helped the emphasis.

'In this life, we want nothing but Facts, Sir; nothing but Facts!'

The speaker, and the schoolmaster, and the third grown person present, all backed a little, and swept with their eyes the inclined plane of little vessels then and there arranged in order, ready to have imperial gallons of facts poured into them until they were full to the brim.

(b) Analysis

Mr Gradgrind takes the classical definition of man as 'a rational animal' to a chillingly logical extreme. His discourse is effect-dominated. The implantation of facts, to achieve the final cause of 'forming the mind' (facts alone being the formal cause of such a mind) totally obsesses him, as the one desirable effect of his philosophy. In cognitive terms, this is his single instrumental goal. Dickens ironically implies the barrenness of mere factuality through the harsh repetitive language (see Chapter 6). The oppositional model of argument is used as Gradgrind instructs his subordinate, M'Choakumchild, to plant nothing else but facts, and 'root out everything else'. The teacher is himself the efficient cause demanded by Gradgrind's educational philosophy. Readers then and now will measure this against their own educational experience (meta-MOP). Metaphor is used to convey the impression of Utilitarianism pervading town and country alike; Mr Gradgrind's forehead is a 'square wall', his eyes 'two dark caves' for cellarage, and his bristly hair 'a [manmade] plantation of firs'. Even a momentarily jocular comparison of his knobbly cranium to 'the crust of a plum pie' continues grimly 'as if the head had hardly warehouse-room for the hard facts stored inside'. The *logos* and *enargeia* of the passage are thus perfectly matched.

Appendix B: Further Rhetorical Devices

This includes a range of tropes and schemes that have not been detailed earlier, covering the same range of persuasive repertoire, and in the same categories as in Chapter 6. Here we have made up most of the illustrations to show the potential of these devices within contemporary English usage. For further definitions and examples of the figures, readers are referred to Puttenham, *Arte of English Poesie* (1968 [1589]), to Richard Lanham, *A Handlist of Rhetorical Terms* (1991) and to Lee Sonnino, *Handbook to Sixteenth-Century Rhetoric* (1968). An invaluable Internet resource is the website 'Silva Rhetoricae', rhetoric.byu.edu (humanities.byu.edu/rhetoric/silva.htm), which covers not only the figures but also all other aspects of traditional rhetoric.

A comprehensive list of modern English rhetorical terms, corresponding to the whole range of devices mentioned in this book, can be found in Appendix C. This list groups the devices in their respective categories and as far as possible provides the Greek or Latin name of each identified device.

Figurative Language or Trope

(a) Allegory

The mode of relationship between source and target domain in metaphor differs from that of allegory in two respects; firstly, metaphor typically compares two objects or two qualities whereas allegory compares two stories; secondly, allegory may be used to conceal similarity, as readily as to disclose it. It thrives on ambiguity. George Puttenham (habitué of Court intrigue and gossip) confirms this when he proposes the equivalent English term for allegory as '*false semblant* [false resemblance] *or dissimulation*' (Puttenham, 1968:

155). Far more clearly than metaphor, the protracted trope of allegory often uses *kairos* to convey the politics of some particular and time-specific relationship between persuader, persuadee and topic; thus allegory can subvert authority, lend itself to subversive creativity, covertly criticise the government (or any other power base) and promote factional intrigue amongst a governing class. Equally, allegory could serve the interests of those in power. Puttenham claims that many of 'the most noble and wisest Prince[s]' used allegory, following the example of the Emperor who said '*Qui nescit dissimulare nescit regnare*' ['He who knows not how to veil the truth, knows not how to rule']. In more recent times, the subversive potential of allegory has also been aimed (to great effect) at the entrenched attitudes of individuals and smaller social groups.

In turning from *why* allegory exists to *how* it functions, Puttenham describes it as 'a long and perpetuall Metaphore' (Puttenham,1968: 156). There are two important sub-varieties:

(i)   Fable

This began with Aesop (*c.*600 BC) and is exemplified in the twentieth century by George Orwell's *Animal Farm*. Thomas Wilson, author of an early English *Arte of Rhetorique* (1560), says that fable involves actions or speeches 'such as are attributed to brute beasts, (or) the parts of a man's body' (Sonnino, 1968: 97). It ends with a clearly underlined moral point. A further example showing its typical use in rhetoric (in this instance, to calm an angry crowd) can be found in Shakespeare, *Coriolanus* (I.i.77–143).

(ii)   Parable

Using a wider range of imagery than fable, the parable is designed to make the audience think, and is typically enigmatic. It exercises the mind in interpretation, engages the imagination, and provokes self-examination. Parable may employ striking dissimilarities, as well as similarities, between the subject of the parable and the allegory itself. For example, in one New Testament gospel (Luke 16: 1–9) the zealous seeker after God's kingdom is mysteriously compared to a dishonest steward short-changing his employer (interestingly, this parable remains a great headache for contemporary preachers when they have to explain it to their congregations!).

Allusive label (antonomasia)

This is a form of metonymy, using the associational link to rename or label someone (or something). Puttenham (1968: 151) calls this device 'the surnamer', implying a formal or poetic usage; it can, however, be used to produce a comic effect. We have identified six variations, but more may be found:

(i)   Offspring identified through the name of the parent: e.g. 'Judy Garland's daughter' (Lisa Minelli).

(ii)   Person identified by place or country of origin, as in a sports commentator referring to players by nationality (e.g. Reyes, 'the Spaniard', playing in England, or Beckham, 'the Englishman', playing in Spain).

(iii)   Some associated attribute (a kind of nickname): e.g. 'Mr Clean' for a politician or 'Mr Fixit' for someone who's good at sorting out problems.

(iv)   Identification of someone by their occupation, profession or skill (past or present): e.g. 'the peanut farmer' for Jimmy Carter (US President, 1976–80).

(v)   Application of a personal name, prominent for some characteristic or accomplishment, to an individual with ambition in the same field: e.g. 'the new Nureyev' (for an aspiring male dancer).

(vi)   Application of the name of a nation, city, neighbourhood or street famous for some characteristic to any person allegedly showing that characteristic. An ancient example is 'sybarite' (meaning any addict of luxurious living) – this name reflects the legendary lifestyle of the former Greek colony Sybaris. Contemporary examples include the facetious 'Sloane Ranger' (from a fashionable square in London) or 'Hampstead type' (associated with a part of London where many 'intellectuals' are believed to live).

Personification (prosopopoeia)

Attribution of a personality to material object, plant, animal, or abstract idea. This device can be of major importance when it is associated with cultural traditions. The obvious example is the ancient custom of personifying ships as 'she' (e.g. Catullus, Melville, Conrad).

Personification, often linked to metonymy, is much used in contemporary advertising; for example, a car (such as the Renault Mégane) is alleged to have 'sexy' attributes, just like the glamorous people who will be persuaded to buy and drive it. Personification is also related to 'amplification' and 'diminution'.

Remote metonymy (metalepsis)

This trope is of great importance in the critical theory and practice of Harold Bloom (see *The Anxiety of Influence*, 1973 and *A Map of Misreading*, 1975). As the English version of the term implies, *metalepsis* involves a chain of associations (often of causation) between the given image and the thing signified, the intermediate links being supplied by the audience's imagination. Thus 'It's her third trip to the registry office, would you believe it!' implies that the person in question has chosen her marital partners unwisely. Puttenham (1968: 152) calls this trope 'far-fet' ('far-fetched').

(e) Transferred epithet (hypallage)

A common term for this version of metonymy is 'transferred epithet'. If we speak of a cat's 'furry purposes' when hunting mice, the quality and texture of the animal's outside is transferred to its inner motivation. The device is also well adapted to deflating pomposity by juxtaposing grandiose pretensions and everyday objects (the 'episcopal dustbins' at the back of a bishop's residence; or 'the royal toothbrush'). Qualities of human experience may also be transferred to some aspect of the physical environment ('it's a perishing cold day').

Schematic Language

This section begins with two categories of devices corresponding directly to the first two sections of Chapter 6 (variation in lexical choice and aural effect), followed by further schemes with examples.

(a) Single words

(i)   Word-coinage or neologism. Words invented or 'coined' to express newly conceived qualities or phenomena, particularly associated with new technology in the fields of medicine, the military and computing, with social change and developments in the media. Examples rapidly become part of accepted usage for as long as they are needed (e.g. 'internet'). All of us can make them up (e.g. 'semi-coloniser' for a punctuation enthusiast) but relatively few will catch on and become part of the lexicon.

(ii)　Split word (*tmesis*). In contemporary English this is most likely to be applied negatively to proper names. The device divides a word, phrase or name and inserts another word or words (e.g. 'Derek Clever-Dick Smith'; 'Ha-blooming-ha!').

Aural devices

Sound-image (*onomatopoeia*). This is a very well-known device that hardly needs illustration. The Greek term denotes 'making a word or a name', but in current usage it means a word whose *sound* directly evokes a sensation (e.g. 'squelch', 'thud').

Syntactic devices

(i)　Cross-over (*chiasmus*). Syntactical elements in a sentence are reversed to achieve a particular effect. An example might be: 'British inventiveness (*A*) I take for granted (*B*) – what strikes (*B*) me more is our failure to exploit our inventions (*A*)'. Here, the reversed syntax emphasises the point the speaker is making.

(ii)　Contrastive series. This is a development of syntactic parallelism involving balanced sentences or clauses, continuing a process of opposition through three or more stages. This might involve a series of shorter or longer ripostes. The following imaginary example is an advertisement for First Class service in the next generation of giant intercontinental aircraft: 'Other airlines put food on plastic trays; we serve ours on Royal Doulton china with silver cutlery and cut-glass. They pre-cook their food; we employ five-star chefs with in-flight galleys' (etc.).

(iii)　Correlative distribution. A series of subjects, followed by a series of verbs, mainly suited to the production of comic or burlesque effects. An example would be 'His head, hat, heart, were punched, sat on, set on fire.'

(iv) Many cases (*polyptoton*). The most famous instance of this in English is Lincoln's definition of democracy as 'Government *of* the people *by* the people *for* the people', which correlates the genitive, ablative and dative cases.

(v) Many links (*polysyndeton*). Multiple use of conjunctions between successive words or phrases: 'Sick and tired and cold and hungry and thirsty.' This is well adapted to conveying a subjective sense of cumulative strain. Compare the anti-type of this device (which follows).

(vi) No links (*asyndeton*). A staccato series of words or phrases without conjunctions. Sharper and more aggressive than the previous device: 'Sick, tired, cold, hungry, thirsty' sounds more accusatory than plaintive.

(vii) Paired series (*scesis onamaton*). A series of nouns each accompanied by an adjective. The noun and adjective may be linked by a repeated preposition, or by a range of prepositions: 'Olive oil – rich in taste, ripe in association, kind to cooks, kinder to the heart.'

Repetition

(i) Staircase (*climax*). One of the most flamboyant of figures. A series of sentences in which the last word or phrase of the preceding sentence is adapted as the first word or phrase of the following sentence: 'Because I lost my season ticket I was late for work; because I was late for work my secretary got in a muddle; because he got in a muddle I lost the vital file on the computer, because I lost the file we lost the contract.'

(ii) Full-circle (*epanalepsis*). A sentence opening and closing with the same word or phrase: 'In the bin is where litter belongs; so make sure you put it in the bin!'

(iii) Prose rhyme (*omoeoteleuton*). Although it involves repetition, this might also be classed as an aural device. A series of words or phrases ending with the same inflection and sound – a prosaic form of rhyme. An example might be 'Your behaviour was careless; you carried on regardless; when it came, the apology was graceless.'

(iv)   Two-track repetition (*symploche*). A series of sentences, each beginning with an identical or slightly varied word or phrase, and ending with *another* word or phrase, also repeated at the end of each sentence of the series. In the following familiar example the device is combined with climax: 'For the want of a nail the shoe was lost; for the want of a shoe the horse was lost . . . and all for the want of a horse-shoe nail.'

Amplification and diminution

In this last major category of schemes, we distinguish between devices relating to the emotive element of graphic actualisation (*pathos*), and devices enhancing *ethos* and *logos* through heightened textual coherence.

(i)   Topics for actualisation in reportage and fiction

The subject-matter or topics suited to the use of amplificatory devices were traditionally divided between (a) evocations of real things or people, and (b) portrayals of imaginary things or people. A modern persuader needs the shortest and clearest possible check-list to serve as a reminder of the main topics or subjects to which actualisation may be applied (This is provided below.) Traditional rhetoric did not always differentiate between actualised description in fact (history) and in actualised description in fiction (poetry). The reason for this is that the rhetorical concepts of amplification/diminution predate modern approaches to history and psychology and the Western concept of individualism. Consequently, traditional rhetoric is relatively uninterested in circumstantial description of time, place, event, individual person, or object. The modern persuader is therefore at liberty to adapt and develop these devices as s/he chooses.

- Action-shot (*pragmatographia*). The Greek term means 'description of an action'. We have an example in the graphic *enargia* of Quintilian's murder scene (Chapter 2).
- Actualisation of real people (*prosographia*) or of imaginary people or personifications (*prosopopoeia*). Examples of personifications include personified abstractions, humanised animals and personified natural objects. Producing an itemised description of the limbs, features and clothing of the person concerned

was a traditional method of actualisation. Today the persuader is more likely to highlight only one or two items of appearance.

- Speech-portrayal (*dialogismos*). The force of such evocations was greatly increased when the actualised person (or personification) spoke, or even held a dialogue with the persuader. For example, in his first oration against Catiline, delivered in the Roman Senate, Cicero anticipates the Senators' doubts about his handling of the affair by putting a long indignant speech into the imaginary mouth of Rome herself, 'this land of ours' (Cicero, 1969: 89–90). Then Cicero himself replies to 'Rome', answering her objections, and (more importantly) those of the Senators. The term *dialogismos* was often applied to this kind of made-up speech, whether or not it involved dialogue in the modern sense (Sonnino, 1968: 168–9). As noted in Chapter 7, rhetorical training included the composition of speeches expressing either the comic reaction (*ethopoeia*) or tragic emotion (*ethopoeia passiva*) of a real or imaginary person.

- Time-portrayal (*chronographia*). This might involve actualisation of the time of day or season of the year, a particular form of vivid description or *ekphrasis*. Its most obvious use is in fiction or poetry, but it can also contribute to a sense of circumstantial reality in functional persuasion.

- Place-portrayal. As we have seen, there was a traditional distinction between the actualisation of a real place (*topographia*) and that of an imaginary one (*topothesia*). (There was even a standard form of itemised description, depicting the *locus amoenus* or ideally beautiful place (see Curtius, 1953: 192–202). Comparable distinctions between the real and the imaginary may be made today with respect to realistic fiction, magic realism and science fiction.

(ii)   Amplificatory frameworks

These include some very distinctive combinations of subject matter, structure and style.

- Antithesis. This important scheme is a means of magnifying and articulating persuasive emotion (see Chapter 2), but it is also linked to the oppositional model of argument (see Chapter 3). Using antithesis as well as syntactic parallelism will greatly enhance the effect of an amplificatory passage.

- Comparison (of kind and degree). Although this device was discussed as a model of argument in Chapter 3, we mention it here as a reminder of its importance in amplification (i.e. in the argumentative structuring of emotional effects).
- Break-down (*merismus*). This achieves impact (emotive, logical or imaginative) by its directness. It avoids introductory or summary statements of ideas by breaking them down into their main aspects or constituent parts. For example, to expand the implicit idea that 'families have arguments', we might write as follows: 'Parents argue about money; children about siblings borrowing clothes without asking; they all argue about when to get in and when to get up; even the cat argues with the dog; everybody argues about chores, duties and privileges.' Such a break-down might also involve schemes of repetition and syntactic parallelism.
- Leading summary (*prolepsis*). Here a brief summary statement is followed by a detailed part-by-part amplification (as above). 'He was the most bigoted man I'd ever met' (to be followed by an enumeration of his bigoted attitudes one by one).
- Terminal summary. A summary may be placed *after* the itemised details of a description or evocation. Where this involves an element of repetition and contrast it is known in Greek as *epanados* (Lanham, 1991: 67; Sonnino, 1968: 158–9). A modern example would be: 'A, B, X and Y walked into my room and sat down around the table; A and B were the most honest men I knew, and X and Y the greatest rogues.'
- Descant (*expolitio*). We use the old term here to express the idea of deliberate elaboration, amplifying a single idea. The word appears in Richard of Gloucester's early, sardonic observation that to 'descant on mine own deformity' might be a way of whiling away 'this weak piping time of peace' (Shakespeare, *Richard III*, I.i.24, 27). Puttenham includes a poem by Queen Elizabeth as an example of this figure, although he doubts whether he should 'terme it a figure, or rather a masse of many figurative speaches' (Puttenham, 1968: 206–8). A full dress version of descant in a sixteenth-century school rhetoric (Susenbrotus, 1570: 90–1) involves: (i) the initial statement of a conventional idea; (ii) two reasons for this; (iii) a moral proposition plus two subsidiary reasons; (iv) a moral observation or *sententia*; (v) a contrary instance; (vi) two more reasons; (vii) another contrary; (viii) two more reasons; (ix) a simile; (x) a comparison of degree; (xi) a

particular example; (xii) another moral observation plus a reason; (xii) a conclusion. Absurd as this seems, parts of the full recipe (such as the sequence of contrary, simile and example) may still be found in modern functional persuasion!

Tricks and ploys

(i)   Apologising (*licentia*). Apologising, sincerely or ironically, for a frank expression of opinion. If sincere, this shows goodwill and tact towards the audience; if ironic, it wrong-foots them and shakes their confidence: 'I must apologise for not deferring to your enlightened views on . . .'

(ii) Conceding (*concessio*). Conceding something to an opponent that is actually damaging to them: 'Yes, the Chancellor spent the whole weekend working on his Autumn Statement; and yes, he really cares about the economy: and look what a mess he's made of them both!'

(iii) Conferring (*communicatio*). Asking the audience what they would do about a problem (implying that they couldn't do any better than the questioner).

(iv) Referring (*permissio*). Showing supreme confidence by referring a matter (as self-evident) to the judgement of an audience.

(v)   Questioning:
      - Rhetorical question (*interrogatio*). A question to which the answer is by implication obvious. Its effects may be various, e.g. shaking the confidence of an audience opposed to the persuader's view, or reinforcing an opinion already formed or forming.
      - Multiple questions (*pysma*). A barrage of rhetorical questions.
      - Question and answer (*subjectio*). Asking a series of questions and answering them ourselves. This might, for instance, show a superior stance in relation to audience and topic, or signal a mutual effort to shed light on a murky situation by working steadily through the ascertainable facts.
      - Open question. A genuine question, to which we don't know the answer. This question tests an audience's undeclared attitude, or expresses a genuine uncertainty on a

matter of common concern. This might be a way into genuinely open, dialogic rhetoric.

- Dodging the question. This is a familiar rhetorical device, much used in broadcast interviews. It can be executed with the aid of any one or more of the models of argument (see Chapters 3 and 4), such as answering a particular point in general terms, or shifting the point at issue to one more favourable to the dodger.
- Making it clear. Claiming to have 'made it clear' often helps to dodge the question, implying that it has been answered already (another useful political ploy).

Appendix C: A Finding List for Rhetorical Devices

In this Appendix we provide a combined list of all the rhetorical devices specified in this book, normally using our own English terminology and adding traditional Greek or Latin terms where applicable. For each entry we indicate whether the device is discussed in Chapter 6 (C6), consigned to Appendix B (AB) or, as with general categories such as questioning, mentioned in both (C6/AB). We also provide a page reference to Lanham (1991), except in the case of devices identified more recently. The devices are listed in the same sections and same order as was followed in both Chapter 6 and Appendix B, but are here arranged in alphabetical order for each section.

NAME OF DEVICE	OUR REFERENCE	LANHAM REFERENCE
1. Trope or figurative language		
Allegory	AB	4–6
includes fable, parable (*fabula, parabola*)	AB	77, 106–7
Allusive label (*antonomasia*)		
Six types	AB	17
Irony	C6	92–3
Includes one-word irony (*antiphrasis*)	C6	14–15
Epigrammatic irony	C6	
Sustained irony	C6	
Metaphor	C6	100–01
Metonymy	C6	102
Includes subject/adjunct	C6	
container/content	C6	
cause/effect	C6	
clothes/wearer	C6	
inventor/invention	C6	
Mislabel (*catachresis*)	C6	31
Personification (*prosopopoeia*)	AB	123–4
Remote metonymy (*metalepsis*)	AB	99–100
Synecdoche	C6	148
Includes whole–part/part–whole	C6	
genus–species/species–genus	C6	

238

NAME OF DEVICE	OUR REFERENCE	LANHAM REFERENCE
plural/singular	C6	
singular/plural	C6	
Transference (*hypallage*)	AB	

2. Schematic language

(a) *Single words (lexical choice)*

Split word (*tmesis*)	AB	151–2
Word-coinage	AB	

(b) *Antithesis (antitheton)*

	C6	16–17

(c) *Puns and word-play*

Deliberate distortion	C6	
Same-sound pun (*antanaclasis*)	C6	12
Similar-sound pun (*paronomasia*)	C6	110
Sound-image (*onomatopoeia*)	AB	105

(d) *Syntactic devices*

Contrastive series	AB	
Correlative distribution	AB	
Cross-over (*chiasmus*)	AB	33–4
Left- and right-branching sentences	C6	(*see* Nash, 1980)
Listings or heapings-up (*synathrismos, accumulatio* or *congeries*)	C6	1, 39–40
Many cases (*polyptoton*)	AB	117
Many links (*polysyndeton*)	AB	117
No links (*asyndeton*)	AB	25
Paired series (*scesis onamaton*)	AB	135
Syntactic parallelism (*isocolon, tricolon*)	C6	93, 154
Verb-based variations	C6	
Includes Hyperactive subject (*colon, diazeugma*)	C6	36, 53
Syllepsis	C6	145
Zeugma	C6	159–61
Word-class variation (*traductio*)	C6	153

(e) *Repetition*

Full-circle (*epanalepsis*)	AB	66–7
Initial repetition (*anaphora*)	C6	11
Instant repetition (*epizeuxis*)	C6	70–1
Prose rhyme (*homoioteleuton*)	AB	83–5
Random repetition (*ploche*)	C6	116
Refrain (*epimone*)	C6	68–9
Staircase (*climax*)	AB	36
Stop-and-start (*anadiplosis*)	C6	10
Switch-around (*antimetabole*)	C6	14
Terminal repetition (*antistrophe*)	C6	16
Two-track repetition (*symploche*)	AB	146

NAME OF DEVICE	OUR REFERENCE	LANHAM REFERENCE
(f) *Amplification and diminution*		
(i) *Modes of statement:*		
Hype (*hyperbole*)	C6	86
Playdown/understatement (*litotes*)	C6	95–6
(ii) *Graphic actualisation:*		
Action-shot (*pragmatographia*)	AB	118
Actualised persons, *includes:*		
Real people (*prosopographia*)	AB	123
Imaginary people, personified things, animals, or qualities (*prosopopoeia*)	AB	123–4
Place-portrayal, *includes:*		
Real places (*topographia*)	C6/AB	153
Imaginary places (*topothesia*)	C6/AB	153
Speech-portrayal (*dialogismos*), *includes:*		
Revelation of character (*ethopoeia*)	AB	71
Characteristic emotion (*ethopoeia passiva*)	AB	
Time-portrayal (*chronographia*)	AB	35
(iii) Structural amplifiers:		
Antithesis	AB	
Break-down (*merismos* or *distribution*)	AB	59–60
Build-up (*incrementum* or *auxesis*)	C6	26–8
Comparison of kind and degree (*comparatio*)	AB	
Descant (*expolitio* or *exergasia*)	AB	74
Leading summary (*prolepsis*)	AB	120–21
Terminal summary (*epanodos*)	AB	67
(g) *Tricks and ploys*		
Apologising (*licentia, parrhesia*)	AB	110
Breaking off (*aposiopesis*)	C6	20
Conceding (*concessio*)	AB	38–9
Conferring (*communicatio, anacoenosis*)	AB	9–10
Doing-down (*meiosis*)	C6	98
Doubting (*aporia*)	C6	19–20
Passing over (*praeteritio, occultatio*)	C6	104
Questioning, *includes:*	C6/AB	
Multiple questions (*pysma*)	AB	128–9
Open question	AB	
Question and answer (*subjectio*)	AB	145
Rhetorical question (*interrogatio* or *erotisis*)	AB	71
Referring (*permissio, concessio*)	AB	38–9
Self-correcting (*epanorthosis* or *correctio*)	C6	42
Whitewash (*paradiastole*)	C6	107
Two modern ploys		
'Dodging the question'	AB	
'Making it clear'	AB	

References

Achebe, Chinua (1958) *Things Fall Apart* (London: Heinemann).

Andrews, R. (ed.) (1992) *Rebirth of Rhetoric: Essays in Language, Culture and Education* (London: Routledge).

Aristotle (1926) *The 'Art' of Rhetoric*, trans. J. H. Freese, Loeb Classical Library (London: Heinemann).

Aristotle (1963) *Poetics*, trans. J. Warrington, Everyman's Library (London: Dent).

Aristotle (1984) *Topics*, trans. W. A. Pickard-Cambridge, in J. Barnes (ed.), *The Complete Works of Aristotle: The Revised Oxford Translation*, vol. I (Princeton, NJ: Princeton University Press).

Aristotle (1991) *The Art of Rhetoric*, ed. and trans. H. C. Lawson-Tancred, Penguin Classics (London: Penguin Books).

Augustine, St (1995) *De Doctrina Christiana*, ed. and trans. R. P. H. Green (Oxford: Oxford University Press).

Austen, Jane (1970 [1813]) *Pride and Prejudice*, ed. F. W. Bradbrook, Oxford English Novels (London: Oxford University Press).

Bailey, D. (ed.) (1965) *Essays on Rhetoric*. New York: Oxford University Press.

Bakhtin, M. M. (1981) *The Dialogic Imagination: Four Essays*, ed. M. Holquist, and trans. C. Emerson and M. Holquist (Austin: University of Texas Press).

Beckett, Samuel (1956) *Waiting for Godot*. London: Faber & Faber.

Belloc, Hilaire (1970) *Complete Verse* (London: Duckworth).

Betjeman, John (1978) *The Best of Betjeman*, ed. J. Guest (Harmondsworth: Penguin).

Biber, D., and Finegan, E. (1989) 'Styles of Stance in English: Lexical and Grammatical Marking of Evidentiality and Affect'. *Text*, 9: 93–124.

Biester, James (1996) 'Admirable Wit: *Deinotēs* and the Rise and Fall of Lyric Wonder'. *Rhetorica*, 14, pp. 289–331.

Billig, M. (1996) *Arguing and Thinking: A Rhetorical Approach to Social Psychology*, 2nd edn (Cambridge: Cambridge University Press).

Bloom, Harold (1973) *The Anxiety of Influence: A Theory of Poetry* (New York: Oxford University Press).

Bloom, Harold (1975) *A Map of Misreading* (New York: Oxford University Press).

Bradbury, Malcolm (1975) *The History Man* (London: Seckcr & Warburg).

Brecht, Bertolt (1981) *The Resistible Rise of Arturo Ui*, trans. R. Manheim, in *Collected Plays*, vol. VI, part 2 (London: Methuen).

Brinsley, John (1612) *Ludus Litterarius: or, the Grammar School* (London: Thomas Man).

Brontë, Charlotte (1996 [1847]) *Jane Eyre*, ed. Susan Cockcroft, Cambridge Literature (Cambridge: Cambridge University Press).

Brown, G. and Levinson, S. C. (1978) *Politeness: Some Universals in Language Use* (Cambridge: Cambridge University Press).

Browning, Robert (1940) *Poetical Works* (Oxford: Oxford University Press).

Burke, Kenneth (1969) *A Rhetoric of Motives* (Berkeley and Los Angeles: University of California Press).

Byron, Lord (1945) *Poetical Works*, Oxford Standard Authors (London: Oxford University Press).

Campbell, George (1963) *The Philosophy of Rhetoric*, ed. L. F. Bitzer and D. Potter (Carbondale, IL: Southern Illinois University Press).

Carter, R. (1987) *Vocabulary: Applied Linguistic Perspectives*, Aspects of English Series (London: Allen & Unwin).

Carter, R. (1999) 'Common Language: Corpus, Creativity and Cognition'. *Language and Literature*, 8 (3), pp. 195–216.

Carter, R. (2004) *Language and Creativity*. London: Routledge.

Church, A. (2004) Website on Teaching using the Classical *Progymnasmata*. http://gemini.utb.edu/achurch/progymnasmata.html.

Churchill, Winston (1941) *Into Battle: Speeches by Winston S. Churchill*, ed. Randolph Churchill (London: Cassell).

Cicero (1942) *De Oratore*, trans. H. Rackham, 2 vols, Loeb Classical Library (London: Heinemann).

Cicero (1969) *Selected Political Speeches of Cicero*, trans. and intro. M. Grant, Penguin Classics (Harmondsworth: Penguin Books).

Cicero (1988) *Orator*, trans. H. M. Hubbell (with *Brutus*, trans. G. L. Hendrickson), Loeb Classical Library (London: Heinemann).

Coates, Jennifer (ed.) (1998) *Language and Gender: A Reader* (Oxford: Blackwell).

Cockcroft, R. (2003) *Rhetorical Affect in Early Modern Writing: Renaissance Passions Reconsidered* (Basingstoke: Palgrave Macmillan).

Cockcroft, R. (2004) 'Putting Aristotle to the Proof: Style, Substance and the EPL Group'. *Language and Literature*, 13 (3).

Cockcroft, Susan (1999) *Investigating Talk*, Living Language Series, gen. ed. G. Keith and J. Shuttleworth (London: Hodder and Stoughton).

Coleridge, Samuel T. (1956) *Biographia Literaria*, ed. G. Watson, Everyman's Library (London: Dent).

Conrad, Joseph (1986[1900]) *Lord Jim*, ed. C. Watts, Penguin Classics (Harmondsworth: Penguin).

Corbett, E. P. J. (1990) *Classical Rhetoric for the Modern Student*, 3rd edn (New York: Oxford University Press).

Coulthard, M. (1985) *An Introduction to Discourse Analysis*, 2nd edn (London: Longman).

Coulthard, M. (ed.) (1992) *Advances in Spoken Discourse Analysis* (London: Routledge).

Coupland, N. and Jaworski, A. (eds) (1997) *Sociolinguistics: A Reader and Coursebook* (Basingstoke: Palgrave Macmillan).

Coupland, N., Coupland, J. and Giles, H. (1991) *Language, Society and the Elderly* (Oxford: Blackwell).

Crowley, S. and Hawhee, D. (1999) *Ancient Rhetorics for Contemporary Students*, 2nd edn (Boston, MA: Allyn & Bacon).

Crystal, D. (1997) *The Cambridge Encyclopedia of Language*, 2nd edn (Cambridge: Cambridge University Press).

Curtius, E. R. (1953) *European Literature and the Latin Middle Ages*, trans. W. R. Trask (London: Routledge).

Damasio, A. (1999) *The Feeling of What Happens: Body and Emotion in the Making of Consciousness* (London: Heinemann).

Demosthenes (1970) *Philippic I*, in A. N. W. Saunders (ed. and trans.), *Greek Political Oratory*, pp. 188–9, 198 (Harmondsworth: Penguin).

Dickens, Charles (1955 [1854]) *Hard Times*, New Oxford Illustrated Dickens (London: Oxford University Press).

Dickens, Charles (1952 [1864–5]) *Our Mutual Friend*, New Oxford Illustrated Dickens (London: Oxford University Press).

Dickens, Charles (1965 [1861]) *Great Expectations*, ed. A. Calder (Harmondsworth: Penguin).

Dollimore, J. (1984) *Radical Tragedy: Religion, Ideology and Power in Shakespeare and his Contemporaries* (Brighton: Harvester).

Donne, John (1967) *Selected Prose*, chosen by E. Simpson, ed. H. Gardner and T. Healy (Oxford: Oxford University Press).

Donne, John (1990) *John Donne*, ed. J. Carey, The Oxford Authors (Oxford: Oxford University Press).

Downes, W. (2000) 'The Language of Felt Experience: Emotional, Evaluative, and Intuitive'. *Language and Literature*, 9 (2), pp. 99–121.

Dryden, John (1987) *John Dryden*, ed. K. Walker, The Oxford Authors (Oxford: Oxford University Press).

Dyck, T/Ed. (2002) 'Topos and Enthymeme'. *Rhetorica*, 20 (2), pp. 105–17.

Eliot, George (1965 [1872]) *Middlemarch* (Harmondsworth: Penguin).

Eliot, T. S. (1963) *Collected Poems, 1909–1962* (London: Faber & Faber).

Ellison, Ralph (1965 [1952]) *Invisible Man* (Harmondsworth: Penguin).

Eramus, Desiderius (1999) *The Sileni of Alcibiades*, ed. and trans. David Wootton (with Sir Thomas More, *Utopia*) (Indianapolis: Hackett).

Erskine-Hill, H. and Storey, G. (eds) (1983) *Revolutionary Prose of the English Civil War* (Cambridge: Cambridge University Press).

Fahnestock, Jeanne and Secor, Marie (1990) *A Rhetoric of Argument*, 2nd edn (Boston, MA: McGraw-Hill).

Fahnestock, Jeanne (1999) *Rhetorical Figures in Science* (Oxford: Oxford University Press).

Fairclough, N. (2001) *Language and Power*, 2nd edn (London: Longman).

Firbas, Jan (1992) *Functional Sentence Perspective in Written and Spoken Communication* (Cambridge: Cambridge University Press).

Fisher, Alec (1988) *The Logic of Real Argument* (Cambridge: Cambridge University Press, 1988).

Gagarin, Michael (2001) 'Did the Sophists Aim to Persuade?' *Rhetorica*, 19 (3), pp. 275–91.

Garver, Eugene (1994) *Aristotle's Rhetoric: An Art of Character* (Chicago: University of Chicago Press).

Gibbs, Raymond W. (1994) *The Poetics of Mind: Figurative Thought, Language, and Understanding* (Cambridge: Cambridge University Press).

Goffman, Erving (1974) *Frame Analysis: An Essay on the Organization of Experience* (New York: Harper & Row).

Goffman, Erving (1982) *Interaction Ritual: Essays on Face-to-Face Behavior* (New York: Pantheon Books).

Gordimer, Nadine (1983) *Selected Stories* (Harmondsworth: Penguin).

Graddol, D., Cheshire, J. and Swann, J. (1994) *Describing Language*, 2nd edn (Buckingham: Open University Press).

Graddol, D. and Boyd-Barrett, O. (eds) (1994) *Media Texts: Authors and Readers*, Multilingual Matters series (Clevedon: Open University Press).

Green, J. (1998) *The Cassell Dictionary of Slang* (London: Cassell).

Grice, H. P. (1975) 'Logic and Conversation', in P. Cole and J. L. Morgan (eds), *Speech Acts*, pp. 41–58 (New York: Academic Press).

Gross, Alan G. (1990) *The Rhetoric of Science* (Cambridge, MA: Havard University Press).

Gumperz, J. J. (1982) *Discourse Strategies*, Studies in Interactional Sociolinguistics, 1 (Cambridge: Cambridge University Press).

Gunner, Elizabeth (1994) 'The Dynamics of Singer and Audience in Contemporary Zulu Praise Poetry', in M. Branch and C. Hawkesworth (eds), *The Uses of Tradition*, pp. 251–63 (London: School of Slavonic and East European Studies).

Halliday, M. A. K. (1973) *Explorations in the Function of Language* (London: Edward Arnold).

Hasan, Ruqaiya (1984) 'The Nursery Tale as a Genre'. *Nottingham Linguistic Circular*, 13, pp. 71–102.

Hawkes, T. (1977) *Structuralism and Semiotics*, New Accents series (London: Methuen).

Heath, Malcolm (ed.) (1995) *Hermogenes on Issues: Strategies of Argument in Later Greek Rhetoric* (Oxford: Oxford University Press).

Henderson, Judith R. (1999) 'Must a Good Orator be a Good Man? Ramus in the Ciceronian Controversy', in P. L. Oesterreich and T. O. Sloane (eds), *Rhetorica Movet* (Leiden: E. J. Brill, 1999).

Heller, Joseph (1962) *Catch 22* (London: Jonathan Cape).

Howell, W. S. (1961) *Logic and Rhetoric in England, 1500–1700* (New York, Russell).

Hume, David (1911 [1738]) *A Treatise of Human Nature*, Everyman's Library series, 2 vols (London: Dent).

Hunston, S. and Thompson, G. (eds) (2000) *Evaluation in Text: Authorial Stance and the Construction of Discourse* (Oxford: Oxford University Press).

Hunter, Lynette (1984) *Rhetorical Stance in Modern Literature: Allegories of Love and Death* (Basingstoke: Macmillan).

Huxley, Aldous (1994 [1932]) *Brave New World*, introd. D. Bradshaw, Flamingo Modern Classics (London: Harper Collins).

Isocrates (2000) *Isocrates I*, trans. D. C. Mirhady and Yun Lee Too, The Oratory of Classical Greece, 4 (Austin, Tx: University of Texas Press).

Jameson, Fredric (1983) *The Political Unconscious: Narrative as a Socially Symbolic Act* (London: Methuen).

Jefferson, A. and Robey, D. (eds) (1986) *Modern Literary Theory: A Comparative Introduction* (London: Batsford).

Johnson, Samuel (1957) *Prose and Poetry,* 2nd edn, selected by Mona Wilson, The Reynard Library (London: Hart Davis).

Jones, P. E. (1995) 'Philosophical and Theoretical Issues in the Study of Deixis: a Critique of the Standard Account', in K. Green (ed.), *New Essays in Deixis* (Amsterdam: Rodopi), pp. 27–48.

Jones, M. V. (1989) 'Bakhtin's Metalinguistics', in C. S. Butler et al. (eds), *Essays in Honour of Walter Grauberg*, University of Nottingham Monographs in the Humanities, VI (Nottingham: University of Nottingham).

Jonson, Ben (1985) *Ben Jonson*, ed. I. Donaldson, The Oxford Authors (Oxford: Oxford University Press).

Kafka, Franz (1959[1926]) *The Castle,* trans. W. and E. Muir (Harmondsworth: Penguin).

Keats, John (1970) *The Complete Poems*, ed. M. Allott, Annotated English Poets (London: Longman).

Kennedy, G. A. (1980) *Classical Rhetoric and its Christian and Secular Tradition from Ancient to Modern Times* (London: Croom Helm).

Kennedy, John F. (1962) *Public Papers of the Presidents: John F. Kennedy* (Washington, DC: Government Printing Office).

Labov, William (1972) *Language in the Inner City: Studies in the Black English Vernacular* (Philadelphia: University of Pennsylvania Press).

Langland, William (1967) *Piers Plowman,* ed. E. Salter and D. Pearsall, York Medieval Texts (London: Edward Arnold).

Lanham, R. A. (1991) *A Handlist of Rhetorical Terms,* 2nd edn (Berkeley, CA: University of California Press).

Larkin, Philip (1988) *Collected Poems*, ed. Anthony Thwaite (London: Marvell Press and Faber).

Lawrence, D. H. (1950) *Selected Essays* (Harmondsworth: Penguin).

Leishman, J. B. (ed.) (1949) *The Three Parnassus Plays* (London: Nicolson & Watson).

Leith, D. and Myerson, G. (1989) *The Power of Address: Explorations in Rhetoric* (London: Routledge).

Levinson, S. C. (1988) 'Putting Linguistics on a Proper Footing: Explorations in Goffman's Concepts of Participation', in P. Drew and A. Wootton (eds), *Erving Goffman: Exploring the Interactive Order*, pp. 161–227 (Cambridge: Polity Press).

Liddell, H. G. and Scott, R. (1973) *A Greek–English Lexicon,* new edn by S. H. Jones and R. McKenzie. Oxford: Oxford University Press.

Lloyd, G. E. R. (1968) *Aristotle: The Growth and Structure of his Thought* (Cambridge: Cambridge University Press).

Lodge, David (1977) *The Modes of Modern Writing: Metaphor, Metonymy and the Typology of Modern Literature* (London: Edward Arnold).

Lodge, David (1988) *Nice Work* (London: Secker & Warburg).

Luce, A. A. (1958) *Teach Yourself Logic* (London: English Universities Press).

MacArthur, B. (ed.) (1996) *The Penguin Book of Historic Speeches* (Harmondsworth: Penguin).

Mack, Peter (1993) *Renaissance Argument: Valla and Agricola in the Traditions of Rhetoric and Dialectic* (Leiden: E. J. Brill).

Mack, Peter (2002) *Elizabethan Rhetoric: Theory and Practice* (Cambridge: Cambridge University Press).

Mandler, J. M. and Johnson, N. S. (1977) 'Remembrance of Things Parsed: Story Structure and Recall'. *Cognitive Psychology,* 9: 111–51.

Marlowe, Christopher (1969) *The Complete Plays*, ed. J. B. Steane, Penguin Classics (Harmondsworth: Penguin).

Marvell, Andrew (1990[1681]) *Andrew Marvell: A Critical Edition of the Major Works*, ed. F. Kermode and K. Walker, The Oxford Authors (Oxford: Oxford University Press).

Mayhew, Henry (1984) *The Unknown Mayhew: Selections from the 'Morning Chronicle', 1849–50*, ed. E. P. Thompson and E. Yeo (Harmondsworth: Penguin).

McLuhan, Marshall (1962) *The Gutenberg Galaxy: The Making of Typographic Man* (London: Routledge).

Melville, Herman (1967) *Billy Budd, Sailor and Other Stories*, ed. and introd. Harold Beaver (Harmondsworth: Penguin).

Milton, John (1968) *The Poems of John Milton*, ed. J. Carey and A. Fowler, Annotated English Poets (London: Longmans).

Milton, John (1974) *Selected Prose*, ed. C. A. Patrides, Penguin English Library (Harmondsworth: Penguin).

Minnis, A. J. (ed.) (1988) *Medieval Theory of Authorship: Scholastic Literary Attitudes in the Later Middle Ages,* 2nd edn (Aldershot: Scolar Press).

Murphy, James J. (1974) *Rhetoric in the Middle Ages: A History of Rhetorical Theory from Saint Augustine to the Renaissance* (Berkeley, CA: University of California Press).

Murray, D. (1987) 'Dialogics: Joseph Conrad, *Heart of Darkness*', in D. Tallack (ed.), *Literary Theory at Work: Three Texts*, pp. 115–34 (London: Batsford).

Nash, W. (1980) *Designs in Prose*, English Language Series 12 (London: Longman).

Nash, W. (1989) *Rhetoric: The Wit of Persuasion* (Oxford: Blackwell).

Norris, C. (1982) *Deconstruction: Theory and Practice*, New Accents (London: Methuen).

Norris, Frank (1964 [1901]) *The Octopus: A Story of California*, Signet Classics (New York: The New American Library).

Nystrand, M. (ed.) (1981/2) *What Writers Know: The Language Process and Structure of Written Discourse* (New York: Academic Press).

Ong, Walter (1958) *Ramus, Method and the Decay of Dialogue* (Cambridge, MA: Havard University Press).

Ong, Walter (1982) *Orality and Literacy: The Technologizing of the Word* (London: Routledge).

Parker, Ann (2003) *The Gasman Dances and Other Poems* (private publication).

Paulin, Tom (1986) *The Faber Book of Political Verse* (London: Faber & Faber).

Perelman, C. and Olbrechts-Tyteca, L. (1969) *The New Rhetoric: A Treatise on Argumentation*, trans. J. Wilkinson and P. Weaver (Notre Dame: University of Notre Dame Press).

Plath, Sylvia (1981) *Sylvia Plath: Collected Poems*, ed. Ted Hughes (London: Faber & Faber).

Plato (1960) *Gorgias*, trans. W. Hamilton, Penguin Classics (Harmondsworth: Penguin Books).

Plato (1973) *Phaedrus* (with the *Seventh and Eighth Letters*), trans. W. Hamilton, Penguin Classics (Harmondsworth: Penguin Books).

Poe, Edgar Allan (1967) 'The Pit and the Pendulum', in D. Galloway (ed.), *Poe: Selected Writings*, pp. 261–76 (Harmondsworth: Penguin).

Polland-Gott, L. *et al.* (1979) 'Subjective Story Structure'. *Discourse Processes*, 2(4): 251–81.

Pope, Alexander (1968) *The Poems of Alexander Pope*, ed. J. Butt (London: Methuen).

Pope, R. (1998) *The English Studies Book* (London: Routledge).

Propp, Vladimir (1975) *Morphology of the Folk Tale* (Austin: University of Texas Press).

Puttenham, George (1968) *Arte of English Poesie 1589*, facsimile (Menston: The Scolar Press).

Quintilian (1920–2) *Institutio Oratoria*, trans. H. E. Butler, 4 vols, Loeb Classical Library (London: Heinemann).

Ramus, Peter (1968 [1574]) *The Logicke of the Most Excellent Philosopher P. Ramus Martyr*, trans. M. R. MacIlmaine, facsimile (Menston: The Scolar Press).

Rhetorica ad Herennium (1954), trans. H. Caplan, Loeb Classical Library (London: Heinemann).

Richards, I. A. (1965) *The Philosophy of Rhetoric* (New York: Oxford University Press).

Ricoeur, P. (1979) 'The Metaphorical Process as Cognition, Imagination and Feeling', in S. Sacks (ed.), *On Metaphor*, pp. 141–57 (Chicago: Chicago University Press).

Ricoeur, P. (1996) 'Between Rhetoric and Poetics', in A. O. Rorty (ed.), *Essays on Aristotle's 'Rhetoric'*, pp. 324–84 (Berkeley, CA: University of California Press).

Sacks, H., Schegloff, E. A. and Jefferson, G. (1974) 'A Simplest Systematics for the Organisation of Turn-Taking in Conversation'. *Language*, 50 (4): 696–735.

Salinger, J. D. (1958) *The Catcher in the Rye* (Harmondsworth: Penguin).

Schank, R. C. and Abelson, R. (1977) *Scripts, Plans, Goals and Understanding* (Hillsdale, NJ: Lawrence Erlbaum).

Schank, R. C. (1982) *Dynamic Memory: A Theory of Reminding and Learning in Computers and People* (Cambridge: Cambridge University Press).

Schank, R. C. (1999) *Dynamic Memory Revisited* (Cambridge: Cambridge University Press).

Schiappa, Edward (1999) *The Beginnings of Rhetorical Theory in Classical Greece*. New Haven, CT: Yale University Press.

Schulman, Grace (2003) *Days of Wonder: New and Selected Poems* (New York: Houghton Mifflin).

Smiley, Jane (1992) *A Thousand Acres* (London: Flamingo).

Semino, Elena (1997) *Language and World Creation in Poems and Other Texts* (London: Longman).

Shaffner, Diana (1998), 'The Shadow of Helen'. *Rhetorica*, 16 (3): 243–57.

Shakespeare, William (1997) *The Norton Shakespeare*, ed. Stephen Greenblatt et al. (New York: W. W. Norton).

Shelley, Percy Bysshe (1934) *The Complete Poetical Works*, ed. T. Hutchinson (London: Oxford University Press).

Shepherd, S. (1986) *Marlowe and the Politics of Elizabethan Theatre* (Brighton: Harvester).

Sheridan, R. B. (1979[1777]), *The New Mermaids*, ed. F. W. Bateson (London: Benn).

Shuger, Debora K. (1988) *Sacred Rhetoric: The Christian Grand Style in the English Renaissance* (Princeton, NJ: Princeton University Press).

Sidney, Philip (1973) *An Apology for Poetry*, ed. G. Shepherd (Manchester: Manchester University Press).

Simons, Herbert W. (ed.) (1989) *Rhetoric in the Human Sciences* (London: Sage).

Sinclair, J. McH. and Coulthard, R. M. (1975) *Towards an Analysis of Discourse* (Oxford: Oxford University Press).

Smith, Adam (1976) *The Theory of Moral Sentiments*, ed. D. D. Raphael and A. L. MacFie (Oxford: Oxford University Press).

Smith, Stevie (1985) *The Collected Poems* (Harmondsworth: Penguin).

Sonnino, Lee A. (1968) *A Handbook to Sixteenth-Century Rhetoric* (London: Routledge).

Speght, Rachel (1985 [1617]) *A Muzzle for Melastomus*, in S. Shepherd (ed.), *The Women's Sharp Revenge: Five Women's Pamphlets from the Renaissance*, pp. 57–83 (London: Fourth Estate).

Spenser, Edmund (1992) *Selected Writings*, ed. Elizabeth Porges Watson, Routledge English Texts (London: Routledge).

Steinmann, M. (1981/2) 'Speech-Act Theory and Writing', in Nystrand, 1981/2.

Stockwell, P. (2002) *Cognitive Poetics: An Introduction* (London: Routledge).

Stubbs, M. (1986) 'A Matter of Prolonged Fieldwork: Towards a Modal Grammar of English'. *Applied Linguistics*, 7, 1–25.

Susenbrotus, Ioannes (1570) *Epitome Troporumac Schematum* (London: Henry Wykes).

Swift, Graham (1984) *Waterland*, Picador edn (London: Pan Books in association with Heinemann).

Swift, Jonathan (1932) *Satires and Personal Writings*, ed. W. A. Eddy (London: Oxford University Press).

Tallack, D. (ed.) (1987) *Literary Theory at Work: Three Texts* (London: Batsford).

Tannen, Deborah (ed.) (1993) *Framing in Discourse* (New York: Oxford University Press).

Tannen, Deborah (1998) *The Argument Culture: Changing the Way We Argue and Debate* (London: Virago).

Tennyson, Alfred (1969) *The Poems of Tennyson*, ed. C. Ricks, Longmans Annotated English Poets (London: Longmans).

Toolan, M. J. (1988) *Narrative: A Critical Linguistic Introduction* (London: Routledge).

Trudgill, P. (1974) *The Social Differentiation of English in Norwich* (Cambridge: Cambridge University Press).

Vickers, Brian (1988) *In Defence of Rhetoric* (Oxford: Oxford University Press).

Walcott, Derek (1990) *Omeros* (London: Faber & Faber).

Wales, Katie (2001) *A Dictionary of Stylistics*, 2nd edn (London: Longman).

Walker, Alice (1983) *The Color Purple* (London: The Women's Press).

Ward, John O. (2001) 'Rhetorical Theory and the Rise and Decline of *Dictamen* in the Middle Ages and Early Renaissance'. *Rhetorica*, 19 (2): 175–223.

Wells, G. (1981) 'Language and Interaction', in G. Wells (ed.), *Learning through Interaction: The Study of Language Development*, Language at Home and at School 1, pp. 22–72 (Cambridge: Cambridge University Press).

Winstanley, Gerrard (1973[1652]) *Winstanley: The Law of Freedom and Other Writings*, ed. Christopher Hill (Harmondsworth: Penguin).

Woods, M. C. (2003) 'Medieval Rhetorical Exercises in the Postmodern Classroom', paper to the International Society for the History of Rhetoric, Calahorra.

Woolf, Virginia (1964[1925]) *Mrs Dalloway* (Harmondsworth: Penguin).

Wordsworth, William and Coleridge, S. T. (1963[1798]) *Lyrical Ballads*, ed. R. L. Brett and A. R. Jones (London: Methuen).

Index